Female Pileated Woodpecker

# Woodpeckers
# of Eastern
# North America

## Lawrence Kilham

DOVER PUBLICATIONS, INC.
NEW YORK

Published in Canada by General Publishing Company, Ltd., 30 Lesmill Road, Don Mills, Toronto, Ontario.

Published in the United Kingdom by Constable and Company, Ltd., 3 Lanchesters, 162–164 Fulham Palace Road, London W6 9ER.

This Dover edition, first published in 1992, is an unabridged republication of the work first published by the Nuttall Ornithological Club ("Publications of the Nuttall Ornithological Club, No. 20; Editor, Raymond A. Paynter, Jr."), Cambridge, Massachusetts, 1983, under the title *Life History Studies of Woodpeckers of Eastern North America*. In this edition the frontispiece, originally in color, has been reproduced in black and white.

Manufactured in the United States of America
Dover Publications, Inc., 31 East 2nd Street, Mineola, N.Y. 11501

*Library of Congress Cataloging-in-Publication Data*

Kilham, Lawrence, 1910–
    [Life history studies of woodpeckers of eastern North America]
    Woodpeckers of eastern North America / Lawrence Kilham.
        p.    cm.
    Originally published: Life history studies of woodpeckers of eastern North America. Cambridge, Mass. : Nuttall Ornithological Club, 1983. (Publications of the Nuttall Ornithological Club ; no. 20)
    Includes bibliographical references.
    ISBN 0-486-27040-8 (pbk.)
    1. Woodpeckers—East (U.S.)  2. Woodpeckers—Canada, Eastern.  3. Woodpeckers—East (U.S.)—Behavior.  4. Woodpeckers—Canada, Eastern—Behavior.  I. Title.  II. Series: Publications of the Nuttall Ornithological Club ; no. 20.
    [QL696.P56K55    1992]
    598.7′2—dc20                                                    91–33227
                                                                                    CIP

# CONTENTS

# PREFACE

I had two plans while contemplating writing this monograph. One idea was to include everything known about the woodpeckers of eastern North America, which would have contained many references; the other plan was for a simpler book built on my own observations. The latter has had more appeal. I have been studying the woodpeckers of eastern North America for 25 years as an amateur and have published 51 articles and notes in *Auk, Condor, Wilson Bulletin, Bird-Banding, Avicultural Magazine,* and *American Birds.* The material in these articles forms the core of this book. The book, however, is more than a summation. An aim in writing it has been to rearrange, add new observations, and to pull all together in a narrative style, simpler and somewhat different than that used in technical journals.

The illustrations and some of the material on the Crimson-crested and Lineated Woodpeckers, and the section on a tame Pileated are reprinted, with modifications, from my *A Naturalist's Field Guide* (1981), with permission of Stackpole Books, Harrisburg, Pennsylvania.

While studying woodpeckers in the south, my wife and I were grateful for opportunities to stay at the Marine Institute of the University of Georgia on Sapelo Island, the Archbold Biological Station at Lake Placid, in southern Florida, and on the Groton Plantation at Luray, South Carolina, thanks to Mr. Frederick Winthrop.

Acknowledgements are due particularly to my wife, Jane Kilham, for making the black and white illustrations in this book as well as for help in locating and watching nests.

# 1

# INTRODUCTION

*"Besides these quadrupeds, there are a whole genus of birds, called Pici Marcii, or wood-peckers, that in like manner have a tongue which they can shoot forth to very great length, ending in a sharp stiff bony rib, dented on each side, and at pleasure thrust it deep into holes, clifts and crannies of trees, to stab and draw out cossi, or any other insects lurking there. . . ."*————John Ray (1627–1705).

The present studies began by chance. I had spent a year in what was then British East Africa doing virus research, but with time to make a study of Black-and-White Casqued Hornbills on the side. But what could take the place of the hornbills when I returned to the United States? The prospect of facing winters with little bird activity, after a year in equatorial Africa, was somewhat discouraging.

After returning with my family to live in Bethesda, Maryland, I was walk-ing, one Saturday, along the Potomac River. Red-headed Woodpeckers were gathering acorns from pin oaks and I stopped to watch. After a time, the thought came to me that here were some beautiful and exciting birds. Why look further? Why not study these woodpeckers as if they were hornbills, whether much happened or not? From then on I went to Seneca Swamp, as I called the place, every weekend and holiday throughout the fall, winter, and spring. Although results were slow to begin, they developed later be-yond expectations. I came to find that the Red-headed Woodpeckers win-tered in small, individual territories determined by the storage of acorns, many of which were sealed in cavities with splinters of wood. My interests soon extended to other woodpeckers. Attracted by the loud *kwirr*s of Red-bellieds in midwinter, I discovered that they had a remarkable courtship ceremony that I termed mutual tapping. By spring I was interested in all of the local woodpeckers. From there I began to entertain a project of studying the woodpeckers of eastern North America.

Of aid was a summer place we had in Tamworth, New Hampshire. We later moved to New Hampshire permanently with a house in Lyme. In studying the woodpeckers of the south, my wife and I visited three main places over a number of years. One was Sapelo, a sea island off Georgia, for Pileateds; another the Groton Plantation, at Luray, South Carolina, for the breeding of Red-headeds; and lastly in southern Florida, the vicinity of the Archbold Biological Station at Lake Placid for flickers and other species.

The woodpeckers proved a happy choice in a number of ways. They form a small group, yet exhibit considerable diversity. Of the seven that I have studied at greatest length, the Hairy, Downy, Pileated, and Red-bellied Woodpeckers have been resident, enabling me to study them in all months of the year. Of the others, the Northern Flickers and Yellow-bellied Sap-suckers are migratory and Red-headed Woodpeckers irregularly so.

The three remaining woodpeckers of eastern North America are ones that

I have not been able to study in a comparable way. I have watched nestings of Black-backed Woodpeckers in northern New Hampshire but have never been able to find a nest of the Three-toed. The Red-cockaded Woodpecker is one I have watched for many hours in South Carolina and in southern Florida. A drawback to studying it at length, from my point of view, has been the impossibility of distinguishing the sexes in the field.

I have been interested in the total behavior of the seven main woodpeckers in this book—how they scratched, preened, foraged, bred, interacted with other species, and communicated by means of displays, drumming, and vocalizations—an approach that I feel essential to understanding any particular aspect of their lives.

In addition to the woodpeckers of eastern North America, I have studied three others in Central America that have some bearing. Of these, the Pale-billed and Crimson-crested are almost identical in behavior. Being of the same genus as the extinct Ivory-billed, they have provided something of a substitute. The third species, the Lineated, is so close to the Pileated in behavior that it could be regarded as being a tropical Pileated.

It might be asked whether sticking to a single species and really getting to know it might not have been a better scheme. While such an objective might work for some, I would have found it difficult. Studying a group of birds offers many advantages. One is the making of comparisons. Tapping, for example, is an important form of communication among woodpeckers, yet I could find few descriptions of it when I first began. For the most part, it registers agreement and acceptance of a nest site by the members of a pair. This was something I had to work out. Tapping became clearer and more interesting when I discovered that it occurs among all of the woodpeckers, from sapsuckers to Pileateds.

Another advantage of following a number of species has been opportunism. A way to make discoveries, in many fields of science, is to follow whatever lead is most favorable. Time and again when I have planned to study one species, I have switched when I stumbled on a better opportunity with another. While this scheme may seem haphazard, it is one that has sustained my interest in woodpeckers over many years.

My studies were not limited to the field. Unable to get to the country and good woods on weekdays, I early established an aviary (Appendix I) where, for nearly 10 years, I was able to learn about woodpeckers seven days a week. This was one of the most valuable things I did. As narrated in many of the following chapters, I not only learned much from my handraised captives but also derived much pleasure in watching them at close range.

## GENERAL REFERENCES ON WOODPECKERS

BENT, A. C. 1939. Life histories of North American woodpeckers. Bull. U.S. Nat'l Mus., **174**: 1–322.

# INTRODUCTION

JACKSON, J. A. 1976. How to determine the status of a woodpecker nest. Living Bird, **15**: 205–221.

LAWRENCE, L. DE K. 1967. A comparative life-history study of four species of woodpeckers. Ornith. Monogr. (Amer. Ornith. Union), no. 5, 156 p.

SHORT, L. L. 1982. Woodpeckers of the world. Delaware Mus. Nat. Hist. Monogr. Ser., no. 4, 676 p.

# DOWNY WOODPECKER

## ROOSTING IN FALL AND WINTER

### MARYLAND

Downy Woodpeckers often excavate roost holes in the fall. Wishing to become better acquainted with this habit when we lived in Maryland, I tried an experiment. On work days I could not go to Seneca Swamp, where I watched woodpeckers, for it was too far. But I had noticed that Downies roosted in dead stubs about 2.5 m tall and 13 cm in diameter. "Why not collect stubs of the right type," I thought, "and wire them to fence posts in the yard?" I collected logs, or segments of broken branches and trunks lying below dead elms and other trees. Not all of these were suitable. I had to inspect to see whether they were a little decayed but not too much so, a kind that a Downy would select naturally.

The experiment was a success. Four Downies came to inspect soon after I had wired the logs in place. After sounding them out, some of the birds started digging cavities. There was no difference in the yard from what I had noticed in the swamp. The Downies did their excavating largely between September and January, with a peak of activity in November.

The Downies worked especially in the middle of the day. A male or a female might toss out as many as 40 billfuls of sawdust once it could get inside a hole. Every now and then one swung out to percuss the outside. I think this was to see if the walls were of equal thickness all the way around.

Times taken to excavate varied. A female that began excavating on November 1, spent her first night in the hole on the sixth. When she became interested in a second log a few months later, the excavating took eight days. The consistency of the wood, as well as the urgency of getting a hole ready, made for such variations. If there was no urgency, a Downy worked only in the middle of the day. But if a bird had lost one cavity and needed another, it might work morning and afternoon.

Having a hole is important. A woodpecker that has to roost in the open will have a harder time retaining heat on a cold night. It will also be more exposed to owls and other predators. I did not expect to see owls in the yard. But in one period of four days, our woodpecker population melted away. It was only after a third day that I noticed a screech owl occupying a box I had set up for squirrels. When the owl left the Downies returned. Woodpeckers generally have more than one roost hole. If something goes wrong at one, they can fly to an alternate before darkness sets in.

Roost holes are important to survival but stubs suitable for excavating are nearly always in short supply. In the competition to occupy the good ones, male Downies appear to have no special advantage over females. A male Downy, after inspecting stubs in September, looked into one that a female was excavating. She struck at him and there was lively exchange of blows before the male left.

On October 29 there was an even more severe encounter when a male and female grappled in midair. Male woodpeckers are dominant over females at feeding places, but when it comes to roost holes, a female Downy is as dominant at hers as a male is at his. I have thus come to think that one reason why male and female Downies, as well as Hairies, are so alike in color, especially when seen head on, is that it puts the sexes on a more equal basis.

A male on December 28 swooped at a female that had ventured within 5 m of his roost hole. The immediate vicinity, as well as a hole itself, is a defended area. I found, however, that my Downies remained peaceful with one another once boundaries and ownership were settled. I even noted, later, that two females roosted only a half meter apart, after making excavations in the same upright log.

Downies drove away competitors ranging from Carolina Chickadees to Hairy Woodpeckers. The Hairies were easily driven off if they came to the yard casually, but if they were interested in the stubs, results might be different. On December 23, when a female Downy attacked, a Hairy swooped at her in return. The Downy persisted and the Hairy left. On another day, a male Hairy drove away a female Downy, inspected her excavation, and flew off.

Downies have reason to fear larger woodpeckers, as I discovered on two occasions. In one a Red-bellied Woodpecker came to a Downy hole and enlarged the entrance with few quick blows. It then flew off, taking no further interest. Such destruction takes only a minute, but is enough to ruin a cavity, for Downies, like most woodpeckers, want entrances fitting their body size exactly.

I witnessed another episode when a Hairy flew to a Downy's roost hole, enlarged the entrance, and popped inside. The Hairy stayed in only a few minutes. Possibly the cavity was too small. In the meantime, the cavity had been ruined for its rightful owner.

It is no small matter to lose a roost hole as darkness is coming on. This is particularly evident if one considers that woodpeckers, like many birds, have no night vision. They are helpless in the dark.

## New Hampshire

I had further experiences with Downies after we moved to New Hampshire. Woods there were deep in snow and trees cracked at zero temperatures when I went out to see how woodpeckers behaved in the shortest and darkest days of the year. My visits were to a wooded slope where numbers of stubs attracted woodpeckers. December of my first year was unusually cold. I dressed in a padded snow suit with a fur hood and wore pack boots to avoid freezing while watching in early morning hours.

The slope provided roosting places for Downies as well as Hairies. I got to know one female Downy well. Like most woodpeckers, she looked forth from the dark recess of her hole for some minutes before emerging. After that she had no set pattern. On December 15 she scratched her head a few times, ascended three straight trees, getting higher on each, then flew over the tree tops in a looping flight that looked like sheer exuberance.

Her line of flight was in the direction of our house some distance away. Could she be one of the Downies that visited our suet? I made sketches of the pattern of the black and white at the back of her head so that I could recognize her, then drove home. I found her on the suet when I arrived. It seemed that she had flown 2.2 km from roost to suet almost directly.

The Downy entered her roost at 16:13 hours on December 22. This was close to the longest night of the year. What is the longest a woodpecker can spend in a hole? This doubtless varies. The Downy emerged at 07:26 the next morning, making a total of 15 hours and 13 minutes. December 31 was possibly the coldest day of the year. How would the female Downy behave at thirty below? Would the cold affect her? She flew out at 07:25. After scratching her head with one foot, then the other, wiping her bill on the bark of a tree and fluffing out and shaking her feathers, she took off on a long flight.

I continued studying Downies some years later in a beaver swamp. The beaver had gone but their flooding had killed many trees. I had to start off in the dark, often by starlight, to be in place at the first light of day. Events on November 8 revealed what a good place it was. Within a few minutes of 06:15 a male White-breasted Nuthatch, a pair of Hairies, and five Downies emerged from holes at about the same time. I wondered whether these birds interacted with one another. Did they compete for stubs?

On January 3 I frightened a male Downy from a cavity it was excavating a meter above the snow. On later visits I found the Downy sharing the stub with a female Hairy that roosted 4 m above. The two appeared peaceful and one might ask how this could happen. Some strategy may have been involved. In experiences with 25 roost holes, I have never found Hairies roosting close to the ground. It is possible, therefore, that the Downy, by digging his hole low, avoided competition.

The apartment stub did not last long. It blew down in February, breaking at the place where the woodpecker had dug his cavity. He, meanwhile, had shifted to a birch stub that had been occupied by a male White-breasted Nuthatch. Such interchanges added interest. After a succession of them, I was never sure, on early mornings, which bird might emerge from what hole.

Downy Woodpeckers and White-breasted Nuthatches are of much the same size and the nuthatches can occupy holes excavated by Downies. On two of three occasions when ownership changed, I noticed that a nuthatch had taken over from a Downy. Which species is dominant, however, is hard to say. I never witnessed a conflict. What may happen is that whichever bird pops into a hole first on a late afternoon, is in a good position to hold onto it.

A practice I developed in the course of studies on roosting has been to make sketches of head patterns (Fig. 1). I have never found two Downies whose patterns were alike; all identifications of individuals in the following sections were based on this method.

## SEXUAL DIFFERENCES IN WINTER FORAGING

### CONCENTRATION ON PAPER BIRCHES

When I started studies in New Hampshire I walked many profitless miles in fall and winter woods. I found few Downies. It was only by ranging far

FIG. 1. Head markings of Downy Woodpeckers showing differences in individual birds. Males, left; females, right.

that I found them concentrating on paper birches of a special kind. New Hampshire has many birches with straight trunks and white bark. But these held little attraction. What the Downies sought were defective birches, ones that were crooked or leaning, had broken branches in their crowns, or with areas of their trunks blackened with cankers. I was almost sure to find Downies once I found trees of this kind. These trees were nearly always on exposed ridges or hillsides damaged by logging. But on what were the Downies feeding? I was fortunate to learn that the defective paper birches had heavy infestations of a coccid, *Xylocculus betulae* (Hubbard and Pergunde, 1898). A coccid is a small insect that embeds itself in bark, feeding on sap. It is important in being a principal winter food of Downies in the north.

The adult female coccid is comparatively large, 3 mm across. Orange-red and soft-bodied, she lies in a cavity just under the outer bark. She extrudes a wax tube that protrudes 3 cm out into the breezes in summer. This is to excrete a saccharine honeydew similar to that produced by aphids. In winter she is dormant. The signs of a birch infested with these insects are the small trap doors made by Downies. Downies make a neat circle of sharp pecks around the adult coccid, then swing the bark open as on a hinge. One can often find dozens of these markers on a defective birch, for the bark of a single tree can shelter hundreds of coccids in places ranging from lenticels to branch stubs. *Xylocculus betulae* infects other trees, including yellow birches and beeches. But it is infected paper birches that attract Downies the most.

I made repeated visits to a number of stands of coccid-invested birches, but not always successfully. Snow made some inaccessible and heavy frost coated others, forcing the Downies to feed elsewhere for weeks at a time. I was fortunate, however, in having one area, a boulder slope, that was lower down and more accessible.

I found three male and six female Downy Woodpeckers feeding within the boulder slope in the winter of 1967–68. I seldom saw all nine on any one of 20 visits, but I frequently encountered five or six of them on a single day. The same individuals were often in the same groups of trees. This suggested territorial behavior and I was keen to watch for further indications.

On January 18 Female C flew 50 m to attack Female A who was at their common boundary. The two circled a tree making *chrr* notes. Female C did a bill-waving dance, a display used in conflicts, then flew at Female A who left. The feeding territory of Female C was of interest. She had defended a concentration of paper birches that appeared to offer the best feeding on the slope. I often found as many as five Downies working in its close vicinity. To my surprise these trees received almost no attention in a following year. I wondered whether the intensive feeding of one winter could eliminate a winter population of coccids from certain groups of trees. Yet the overall suppy has seemed inexhaustible. I have found Downies feeding on birches over many winters.

By January 1969 I was following the activities of Downies for periods of 30 to 40 minutes, noting their relations to each other and to the parts of trees on which they fed. A circumstance favoring watching was that the Downies had little else to do except to feed on paper birches. After leaving one they usually flew to another. Of the Downies watched, two were unique in being members of a pair (Pair A) that was to nest near the boulder slope the following spring.

In observing the parts of trees that were fed upon, I found, in repeated observations, that male A fed on upper trunks, limbs, and smaller branches while his mate fed on the middle of trunks and lower down. A typical pattern was for Male A to progress up the trunk into the crown, move out along a branch, often clinging upside down, until he neared the end, then to drop to another branch. He was apt to choose the largest and tallest birches or, if he worked on the trunk, those most blackened by defects.

Female A, in contrast, fed mostly on the mid-third of trunks. Here she had to flutter wherever smoother bark made clinging difficult. She occasionally failed to establish a grip and fell. Her mate rarely had to flutter in this way. The places where he fed had rough spots as well as smaller branches that made clinging easier.

I was not sure what factors led Male A to occupy the upper portions of birches. Both members of the pair pecked steadily and appeared to find food at equal rates. If he preferred the upper parts for feeding, as he apparently did, it could have been for other reasons than abundance of prey. Possibly the higher positions gave him greater dominance.

## Sexual Dominance

Supplanting attacks of males on females in feeding situations are frequent among Downies. Male A flew to Female A at least once an hour in January and February and frequently at lesser intervals. Female A's reaction was to drop away and fly to an adjacent tree. Male A usually pecked briefly where she had been, then moved to feed at a higher level on the same or another paper birch. Thus, on most occasions, he did not seem to be supplanting her merely to take over an especially favorable feeding place. He appeared, rather, to be forcing her to stay lower.

On February 9 I followed Female A as she worked high in several birches. This was early in the day before Male A arrived. When he did so, he flew at her immediately, displacing her four times in seven minutes. Female A

10

then worked low on three yellow birches, trees on which Male A almost never fed. After an interval she resumed her feeding on the middle and lower thirds of paper birches.

Female A's behavior was even more striking on February 28. This time following attacks by Male A she fed at the bases of seven birches in succession; even going below snow line into wells formed by action of wind and sun.

I never saw Male A feed at the base of paper birches. I was surprised, therefore, on March 8, to see a second male, Male B, feeding at the bases of 12 paper birches in succession. All of these were within Male A's territory. My interpretation was that Male B, as a trespasser, was cautious. Insecurity led him to stay where he might escape notice. Male A and his mate were at the opposite side of their domain at the time and seemingly unaware of the intrusion.

The behavior of a single female on March 21 was at the opposite extreme. She fed almost entirely on the top branches of paper birches as she moved from one to another, well outside the territory of Pair A. With no male to keep her down, she fed higher up.

In summary of the sexual differences in feeding behavior, what was striking was that the differences were purely facultative. The males and females feed on the same kinds of trees. It was only when they were together that the male forced the female to feed lower.

The members of Pair A were somewhat special for, in seven years of winter observations, these were the only Downies that I found traveling as a pair in winter. I think it was because their winter territory, which contained many coccid-infested birches, was also their breeding one in spring. They had no occasion to separate in cold months, which is the usual situation with this species, at least in New Hampshire.

My findings in New Hampshire are not unique. While I was making my observations, Jackson (1970) was studying similar situations in Kansas. He also found that male and female Downies partitioned their trees. Papers by others have followed, showing that sexual dimorphism in foraging is widespread. But it is not restricted to Downy Woodpeckers. Ligon (1968) described sexual differences among Red-cockaded Woodpeckers feeding on pines in Florida that are surprisingly similar to those that I noted for Downies on birches in New Hampshire. The males fed on upper branches and the females on main trunks and lower. The value of such partitioning lies in a spacing out of woodpeckers and prey, a kind of insurance against too many birds concentrating in one area.

## DOWNIES IN MIXED FLOCKS

### FORAGING IN WINTER

Although observations in Maryland were limited, I noted 19 flocks containing Downies by the Potomac River between November and March. All contained Carolina Chickadees as well as Tufted Titmice. White-breasted Nuthatches, Golden-crowned Kinglets, and Brown Creepers were the only other species present with any regularity. The flocks included from one to three Downies. I came to find that the easiest way to locate Downies was to listen for the call notes of the titmice, so constant was the association.

Freedom from snow favored diversity in foraging. Downies moving with flocks fed on the ground, among bushes, and at the bases of trees, seemingly on insect populations in various stages of dormancy. They also fed at higher levels in trees. Their ability to forage in varied situations was notable.

I found Downies in mixed flocks with Black-capped Chickadees and other birds 89 times in New Hampshire. This was from October through March. Only a single Downy was present in 65 of the flocks and two Downies, a male and a female, in each of 24. Hairy Woodpeckers, as in Maryland, were only one-sixth as frequent. They were, however, more apt to be together as a pair, as I found on seven of the 13 occasions.

A striking fact was that the Downies were specializing almost exclusively on paper birches in 58 of the 89 flocks. When the flock moved, the woodpeckers sometimes followed only as long as they could continue to feed on their special trees. On February 2, for example, a single female fed on 11 paper birches in the 45 minutes I followed a flock.

The interrelations of Downies and Black-capped Chickadees were of interest from several points of view. While chickadees were predominant in most flocks, five contained only a single chickadee, a situation also noted by Morse (1970) for flocks in Maine.

The attraction between Downies and chickadees appeared to be mutual. I had been watching a female Downy for some time one day when she suddenly flew over 20 m to join a flock of chickadees that had just arrived. On the over hand, I watched a pair of Downies feeding on paper birches for 40 minutes on February 6 with a lone chickadee staying close by the whole time (Fig. 2). Interactions between the two were limited to displacings. These were rare, possibly because chickadees feed on prey so small that a Downy has little to gain.

The chickadees were attracted to paper birches as well as to the Downies, feeding around buds in terminal twigs or fluttering up trunks and larger branches to pick and glean. There thus appeared to be some overlap in feeding habits, but I was not sure how much.

I only once saw a chickadee endeavoring to dig into the bark·like a Downy. This was on the top of a wind-blown ledge. Feeding conditions had become particularly unfavorable when sleet and snow coated twigs as well as the boles of paper birches with ice and frost. The number of birds I saw on the ledge under these conditions fell to almost zero. All I saw on December 15 was one chickadee and one Downy. Two days later there was a single chickadee associated with two Downies.

White-breasted Nuthatches were the commonest members of winter flocks

FIG. 2. Male Downy looking for coccids at a canker on paper birch in winter. Lone chickadee staying by Downy in a "mixed flock."

after the chickadees, and Downies occasionally displaced them. A male nuthatch carrying a piece of acorn on February 4 had hardly arrived at a rough spot when a female Downy supplanted it, then worked at the place for nearly four minutes. It seemed from such observations that the Downies benefited from robbing the nuthatches. On March 20 I saw another female Downy fly to three trees in succession, visiting, on each the exact spot where a White-breasted Nuthatch had been working. As Hairy Woodpeckers displace Downies and Downies displace White-breasted Nuthatches, one can, as described by Wing (1946), arrange these birds in hierarchies of dominance.

## SURVIVAL VALUES

As a result of watching mixed flocks, I have come to feel that all creatures, whether bushmen in the Kalahari Desert or Downies in New Hampshire, survive because of a close and extensive knowledge of where they live. Such knowledge is not just of feeding places. It includes shelter, sources of danger, and many things difficult for an observer to appreciate. Situations may change from day to day with weather and season. A creature familiar with where it lives will, one may presume, be better adapted to emergencies.

How can such a familiarity be maintained? A lone Downy will undoubtedly find out much. On the other hand, watching lone Downies as they feed for long stretches of time, gives one an impression that life can become monotonous. Joining a passing flock may be a way of breaking things up. The flock gives variety and this may be needed by all animals. A Downy Woodpecker associating with other birds is led to range more widely. It explores and investigates a greater variety of cracks, crevices, holes, and types of trees, even within its home range, than it would on its own.

A wider knowledge, it is true, may have no immediate benefit. A Downy might find more food by sticking to one good tree and letting the flock move on. The biological advantages of flocking, however, may be more general and long term. Enlivened by being with other birds, a Downy may gain knowledge that will be lifesaving in times of sudden change, such as an ice storm that forces it to alter its mode of life. The essence of survival is knowledge of resources.

A question is, Why should Downies join flocks more readily than do Hairies? This could be a matter of size. Downies, with their small, finer bills, are closer to such birds as chickadees and nuthatches in manner of feeding than are Hairies. This probably enables them to forage more effectively in those kinds of areas sought out by the mixed flocks.

Other reasons, however, are conceivable. Hairy Woodpeckers begin courtship in late December and travel through the woods together for at least part of each day during the winter. Sociability and its attendant variety is thus built into their lives. Downies, in contrast, do not begin pair formation until March. They begin earlier, in intermittent fashion, in Maryland, but wherever they are, they do not appear to have as close a pair bond as Hairies. They tend to become separated by the frequent displacings of females by males. It is possible, therefore, that by shunning their own kind in winter, they are the more attracted to mixed flocks.

The reasons for joining mixed flocks is a complex biological problem. I have only cited advantages that have occurred to me in the course of my own observations. I have never witnessed predation on small birds in winter in New Hampshire, so I do not know whether birds are safer in flocks or not. A predator might be even more attracted to numbers of birds than to single individuals.

It has been said that birds moving through woods together flush more prey and improve the foraging. But how can this hold for winter woods in New Hampshire when insects are dormant? My own feeling is that the advantages of flocking differ for different species and for different localities. No one rule holds and this makes the subject worthy of continued study.

# DOWNY WOODPECKER

## CONFLICTS AND TERRITORY: EARLY SPRING

### DRUMMING AND BILL-WAVING DANCES

Downy Woodpeckers generally do little drumming from September until midwinter, then drum with increasing frequency as reproductive behavior develops. Drumming is long distance communication and can convey a variety of meanings. Delivered from a tall dead tree of good resonance, it can proclaim territory as well as attract a mate. After pair formation it can serve to bring the partners together.

A female began drumming at 05:11 on April 14 at a rate of 18 bursts a minute. Her mate came from his roost hole three minutes later. He immediately flew in her direction, but stopped to drum on the way. After more drumming, she flew to him.

Drumming might be compared to the song of a passerine. A confusing difference, with Downies as well as with Hairies, is that females can drum, at times, as much as their mates.

### TERRITORIAL CONFLICTS

Other signs of early breeding behavior are territorial conflicts. One of the more puzzling experiences I had when starting to study woodpeckers, was with the dances of Downies as well as Hairies. It was always a pair of either species that was involved, and usually low on the trunks of trees. With heads and bills pointed upward, or even backward, and swinging back and forth like conductors' batons, they jerked heads and bodies while making half-starting motions with their wings (Fig. 3). The jerking made me think of mechanical puppets. Although some have objected to the term dances, the term seems apt to me, a dance being "a rhythmic and patterned succession of movements."

What did these displays mean? My first thought was courtship, the male pursuing the female up a tree. But were the woodpeckers male and female? As the heads of the woodpeckers were bent back and the nuchal patches were obscured, it took time to find out that the dances were always between two birds of the same sex. Instead of being courtship, as a number of observers in Bent (1939) have averred, the displays are aggressive and used, most frequently, in territorial conflicts.

A territory is a defended area. The breeding territory of a pair of Downies, which in early spring may cover up to 10 or more hectares, has boundaries that are seldom well defined. One can, however, learn something by the location of conflicts.

Two males in New Hampshire fought on trunks of small saplings along their common border from 07:20 until 07:55 on February 10. They were within 18 cm of each other in bouts of bill-waving, as well as in intermittent pauses of resting in strained postures. The section of woods where they fought

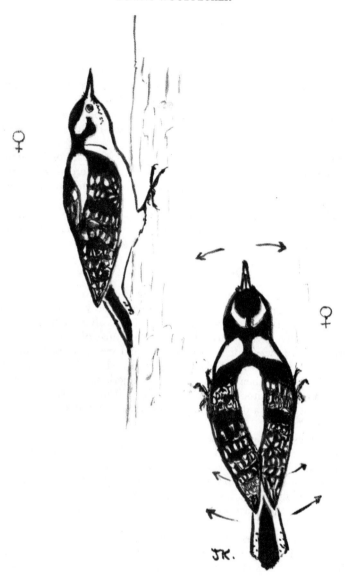

FIG. 3. Bill-waving dance between two female Downies in early spring.

was within 50 m of where one of them nested the following May.

On 28 March, also in New Hampshire, two males fought for 65 minutes. Features of the conflict were: (*i*) that nearly all of the fighting was low on small saplings; (*ii*) that one male might swoop at the other, who was usually able to shift around the tree in time to avoid contact; and (*iii*) that one male seized the other, coming away with a bill full of small feathers and these stuck to his bill as he continued a bill-waving dance. A female remained in the vicinity and, whenever she came close, the fighting was intensified.

Fights between Downies, as with Hairies, are practically always between members of the same sex, and intensify when a mate comes close. When two females were engaged in bill-waving, a male, drumming in a tree above, floated down on outstretched wings. His approach lead to a renewal of the conflict.

One wonders why territorial conflicts should, at times, be so prolonged. Here I think a passage in Thoreau, not on birds but on a farmer, is apropos. The farmer was seeking to establish a tree, one that Robert Frost would have called a "Witness Tree," as marking the boundary between his farm and that of a neighbor. The neighbor was a widow. She sent her boy out to do the job. When he arrived the farmer asked for his knife and started to cut a switch. The boy, seeing what was coming, ran away. The idea in the farmer's mind, as the boy forsaw, was that if the youngster was whipped he would remember where the line was for the rest of his life. Possibly Downies, facing one another in prolonged encounters, imprint the location of boundaries on their minds for the length of a breeding season.

### Types of Conflicts

A feature of conflicts among Downies is that although they may grapple beak to beak in midair, they do not injure each other. Their bills could be powerful weapons. But Downies, like all woodpeckers, seem to have an inhibition against striking with them. They bite instead, pulling out feathers if they can. Physical contact, however, is not common. The dances with bills held in positions where they cannot possibly strike, are battles of persuasion, efforts to get an opponent to go away.

When buds begin to unfold and the time of nesting approaches, the territory of the Downy becomes limited to a smaller area around the nest stub. Conflicts can then be brief and intense. At 06:30 on April 25, I watched two pairs of Downies approaching a stub that looked suitable for nesting. The males began fighting immediately. Their conflict was direct, accompanied by little display, and soon over. The owning male carried on exaggerated pecking (a displacement activity) after his rival had left.

I think that displacement activity following encounters is an indication of their intensity. Woodpeckers, whether Hairy, Downy, or Pileated, can reach high levels of excitement. When an opponent leaves, the emotional level remains. The result is a burst of unrelated activity—usually exaggerated pecking and, sometimes, a quick, nervous, type of preening.

Two females sometimes contend for a male in another type of conflict. A male on April 16 kept returning to drum on a high maple while two females fought in hemlocks below. They went through the whole gamut of bill-waving, grappling in midair, giving *peep, peep, peep* alarm notes, as well as a number of floating threat displays. An occasional flight was accompanied by *check, check, check* notes. The flights seemed an intermingling of courtship and conflict. They occurred, I think, because the male was close. At one time he floated down in an irregular, bat-like flight.

The fighting was renewed two days later with the females engaging in long circular pursuits through the woods, some accompanied by *queek, queek, queek* vocalizations. A feature of the conflicts was that they took place well within the territory and in the vicinity of a nest site to which the male flew in his courtship flights.

## EARLY BREEDING BEHAVIOR

### SEARCH FOR A NEST SITE

If a territory comes to mean less as the time of nesting approaches, one might wonder at its original purpose. From watching over a number of years, I feel that stubs suitable for excavating are scarce. A pair of woodpeckers needs an extensive area in which to search. Once a stub is found, however, and a nest excavated, the large territory is no longer needed.

Woodpeckers of both sexes have a search image of the kind of place they want to excavate. This, for Downies in New Hampshire, appears to be a live tree with a trunk that has broken off, leaving a stub projecting. Suitable stubs are ones about 15 cm in diameter that have fungal decay. If a Downy finds a stub, it then seeks to get its mate to come for a look.

A female on April 24 moved over the broken trunk of a butternut, percussing here and there, as if testing the soundness or decay of the underlying wood. She drummed a few times, then tapped upon seeing her mate. He flew to the stub as she left, to inspect in his turn.

Members of pairs of Downies do not always appear friendly toward each other. One bird always leaves a stub before the other arrives and it is rare to see the two at all close. I think this hostility, if such it is, is the result of males displacing females so often in winter. The male is dominant and finds it difficult to have another Downy close by. Pairs of Downies, however, can vary.

The members of Pair A, that remained in the vicinity of their breeding territory all winter, exhibited many of the characteristic forms of courtship. The first sign I saw of a renewed pairbond was on January 11 when the two fed only 15 cm apart. When he flew, she followed. Female A was still staying in the vicinity of her mate a week later, in spite of his supplanting attacks. He flew to her in a floating courtship flight on February 4. Seemingly uncertain of his intentions, she faced him with bill pointed forward, as if to meet an attack.

The two were together from 06:50 to 07:15 two weeks later. He drummed briefly and his mate, moving upward on a possible nest stub, gave a series of loud taps, mixed with drum taps, near the top.

When Male A alighted on the dead top of a live red maple on March 11, he was displaced by his mate. Female A then preened in a leisurely fashion, a further sign that the stub had been accepted as a nest site. Female A was more dominant than is usual for female Downies. When a Hairy Woodpecker came near on March 30, both of the pair attacked, but Female A was the more aggressive and persistent.

A variety of behavior now indicated that the bond between Male A, Female A, and their nest site was close. On 30 and 31 March, the male flew from the stub with wings held at a V as he tilted from side to side in courtship flight. Later Female A preened close to the stub while Male A rested motionless not far away. Resting motionless can be a striking form of behavior, considering how active woodpeckers generally are. On April 6 the pair had a duet of drumming, and on May 2 I witnessed copulations. As also noted by Lawrence (1967), pairs of Downies that remain in or near their breeding territory in winter, may nest several weeks earlier than those that have wandered away.

Breeding seasons do not always progress as smoothly as that of Pair A. Two pairs of Downies nested successfully in a wood in 1968. I sought to follow the nesting of these pairs in another year without success. The pairs inspected every possible stub in their territories in vain. It seemed that, in young woods growing up after lumbering, there were no longer any stubs of the right type.

The male of one pair, in the absence of a nest site, used a slanting maple as a center for preening and drumming. It was there that he met his mate at dawn. There was a dead stub nearby, obviously inadequate, but on 14 May the two flew to it in courtship flight. This was the last I saw of them together. The behavior of the male changed by the following day. He was resting on his slanting maple with feathers fluffed out and head drawn in. His mate did not appear then, or on the following day when he began prolonged drummings that went on well into June when Downies in other woods were nesting quietly.

## EXCAVATION

A pair of Downies can select a site as early as mid-April, yet be in no hurry to excavate. With egg laying not beginning until the first week in May, it may be safer not to complete a cavity until it is needed. The time taken to excavate can thus vary. Pair B had selected its stub by April 16, and Male B had started a small hole. But he did not really begin to work until 13 days later.

He was working at full intensity by May 6, excavating nearly all of the three and a half hours my wife and I watched. His pecks came at rates so

19

fast as to sound like a small motor within the stub. He took little time for feeding or resting, five minutes being the limit that he stayed away. His mate came to the hole five times, as if to relieve him. But he did not come out and she left. The longest single period I noted him working was 76 minutes.

On May 7, instead of tossing sawdust from the entrance, he flew to discard a billful at a distance. This behavior, that is common to other woodpeckers, is what I consider a symbolic removal of feces, an awakening of an instinct for nest sanitation before it is needed. At another nest a male carried sawdust away ten times in 48 minutes.

Male B did not work undisturbed. From May 7 on he had to leave his cavity every hour or two to drive away either a male Yellow-bellied Sapsucker or a male Red-breasted Nuthatch, both rival hole-nesters that can use cavities built by Downies.

The excavation was completed by May 12, two weeks after Male B had begun in earnest. A change now took place. Whereas Male B had more or less monopolized the stub for some weeks and I had seen little of Female B, she now stayed by it and he stayed away. Both gave low *whinny*s or *chipper*s from time to time. Although Female B clung to the hole occasionally, I never saw her enter until May 16. With copulations going on, I supposed that she was about to lay. But a disaster intervened. On May 18 a pair of Yellow-bellied Sapsuckers appropriated the hole, making it over to suit their larger size.

The Downies were thus left without a nest at the peak of mating activities. Female B was the first to react. By afternoon she was starting holes at three different sites and by the next morning her mate was working at four others. I could hear both birds excavating at the same time. When Male B came to a stub being worked by his mate, he drove her away, then worked on the excavating himself. In spite of his seeming hostility, the two copulated five minutes later.

Male B had selected a single site by May 20 when he could get into the cavity except for his tail. Female B was still excavating one of her holes, but flew over to replace him. When he left she excavated briefly and then flew off. On her next visit she tapped and drum-tapped. In none of her visits, over the next few days, was her excavating more than token in nature. Like the tapping, however, it demonstrated that she accepted the male's choice of a stub.

Male B now worked so hard that it was difficult to see when he had time to feed. At one stretch he tossed 23 billfuls of sawdust from the entrance, worked down inside five minutes, tossed 28 more, then, after about another five minutes of work, tossed 36. His elm stub had many small conks, or fruiting bodies of fungi, indicating that it was well-decayed.

When Female B came by silently and squatted on a limb, he flew out, copulated, and returned to his work, all within 15 seconds. His display of energy, in the three days it took to complete the excavation, seemed remarkable. Egg laying began a few days later.

Although I have noted male Downies doing almost all of the excavating, as has Lawrence (1967), I have encountered a few females that did more than their mates, as noted also by Shelley (*in* Bent, 1939). Reversals of this sort reflect the flexibility of Downies. When one partner does more of a task than is usual, its mate is apt to do less, and vice versa. Females have the potential for excavating but seldom have to exercise it to any extent. This arrangement would appear to have survival advantages. It saves females from expending energy at a time when they are building reserves for egg laying.

A possible result of a female's building reserves is that she comes to have a body diameter greater than that of her mate. This would not be discernable were it not for the habit of males of making nest entrances that fit themselves. An entrance carved by a smaller male may not fit his mate. On May 16 I watched a female bow into a nest 27 times in an effort to enter, then return to try 45 more times before being able to do so. She had forced her way in five days previously, but had had to struggle vigorously, bobbing her head up and down, to get out.

### COPULATORY BEHAVIOR

I visited Pair B every day, except one, between May 6 and June 22, spending several hours a day. All of the 24 copulations witnessed in this time took place within 7 m of the nest, 17 times on a "copulation branch" that extended within .5 m of the entrance. Most of the copulations, 18 of 24, were in the morning. They took place, however, at all hours, from 10 minutes after the male emerged from roosting, until 17:40.

The greatest frequency was at time of laying. A copulation at 10:45 on May 11 was followed by a second one two minutes later and a third at 11:00. This burst of activity was exceeded on May 15 when the Downies copulated three times in 17 minutes. A copulation on the next day was followed by another in two minutes. I timed these at 14 and 10 seconds respectively, the usual range of Downy copulations. Considering that I was by the nest only a few hours a day, the total number of copulations must have been well beyond the numbers recorded.

Although copulations could be initiated by either sex, the sexes usually seemed in an equal state of readiness. Circumstances precipitating matings were the following: (*i*) Male B was alone by the nest excavating in the first days of the copulation period (6–8 May). I seldom saw Female B except when she came for copulation. If he was in the nest, she would fly to it, then to the copulation branch as he looked out. Oddly, if Male B was out of the hole when she arrived, she still flew to the nest, then to the branch, in what seemed to be a strengthening of attachment to both mate and nest. (*ii*) At the time of laying, when Female B stayed by the hole and Male B was away, he flew to the copulation branch and she to him. (*iii*) Either sex might drum in seeking copulation. Female B drummed for three minutes on May 8, then flew to the branch where she was joined by her mate. On May 16 the male

Fig. 4. Copulatory behavior of the Downy Woodpecker showing the flight and hover of the male as well as the invitation pose of the female.

spent much time idling by the nest. After 50 minutes, he drummed for several minutes. His mate arrived and a copulation followed. Vocalizations common at this period were a *chipper* or low *whinny* and a *chirr*.

A female Downy, when ready for copulation, perches crosswise or occasionally lengthwise on a horizontal limb (Fig. 4) and raises up on her legs with, as Lawrence (1967:87) described, "her tail pointing straight out, her head up and tilted backward, her . . . breast thrown out, her wings slightly dropped and motionless." The male then lands on her back in a hovering approach.

Male B was perching on the copulation branch on May 6, when his mate flew to him. He immediately moved away from her, then launched into a low, hovering, turning flight (Fig. 4). When behind and slightly below, he rose, hovering to land on her lower back. Copulation then followed, the hover preceding it having taken about two seconds. Although hovering appears to be unique for Downies, it does occur among passerines. Hinde (1954) describes it for the Greenfinch, and I have noted it repeatedly in the House Wren.

Once mounted on the back of a female, a male Downy falls gradually to the left, as he moves his tail under hers. By the time of cloacal contact, he lies along her right side, holding balance by spreading his wings. The period of contact is relatively long. Whereas in the House Wren it is only two seconds or less, I have timed Downies as ranging from 10–16 seconds. A male may mount a female as in full copulation, then both birds fall away, as if one or the other were not in readiness. I noted seven of these abortive copulations to 24 complete ones for Pair B and, in a following year, five abortive to 15 that were completed.

Copulations may extend from the start of a nest excavation until well into incubation, a period of 2–3 weeks. Pair B copulated on the third, fourth, and fifth days of incubation. Copulatory behavior was fragmentary thereafter. Male B drummed on coming by the nest on the eighth day, then alighted on the copulation branch. His mate flew to join him, then flew off. On the following day, Male B chased his mate after a similar episode.

Although infidelity has been described for many birds, I have seen it but once among woodpeckers. This was at a time when Female B disappeared for a few days; seemingly as a result of a retained egg. Another female (New Female) arrived by the afternoon of the day Female B disappeared and started an excavation of her own. Male B did not interfere. But when she came to his nest, on two occasions, he was quick to drive her away. Not long after being ousted the second time, New Female took an invitation pose and Male B hovered over her back. A copulation probably followed, but I was not in a position to see. I did see a copulation on the following day. New Female remained in position and Male B returned to hover again. She then circled his nest stub, but he would not tolerate her coming close. He not only attacked, but pursued her in a long flight. His mate, Female B, returned the next morning and I saw no more of the foreign female.

It was of note that Male B, although willing to copulate with the new female, would not tolerate her by his nest stub. Fidelity to nest was bound up with fidelity to mate, even when she was not around.

## EGG-BINDING

Egg laying can be a period of idleness for males. Male B spent the larger part of his time between May 10 and 19 within a radius of 12 m of his nest, resting, preening, driving away other hole-nesters, and copulating with his mate. This staying by the nest is important. It was in the following year, when the weather was wet and cold, that Male B, failing to stay on guard, lost his cavity to a pair of sapsuckers.

I had an unusual experience with Female B during the period of egg laying. Pair B had copulated on May 6, 7, and 8 when, at 06:30 on May 9, I found Female B clinging to bark, drooping as if about to fall. After a few minutes she ascended to an open cavity, one made by a Pileated Woodpecker, to rest at the bottom of it, with bill tucked in her feathers.

I would not have found her later if her mate had not disturbed her. She was clinging to bark as weakly as before. On my next glance, her white belly was uppermost as she fell into the swamp. There she made feeble efforts to reach a tree. With head back and having difficulties breathing, she would have drowned had I not picked her up.

I took her home where my wife and I felt a hard mass, the size of an egg, distending her abdomen. She appeared to be in spasm and made no effort to resist. Forty minutes later she was stronger and attacked my finger for the first time. Her abdomen was no longer distended, but I could find no trace of her having laid an egg. I presumed that she had either laid one and eaten it or that it had broken inside.

I now took her back to the swamp. She was barely able to flutter to a tree where she clung without moving. Although I made repeated efforts, I did not see her again until two days later. She was now in excellent condition. After further copulations, she must have laid four eggs for, on June 21, there were four fledglings in the nest.

Five years later I noticed another female, feathers fluffed and looking as if about to fall asleep, not far from her nest hole. This was at 06:38, nearly the same hour that I discovered the first female. The second female gave a feeble drum every five minutes or so. Her mate came three times as if trying to copulate, but she moved away. On the following morning she looked alert and unaffected.

How often do birds suffer from egg-binding? I have noted an egg laying lethargy for a flicker, a Common Grackle, and a handraised White-breasted Nuthatch that laid eggs in an aviary in two successive years. But I have been able to find few accounts in the literature. One is given by William Harvey (1654:57), the discoverer of the circulation of the blood. Writing of a parrot that had long enjoyed the best of health, he wrote that it fell sick not long after being caressed and died after repeated convulsions. Harvey had presumed the bird a male. But said he, "on making a post-mortem . . . I found an almost complete egg in its oviduct, . . ."

## NESTING

### INCUBATION

May 22 was the first day I noticed that one or the other of Pair A was in the nest nearly all of the time. Male A had the most drive. His sessions of incubating were two to three times longer than those of his mate. On May 23 he did not come out when she came to relieve him, even though he had been incubating 62 minutes. Another indication of his zest were his fluttering courtship flights. He came to the hole in this manner on four of 12 times he changed with Female A. In my 12 hours of watching, Male A stayed at the nest 60 and his mate 40 percent of the time. Both were nearly 100 percent attentive while on the job.

With Pair E, Male E was in charge of the nest 53 and his mate 42 percent of the 16 hours I watched. But being in charge, what I call a session or the time between changeovers, can be different from actual attentiveness. Thus

Female E spent only 57.4 percent of her time at the nest actually incubating. She was extremely restless for the first few days, entering, putting her head out, flying to forage in trees nearby, then re-entering to stay another 2–10 minutes. Out of a total of 80 minutes one morning, she spent only 15 on the eggs.

Male E, in contrast, spent most of his time (79.4 percent) incubating. His attentiveness might have been higher had it not been for his chasing away other hole-nesters that included flickers, a pair of Hairies, and a male White-breasted Nuthatch.

Heinroth (1958:51) remarks that woodpeckers are "not particularly fond of their mates." Downies are the only ones I have wondered about. When the two of Pair A changed, the incoming partner looked into the hole, then withdrew well to the side, as if avoiding contact when its mate came out. But situations vary. With some pairs a mate coming out may even brush against its partner waiting to enter. On one occasion, both members of Pair B entered their nest at the same time.

Downies frequently make a low *chirr* when changing over. The note sounds much the same as the *chrr* heard in conflicts. It was only after hearing the notes repeatedly in the aviary that I found the *chirr* to be a pleasanter and less harsh sound than the *chrr*.

## Care and Feeding of Young

I could see that incubation ended after 11 days when Female A arrived with prey and Male A left carrying a small fecal sac. Brooding, with each parent staying on the nest until relieved, continued for four days. It ceased on the morning of the fifth, in spite of the weather being cool with frosts at night. The length of brooding varies among pairs. When there are four nestlings, as in Nest A, they may warm each other by huddling together. Pair E, with only a single young one, brooded it for 10 days.

In 39 of 41 observations I found parent Downy Woodpeckers gleaning when foraging for their young. A frequent practice was to start at the base of a tree, move rapidly up into the branches, then drop to the base of another. On some days almost any surface seemed to do. Although attracted to clusters of leaves and flowers in crowns of white ash and sugar maples, the Downies also gleaned along dead trees. An impression was of constant hurry. The speed with which a Downy can fill its bill is remarkable. I was sitting below Nest A on June 21 when Male A appeared. He was close and I could see that his bill was empty. In less than a minute he had it stuffed with small grubs from the terminal branchlets of a bush and was flying to the nest.

Males do the larger part of nest sanitation. Of six nests followed, the females removed 17 to 26 percent of the fecal sacs in three nests and none in the others. Removal of a sac can be a delicate operation. When Female A came from the hole, she emerged slowly, without wriggling, then flew off with shallow wing beats as if afraid the sac might break before being dropped. Males can have bursts of nest cleaning, removing a number of sacs in a short time.

One sometimes hears Downies pecking inside their nests. This excavating seldom goes on for more than a few minutes and seems to provide sawdust for nest cleaning. Some fecal sacs are covered with it.

Male and female Downies feed their young about equally. Nest A was exceptional in that Male A made 69 percent of the 147 visits made by the pair and Female A only 31. The number of feeding visits per hour varied from six to 22. Considering all pairs of Downies observed (n = 6), the males, in addition to spending nights on the nests, did by far the larger share of incubating and nest sanitation, the females sharing the tasks of brooding and feeding nestlings more equally.

A difficulty at some Downy nests is that parents come and go so fast that it is hard to identify the sex. It is here that their manner of feeding their young, by hanging downward with undersides of tails visible within entrances, can be of help. As shown in Figure 5, the patterns of black and white of undertail feathers vary enough among individuals to furnish markers.

## BEHAVIOR OF NESTLINGS

I took four young from a nest on May 23 to raise by hand. With pin feathers emerging and eyes slightly opened, I estimated that they were 11 days of age. They remained quiet and cowered down until I shielded them from the light. Their heads and necks then shot up. Each had fleshy knobs at the basal ends of its lower mandibles and gaped when these were stroked. My wife and I fed our captives bits of raw chicken, wetted to take away the stickiness, half meal worms, and bread soaked in a vitamin mixture, using toothpicks for handling.

The nestlings struck at each other in eagerness to get food. Hadow (1976) described nestlings as making rasping notes when gaping. I do not know why we did not hear more of this. Once fed and shut in a darkened cabinet, our nestlings made pleasant sounds that reminded us of spring peepers or terns fishing in the distance.

FIG. 5.   Individuality in undertail markings of Downy Woodpeckers.

## DOWNY WOODPECKER

### Fledging

Neither parent at Nest A fed the young for an hour and a half on June 21, the twentieth day after hatching. It was not until about 08:00 that Female A arrived with a billful of prey. She alighted to the side and below the hole to avoid being struck by a fledgling who was leaning out and jabbing at her. Female A's position forced the fledgling to lean well out and down. When she flew, the young one, as if eager for more, flew after her. Twelve minutes later a second young one left in a similar manner. Male A arrived not long afterward. It was almost like clockwork the way a third fledgling followed him. I have not seen Hairies or other woodpeckers leave a nest in such close order. Possibly the long stretch of no feeding had increased the readiness of the young to leave.

A single fledgling remained. Male A fed it four times in 15 minutes on the following morning before it left. By making sketches of head patterns of the young as they looked out of the entrance on previous days, my wife and I had surmised that there were four nestlings, the number that were subsequently fledged.

### Postnesting

### Behavior of Juveniles

Fledgling Downy and Hairy Woodpeckers, instead of fluttering their wings and begging as many juvenile birds do, are apt to attack their parents. This is at the end of nesting when a parent has to stay low and to the side of an entrance to avoid being struck. Fledglings free of a nest can be even more aggressive. When a male Downy came to feed a juvenile, the latter attacked. This was done so vigorously that the male had to back away three times. The juvenile even held its wings out in threat. When the male flew, the young one followed.

On another occasion, a male, gleaning rapidly through trees and bushes, fed a juvenile twice in five minutes. After the last feeding, the juvenile flew at its parent as if not getting enough. Smith's (1980) term "demand behavior" is a good one for fledgling Downies.

Methods of feeding can vary. The male fed the juvenile by turning his head so that the opened bills of the two interlocked. This is the type of feeding observable between parents and well-grown nestlings. At a feeder, a fledgling took suet by grabbing its mother's entire bill into its own.

While it is difficult to keep track of parents and juveniles away from nests in wooded country, Downies appear to feed their young for from two and a half to three weeks after nest-leaving. The best place I have found to watch after this time has been by beaver ponds. In middle and late July I found a family staying in the vicinity of the nest the young had left early in June. The mother was going up the trunk of a paper birch on July 13, when a juvenile flew over, landed, and backed down to within a meter of her. She flew at it, driving it away. But the juvenile was like a leech. Hardly had the mother started to feed again, then the juvenile returned. This time the mother did a bill-waving dance. The juvenile, seemingly undisturbed, stayed where it was. She then drove at it again. The young one was so persistent that it was hard to see how the mother got time to feed. The last I saw of the two was the mother chasing her young one in a fast, circular pursuit through the trees.

Juveniles were still around in a following week but were no longer pestering their parents. They idled about, exploring holes and crevices, giving an occasional drum, or playing dodgeball by swinging under a branch, with wings out, when a chickadee came by. They also exhibited curiosity. I was sitting on top of a beaver lodge when a juvenile came within less than two meters to look down at me, a phenomenon that has happened to me several times.

### RECRUDESCENCE OF BREEDING BEHAVIOR

Many woodpeckers experience a recrudescence of breeding behavior at the end of nesting. Except for a courtship flight by one male, I have seen little of this among Downies. But I may have looked too early. When an intruding female came close to the old nest hole of Pair A in late July, Female A did a bill-waving dance. Her mate, Male A, then intervened with the same display, driving the intruder away, one of the few occasions when I have seen a male in conflict with a female.

At a second beaver pond a male did much drumming at the end of July, as much as in early spring. When another male came to his drum stub, he spread his tail and waved his bill. What I took to be his mate appeared shortly afterward. He then floated down to an old, used woodpecker hole in courtship flight and tapped. But instead of his mate coming, the second male interfered. This triangular contest continued into August.

### HAZARDS OF HOLE-NESTING

Hole-nesting birds form a special category. According to Nice (1957) they have a 65 percent chance of their eggs resulting in fledglings compared to only 43 percent for open-nesters. But only a minority of passerines have evolved the habit. A reason, according to von Haartman (1968:3) is that the ecologic niche is saturated. It is impossible for a new species to move in. "Probably with no other birds," continues von Haartman, "will the competition for breeding places be so severe as in hole-nesting birds." A robin or other passerine can find many sites for building in trees and bushes, but a hole-nester may have to search a long time to find a suitable hole.

One might consider woodpeckers different. They, after all, excavate their own holes. But this does not make the problem easier. Trees or stubs suitable for excavating are hard to find. Of the species that I have studied in Maryland and New Hampshire, none have been able to excavate a cavity in a live tree with sound heartwood. The requirements for each species are exacting and even if a pair excavates a cavity of the kind it wants, there is no insurance that it can hold on to it. A pair of Downies, as already described, had their newly finished cavity taken away by a pair of sapsuckers. Hole-nesters chased away by Downies while I was watching included Hairy and Red-bellied Woodpeckers, flickers, Red-breasted and White-breasted Nuthatches, Black-capped Chickadees, starlings, Eastern Bluebirds, House Sparrows, and once a Brown Creeper.

Of all these, starlings are a particular menace. They are relentless in dispossessing woodpeckers such as flickers and Hairies. It would seem that Downies might be safe, considering that their nest entrances are too small for starlings to enter. But starlings may put their heads into Downy nests and keep returning, in spite of persistent efforts of the Downies to drive them away. Howell (1943) watched starlings that broke up nestings of a pair of Downies in three successive years by jabbing through the entrance and wounding the young. I once opened a Downy nest to find that all of the young were maimed. Of the two smallest, one had one wing half the size of the other, and the other, a shriveling of both wings, one of which was only a well-healed knob. The injuries, I presumed, were done when the nestlings were still naked. While I had no way of knowing whether starlings were responsible, it seemed that the injuries must have been the result of some bird striking in with its bill.

## THREE- vs. FOUR-WEEK NESTLING PERIOD

The nestling period of Downies is of three weeks duration while those of other woodpeckers with which they are sympatric, the Hairy, Pileated, flicker, and sapsucker, are from four to 4+ weeks. One might say that this is a matter of Downies being able to develop faster because they are smaller. But this is unlikely as is shown by four European woodpeckers of the same genus. Of these, three, the Lesser, the Middle, and the Great Spotted Woodpecker all have a three-week nestling period, even though the Great Spotted is of the same approximate size as the Hairy. Furthermore, if size made a difference, why should the Pileated and its European counterpart, the Black Woodpecker, have the same four-week nestling period as the smaller Hairy and sapsucker? In attempting to answer this question it might be well to consider, first, why woodpeckers have nestling periods that are longer than those of many open-nesters. A probable reason is that holes are relatively safe places in which to nest. With little selection pressure to get away, nestlings can become more mature and better able to look after themselves.

A point to make is that although holes are relatively safe from predators, some types of cavities are safer than others. Woodpeckers with stronger bills can build nests in tough living trees that have heartrot at the center. Species building nests of this type are the Hairy, the Red-cockaded and the White-backed Woodpeckers, and the Yellow-bellied Sapsucker. All of these have four-week nestling periods.

Seemingly less secure nests, in terms of susceptibility to wind damage or to predators chewing their way in, are ones built in decaying wood by species with weaker bills. These, that include the Lesser, Middle, and Great Spotted Woodpecker of Europe, as well as the Downy, all have three-week nestling periods.

An objection is that Hairy Woodpeckers and sapsuckers sometimes nest in dead, decaying stubs. But from years of watching I believe that they do this by necessity. There are often not enough trees large enough, of the kind they want, in present-day forests. As far as the White-backed Woodpecker goes, I hazard a guess that the same situation holds. Ruge and Weber (1974) describe this species as having the strongest bill of all the European species of *Picoides*. It, like the Hairy, would not nest in a completely decayed stub unless it had to.

A further point regarding the safety of nests is that a small woodpecker, having a relatively weak bill, will be less able to defend itself against predators. As described later on, a Hairy, even though nesting in a well-decayed birch, was able to defend its nest against a raccoon. It seems doubtful if a Downy could have survived under the circumstances.

Hadow's (1976) study of Downies is one of the few ever made of the growth and development of nestling woodpeckers. In reply to Lack's (1968) hypothesis that woodpeckers hatch in a relatively underdeveloped state compared to passerines in open nests, he points out the lack of evidence. What actually happens is differential development. Young Downies have a rapid development of leg parts, balance, and the strength needed to reach up and take feedings from a parent coming down the nest cavity in a vertical position. These developments come at the expense of feathers and sense organs that, in a dark and insulated nest, are not needed initially. It takes more strength, Hadow points out, to cling to a vertical surface and to climb, then to perch. Hole-nesting woodpeckers, therefore, have different priorities than open-nesting passerines.

## METHODS OF COMMUNICATION

### VOCALIZATIONS

*Whinny.*—A *chick, chick, chick, chrr-rr-rr* given only once without repetition. When given as mild *chipper* at the height of courtship, it appears to be pair-bonding. At other times, when delivered as a loud sputter, it expresses dominance.

*Chip or kick.*—This is a common expression of excitement from any cause. Parent Downies gave many *chip*s when I stood below their recently emerged fledglings. Greater alarm is expressed by a shrill, whistle-like *peep-peep-peep*.

*Chirr.*—An intimate greeting exchanged by members of a pair at times of changeovers by a nest.

*Chrr.*—A harsh note heard in conflict that can be difficult to distinguish from the *chirr* at a distance.

*Check, check, check, check.*—A rapid series of notes that accompany courtship flights. At higher intensity the call sounds like *queek, queek, queek, queek, queek.*

*Vocalizations of nestlings.*—Musical twitters when settling down after being fed. A harsh rasp when hungry and gaping (Hadow, 1976).

### Drumming and Tapping

*Drumming.*—The rate and intensity of drumming varies with circumstances. It usually comes in bursts of 1.5 seconds, delivered at rates of nine to 14 bursts a minute, but can consist of as many as 24 bursts. There is little that is stereotyped about the drumming of Downies. It varies in rate with a bird's emotional intensity and in carrying power with the type of substrate, e.g., whether this is a hollow place, one of solid hardwood, or an indifferent one of no particular resonance. Both sexes drum, with females sometimes drumming as much or more than males. The total amount varies with circumstances. A pair that has found a nest site early, drums relatively little, while a pair in woods deficient in suitable stubs, drums a great deal. Among types of drumming distinguishable in relation to circumstances are the following:

a. Territorial. Drumming from a high place proclaims territory in the early breeding season. It can, as a side effect, attract rival males and precipitate conflicts.

b. Dawn rendezvous. The efforts of a Downy to locate its mate at the start of a day can be prolonged, especially where roost holes are far apart.

c. Mate location. This usually consists of only a few bursts, needed when members of a pair are feeding separately over a wide area.

d. Displacement or demonstrative. Downies, like Hairies, often drum in the presence of an intruder, conspecific or otherwise. The drumming is usually done wherever the woodpecker happens to be. After bouts of intense conflict, a Downy may drum as a displacement activity, a working off of high emotion.

e. Contentment. When Downy Woodpeckers are under no pressure to find a nest stub, either because it is early in the season or because they have already found one, one or the other of the pair, but particularly the female, may rest in the sun on some high dead limb, preening in a prolonged, leisurely fashion and drumming in pauses in between. Such activities may promote the pairbond in relation to a particular locality.

f. Duetting. There are two kinds of answering drumming. One promotes the pairbond. When things are going well, each bird drums, in unhurried fashion, in response to the drumming of the other. Another kind of duetting is the tug-of-war type. When relations between members of a pair are disturbed, the male preferring one nest stub and the female another, each drums in an effort to entice its mate to inspect the site. Drumming can then be prolonged and the rate expressive of the intensity of the disagreement.

g. Whisper. When a nest excavation is on its way to completion, the members of a pair may respond to each other with low, brief drumming, not always a matter of duetting. A female near a completed nest cavity may drum softly wherever she happens to be.

h. Copulatory. A Downy of either sex, but chiefly the male, may drum when ready for copulation.

Downies, like other woodpeckers, have drum trees (such as the hardwood at the top of a dead maple) of special resonance. Here Downy may ascend, trying successive spots with a few bursts on each, extracting a variety of sounds, some flat, some deep, others loud and sharp, the effect being like playing a xylophone.

*Tapping.*—Either member of a pair may try to attract the other to a potential nest site by drumming, tapping, or drum-tapping. In drumming the individual blows of the bill come too fast to be detectable by the unaided ear. In tapping, they come at a slow, detectable rate of about three per second, in bursts of nine to 10 taps. Drum-tapping is between the other two in sound.

## Displays

*Crest-raising.*—This may be performed alone or in association with other displays. It is expressive of excitement from any cause.

*Bill-waving dance.*—Two Downies of the same sex jerk heads, bills, and bodies from side to side while making starting motions with their wings and fanning their tails, when facing each other in territorial conflicts. The display can also be used against unrelated birds.

*Full wing-threat display.*—One Downy in conflict with another, may raise its wings outstretched, above its back and fan its tail, as if trying to appear as large as possible.

*Wing ruffle.*—Downies usually fly silently, but can fly with a loud ruffle noise expressive of excitement.

*Frozen pose.*—In response to some immediate danger or threat, whether another Downy or a passing hawk, a Downy may flatten itself against a trunk or limb with bill pointed forward, remaining as if frozen.

*Courtship flight.*—This may be performed by either member of a pair. It ranges from a floating on outstretched wings to a slow, fluttering, bat-like flight. The flight is accompanied at times by a *check, check, check,* or, at higher intensity, *queek, queek, queek* vocalizations.

*Resting motionless.*—One or both of a nesting pair may rest motionless for minutes at a time in the presence of its mate when an excavation is nearing completion. The pose is a sign that things are progressing and that the pair-bond is close.

Downy and Hairy Woodpeckers have a number of comparable vocalizations including the *whinny,* the *kick,* and the *jeek* or *queek* given in series. The displays of the two species are nearly identical. It is virtually impossible, on some occasions, to distinguish the drumming or the tapping of the two species.

## Literature Cited

BENT, A. C. 1939. Life histories of North American woodpeckers. Bull. U.S. Nat'l Mus., **174**: 1–322.

HAARTMAN, L. VON. 1968. The evolution of resident versus migratory habit in birds. Some observations. Ornis Fenn., **45**: 1–7.

HADOW, H. H. 1976. Growth and development of nestling Downy Woodpeckers. No. Amer. Bird Bander, **1**: 155–164.

HARVEY, W. 1651. Exercitationes de generatione animalium. Transl. by R. Willis (1847). London.

HEINROTH, O., AND K. HEINROTH. 1958. The Birds. Univ. Mich. Press, Ann Arbor. 181 p.

HINDE, R. A. 1954. The courtship and copulation of the Greenfinch (*Chloris chloris*). Behaviour, **7**: 207–232.

HOWELL, A. B. 1943. Starlings and woodpeckers. Auk, **60**: 90–91.

HUBBARD, H. G., AND T. PERGUNDE. 1898. A new coccid on birch. Bull. U.S. Dept. Agric., Div. Entomol., **18**: 13–26.

JACKSON, J. A. 1970. A quantitative study of the foraging ecology of Downy Woodpeckers. Ecology, **51**: 318–323.

KILHAM, L. 1961. Downy Woodpeckers scaling bark on diseased elms. Wilson Bull., **73**: 89.

——. 1962. Reproductive behavior of Downy Woodpeckers. Condor, **64**: 126–133.

——. 1970. Feeding behavior of Downy Woodpeckers. I. Preference for paper birches and sexual differences. Auk, **87**: 544–556.

——. 1972. Retention of egg in a wild Downy Woodpecker. Wilson Bull., **84**: 493–494.

——. 1974a. Copulatory behavior of Downy Woodpeckers. Wilson Bull., **86**: 23–34.

——. 1974b. Early breeding season behavior of Downy Woodpeckers. Wilson Bull., **86**: 407–418.

——. 1974c. Play in Hairy, Downy, and other woodpeckers. Wilson Bull., **86**: 35–42.

——. 1979. Three-week vs 4-week nestling periods in *Picoides* and other woodpeckers. Wilson Bull., **91**: 335–338.

LACK, D. 1968. Ecological adaptations for breeding in birds. Methuen & Co., London. 409 p.

LAWRENCE, L. DE K. 1967. A comparative life-history study of four species of woodpeckers. Ornith. Monogr. (Amer. Ornith. Union), no. 5, 156 p.

LIGON, J. D. 1968. Sexual differences in foraging behavior in two species of *Dendrocopos* woodpeckers. Auk, **85**: 203–215.

MORSE, D. H. 1970. Ecological aspects of some mixed-species foraging flocks of birds. Ecol. Monogr., **40**: 119–168.

NICE, M. M. 1957. Nesting success in altricial birds. Auk, **74**: 305–321.

RUGE, K., AND W. WEBER 1974. Biotopwahl und Nahrungserwerb beim Weissruckenspecht (*Dendrocopos leucotos*) in den Alpen. Vogelwelt, **95**: 138–147.

SELANDER, R. K., 1966. Sexual dimorphism and differential niche utilization in birds. Condor, **68**: 43–151.

SMITH, S. M. 1980. Demand behavior: a new interpretation of courtship feeding. Condor, **82**: 291–295.

THOREAU, H. D. 1960. H. D. Thoreau: A writer's journal. (L. Stapleton, ed.) Dover Publ., New York.

WING, L. 1946. Species association in winter flocks. Auk, **63**: 507–510.

# 3

# HAIRY WOODPECKER

Hairy Woodpeckers, with their relatively longer bills, are far from being only a larger edition of Downies. Although often found in the same woods, the two differ in feeding habits, courtship, and nesting. No bird seems sharper or more alert in the winter than a Hairy Woodpecker. They are relatively tame in northern forests and make an excellent bird for year around study. The same cannot be said for the southern Hairy. I have found them shyer, less common, and far more difficult.

## FEEDING BEHAVIOR

### SEXUAL DIFFERENCES

Woodpeckers in general are not attracted to young, healthy woods. They prefer mature ones, such as harbor wood-boring larvae in dead and dying limbs. Sometimes wind storms or tree diseases provide similar situations. This is eminently true of the Dutch elm disease which, however unfortunate for man, has been a boon to woodpeckers. Their benefactor is the elm bark beetle (*Scolytus multistriatus*), a few millimeters long invader that was harmless until it joined up with the fungus *Ceratocystis ulmi*. The team of beetle plus fungus then set out on a joint career that, in its wake, has provided woodpeckers with larvae on which to feed as well as a supply of stubs for nesting, a supply that has lasted for many years.

All this turned out providential for me, 25 years ago, when I set out to learn what I could about woodpeckers. It was the feeding of Downies that first caught my attention. Diseased elms are recognizable by the engraving of multi-branching tunnels that the beetles provide for their eggs and larvae. Between 1956 and 1961, while living in Maryland, I sometimes noted as many as four Downies feeding on a single elm. Wherever the woodpeckers were working, they chipped off outer layers, revealing a bright, fawn-colored, inner bark.

When we moved to New Hampshire in 1961, I became interested in studying the breeding, feeding and other habits of Hairy Woodpeckers. It was not long before I found that the more northern elms, which are tunneled by the larger American elm beetle (*Hylorgopinus rufipes*), were an optimal place to find them. I kept records of what I saw and a remarkable fact soon emerged. In an initial study from August through November, I found that 19 of 20 Hairy Woodpeckers feeding on diseased elms were females. The trees were not visited much by the woodpeckers in December and January, but they were coming to them again in February and from then, through April, when nesting began, I found females on 31 occasions and males on only two.

The female Hairies were energetic when working on elms. They pecked, hewed, struck glancing blows, and seized bits of bark in their bills in an almost furious manner. This was all at a faster, less interrupted pace, than was usual on other trees. The tempo might be maintained for as long as half an hour. During this time, a female progressed slowly along a limb, leaving it light brown in color due to an almost uniform removal of outer bark.

When male Hairies fed on elms, as they did on two occasions, their feeding was never as vigorous or prolonged. A male displaced his mate, on February 8, from a place where she had been working. He pecked at the light brown bark for several minutes, then flew away, apparently uninterested.

On April 4, I found a pair of Hairies working together on an elm. As the two were only 2 m apart, I had an opportunity to compare their feeding behavior. The female progressed rapidly as she percussed and scaled strips of bark. The sound of her activities was fast and regular. Her mate, in contrast, gave deliberate blows, each accompanied by a swing of the head. He progressed only 15 cm up the trunk in 15 minutes before flying away. It was noteworthy that he and his mate had used different patterns of feeding when under essentially the same conditions. It appeared as if he, by habit or innate behavior, had been unable to work on the elm in the effective manner of his mate. This might explain why males seldom came to the elms. Unable to work effectively, they moved to trees where their methods uncovered more food with less effort.

My observations on Hairies were made almost entirely in woods away from houses and feeding stations, in an effort to have conditions as natural as possible. In covering these wilder areas I found that the situations noted on elms obtained for other trees. Thus, of 24 observations on white pines, 23 were of females and only one of a male. The feeding was of several types. In three instances the females sought prey by peering and poking as they moved up the rough bark of field-grown pine. In the others, the females knocked off bark with glancing blows from pines that were dying. When I found males feeding, they were usually excavating the dead trunks or limbs of mature aspens, black cherries, red oaks, or maples.

The Hairies were especially interesting to watch following pair formation in January. They then fed through the woods together. The females percussed, pecked, poked, or scaled bark to reach their prey in 87.7 percent of observations and excavated or dug more deeply into wood in only 12.3 percent. The males came out just the reverse.

The male's preference for excavating leads him, at times, to uncover relatively large prey. I watched one male, working on a well-rotted birch, pull out a larva so large that he was unable to swallow it on a first attempt. He made no effort to dismember it. He just kept trying to force his prize down. When he finally succeeded, he remained motionless for some minutes. With eyes closed, he looked as if the immediate effects of swallowing so much in one gulp was anything but comforting.

On June 5 a male flew to his nest with a grub 5 cm long and 1.3 cm wide. He tried to poke it down the throat of an awaiting young one, but without success. The larva may well have been that of the sugar maple borer, *Glycobius speciosus*. The male next flew to the woods. He soon returned, still carrying the grub and made a second attempt. More tries followed, interspersed with efforts to lodge the larva in crevices and to shake it, as if into smaller pieces. He was finally able to force the grub into the youngster on a fifth attempt. I was struck again by how ineffective a Hairy is in efforts to handle large prey. It has none of the talents of Red-headed Woodpeckers that know how to put insects in an anvil and knock them to pieces.

There are resemblances between the smaller excavations of Pileated Woodpeckers and the larger ones of Hairies. This is especially so when a Hairy has been working in soft wood. I located a male on November 17 by the blows he was making on a dead swamp poplar. He would loosen a chip in vigorous fashion, seize it in his bill, then toss it away. Some of the chips were 5 cm or more in length. The result was a sizeable hole that I might have mistaken for the workings of a Pileated had I come by at a later time.

Hairies occasionally enter bathtub-like excavations made by the larger woodpeckers. It gives them a chance to feed more deeply in some trees than they could on their own. A male on March 16 flew to the excavation of a Pileated that was about 13 cm wide and 10 cm deep. After tossing out a few chips, he enlarged the hole with blows of his own, making feeding motions as if finding prey. He may have been finding larvae of the pigeon horntail (*Tremex columba*). Whatever his prey, the Hairy did not feel much at ease. He came out several times as if fearing that the Pileated might return. Maxson and Maxson have recently (1981) described other relations between Hairies and Pileateds.

## SURVIVAL VALUES OF SEXUAL DIFFERENCES

One may ask why there should be sexual differences in feeding behavior. Of what advantage are they to Hairy Woodpeckers? I think that they enable them to exploit the resources of a particular piece of woodland more effectively. The male's habit of excavating for larvae deep in wood taps a food supply from dead limbs and trunks. No environments, however, are completely stable. Trees weakened by wind or disease lead to proliferation of bark beetles, and the female, the opportunist of a pair, is able to take advantage of these.

Another benefit, I feel, is a lessening of competition between the members of a pair. Male Hairies, like the males of other woodpeckers, dominate their mates by supplanting them when feeding. They may have less opportunity to dominate when the feeding habits of the two are different, the lessened competition serving to promote the pairbond and with it, a greater degree of breeding success.

A remarkable thing I learned about Hairies, after making my observations, was that there is a 10 percent difference in bill length between males and females (Selander, 1965). This almost puts them, in regard to sexual dimorphism, in a class with the extinct Huias of New Zealand. Males of these birds had shorter, straighter bills, good for digging into decaying wood while females had longer, curved ones, better for extracting prey.

## Roosting

### New Hampshire

It is not always easy to find something to watch in bird behavior the year around. Roosting fits in well with winter, for it is in the darkest days of the year, when days are shortest, that it is easiest to be out in the woods at dawn and dusk. My watchings of Hairies began on the same slope where I watched Downies. Two Hairies roosted there. I could watch both of their holes, as well as that of a Downy, from the same spot. This was a boon, for it increased my chances of having something to watch, even on mornings when little was going on.

I always keep a record of head markings of Hairies by means of sketches (Fig. 6). As with Downies, I have never found two with the same pattern of black and white, or of red in the case of males. Nature has thus provided Hairies with natural markers, ones that can be of aid in studying behavior.

I followed the Hairies for five weeks between December 11 and January 15. Times of going to roost varied between 15:25 and 16:40, a difference of over an hour, and of emerging, from 07:20 to 07:35, a difference of 15 minutes. The Hairies were thus more variable about retiring than getting up in the morning. What led them to go to roost was not always clear. It did not seem to be solely a matter of light. Some of the earliest roostings were on bright sunny days. The male even entered his roost at 15:38 on January 8 when sun was shining into it. He made *speak* notes, then swung out. I realized that I was standing too close. When I moved away, he re-entered and remained inside. On January 22 I saw the female enter her hole at 15:25 when a male was near. I felt she was entering to protect it, in case the male had ideas of taking it over.

A question with Hairies, as with Downies, is how long they roost on the shortest days of the year. On December 22 I found that the female retired at 15:52 and did not get up until 07:35 the next morning, a total of 15 hours and 26 minutes. The female Hairy thus spent about the same amount of

## MALES        FEMALES

FIG. 6. Variations in the black and white markings on the heads of four Hairy Woodpeckers, which aided in recognition of individuals. The Male H and Female H are represented by the two central figures.

time as the female Downy on the same night. It is possible that male Hairies are more efficient at finding food in winter than either Downies or female Hairies. If this is so, it might account for their roosting for a longer time, as I think is generally the case. On January 16 a male roosted for three minutes short of 16 hours. This meant a working day of close to eight hours, the shortest that I have noted for any species of woodpecker.

The Hairy Woodpeckers nearly always entered their holes directly. Once they had popped inside, I saw no more of them. Coming out the next morning was another matter. The first I saw of a Hairy in dim light, before dawn, was the white markings of its head. The woodpecker dropped out of sight, bobbed up, put its bill out, then withdrew. Two to 15 minutes of these bobbings often went on before the bird could make up its mind to come out.

The activities of Hairies on emerging, varied. On some mornings they ascended a series of trees, getting higher on each before flying off. On others, they appeared in no hurry. They pecked here and there, preened, and sometimes engaged in conflicts. The female flew over to have a look at the male's roost on December 25. He hastily re-entered and when she looked in, he struck at her. She jumped back, then returned for two more looks, the male striking as before. He was not tolerating intrusions, even from her.

Conflicts over a roost hole are territorial and do not mean per se that a male and female are hostile to each other. I supposed that the two were a pair. In January, however, I noted a second male. From the courtship that went on between him and the female, as well as the attacks he made on the first male, it was soon apparent that he was the actual mate. The first male was thus an intruder, roosting in the territory of a mated pair.

I followed the male of the pair for several years. In a second one he and his mate nested in an aspen with a rotten center. He later roosted in the hole until October, when a squirrel enlarged the entrance and took over. I did not locate him again until December. This time he was back on the wooded slope in a stub with many rotten holes. I was surprised, because male Hairies usually roost in sound holes. But the male, I found, was only using the stub temporarily. He had started an excavation in a sounder stub and was looking out from it at 07:40 on December 16. Instead of being disturbed by my being close, he simply pulled back to resume excavating. I watched as he appeared at the entrance intermittently, to toss out from 30 to 40 billfuls of sawdust. He finally flew out at 08:10.

The male roosted in the hole on December 21 and 22 but on the 23rd I found him roosting elsewhere. What had happened? There had been a thaw accompanied by a heavy rain. I believe that the birch stub, solid enough when it was frozen, had let in rain when it thawed. By December 30, with the return of cold weather, the male returned. I now watched him until February when he disappeared.

I generally noted that Black-capped Chickadees and White-breasted Nuthatches became active on winter mornings earlier than Hairies or Downies.

I was interested, therefore, to read of Hinde's (1952) observations on European counterparts of some of these birds. Hinde watched the roosting of four of them—the Great Spotted Woodpecker, comparable to our Hairy; the European Nuthatch; the Great Tit; and the smaller Blue Tit. What he found was (i) that the length of a day's activities increased with a decrease in body size, that is the Great Spotted Woodpecker went to roost first and the Blue Tit last; (ii) that all four emerged at dawn at a lower light intensity than that at which they went to roost in the evening; and (iii) that in all the species, as I have noted with American woodpeckers, roosting times were more variable than arising times.

## SURVIVAL VALUES OF ROOSTING IN CAVITIES

What determines when a woodpecker goes to roost? Undoubtedly a variety of factors. One relates to the need of Hairies and Downies of an entrance and cavity that fit their body size. They excavate their own holes and each represents an investment of time and energy. But there is always the danger that some competitor, a squirrel or other hole-nesting bird, will get to the hole first. Hence the wisdom of occupying a roost early before some competitor takes it over.

Von Haartman (1968) has pointed out that a large number of the birds resident the year around in colder climates are hole-nesters. This is presumably because they also roost in holes. Roost holes offer special advantages. One is insulation against cold. Kendeigh (1961) has shown that at an ambient temperature of $-8°$ C the temperature inside a nest box can be 6.2° C higher than outside. This inside temperature might be even higher for a woodpecker, say a Hairy, roosting in a hole fitting its body size, especially when its contour feathers are fluffed out and its head is turned back into its scapulars. The surrounding wood gives insulation as well as shelter from the wind. As stated by Kendeigh (p. 145) "the amount of energy . . . conserved may make the difference between survival and death during periods of extreme weather during winter. Likewise, roosting in cavities may enable a species to occur farther north during winter than it otherwise would."

The most convenient thing that I have found about roosting is that it enables me to go into the woods and find the woodpeckers I am studying in a predictable fashion. Just wait until an hour after sunrise and the chances of locating a Hairy or Downy in a reasonable time can be slim. These birds move over large areas in winter and one can easily come back empty-handed in places like New Hampshire. But, in taking the trouble to be by a roost hole at dawn, I have had some of the best of birdwatching. It is in the first half hour of day that woodpeckers can be most active in foraging, courtship, play, and other aspects of their behavior.

# HAIRY WOODPECKER

## Conflicts and Territory

### Males in Early Spring

Some of the most varied conflicts that I have witnessed among woodpeckers have been between male Hairies in winter in Lyme. I had followed the activities of Pairs A and B in a previous year; with the exception of Male A. Female A had lost her mate of the year before and had acquired a new one. The newness of Male A and his unfamiliarity with both mate and territory, may have accounted for his poor showing at first. He fled on January 31 when Male B first appeared. But within a month he had become a match for Male B, as was seen in a conflict that lasted for an hour on February 28. Events began when Male B arrived at 07:00. Female A was alone. She made sharp *speak*s as if nervous, but did not attack. Her mate, Male A, was drumming 200 m away. Bill-waving dances began when he arrived at 07:25. The two males resembled puppets operated by strings as they faced each other, jerking their heads and half-starting their wings. Bursts of dancing lasted for several minutes. The two then rested, bills pointed forward until another round began.

A renewal of the conflict was precipitated when one of the females came closer. Male B then floated to another perch on outstretched wings, followed by his opponent. A common tactic was for one male to get below the other on a tree trunk. The upper male then swooped as the latter evaded by swinging around with his wings out. Such maneuvers brought the two close to the ground. The two persisted until signs of fatigue began to appear, i.e., the pauses were longer and there was more flying from tree to tree.

The four Hairies returned to the same area on successive mornings. As the zone (Fig. 7) straddled a dirt road, I had no trouble watching. Activities, however, tapered off in March. On March 2 the meeting lasted for only 20 minutes. Male A had now come into his own. He swooped repeatedly at Male B. But most of the time the two males just rested motionless. Female B, in one pause, flew toward her mate in a courtship flight, making *chewk* notes. This precipitated a renewal of displays. At the end of the encounter, Female B assumed a position crosswise on a limb, inviting copulation. Male B came within a meter. The two then flew off. With the breeding season advancing, both pairs were now more interested in courtship and nest sites than in conflicts.

I watched conflicts with other pairs that were less prolonged but more intense. One set took place in a somewhat open area on a slope where winds swept over a ridge. Male E and his mate had worked on the wind-blown trees for 20 minutes on March 13 when he flew at Male F, who had just arrived. The two engaged in a bill-waving dance accompanied by *wick, wick* vocalizations. They separated after a few minutes to feed near their respective mates. The pause was broken when Male F suddenly flew at Male E, knocking him from his perch. The two grappled as they fell toward the

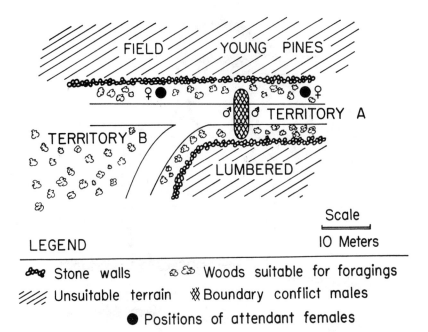

FIG. 7. The site of ritualized, early morning conflicts of two male Hairy Wood-peckers in February along a portion of their common territory boundary, showing positions of attendant females.

ground. There were more clashes in the next three to four minutes. Between several of them I noted one male or the other assume a combat pose, with bill open, wings held out slightly and tail fanned (Fig. 8), with the outer tail feathers sometimes twitching independently.

Female E had meanwhile flown to a dead stump and started drumming. When Male E flew to her after his last clash, she broke into a medley of *tewk*, *tewk*s, moved out to take a copulation pose, then broke into frog-like *quares* as he mounted in coition. There was thus a change, within seconds, from conflict to sexual behavior. The drive built up in one seemed transferable to the other.

That conflicts between males can vary was brought out in 1964 when Female A acquired an odd mate, Male A'. One of his peculiarities was that he was not interested in territorial fighting. This was shown on February 13 when Male B invaded A''s territory at 07:20. Male A' was resting on an aspen 40 m inside the boundary. Male B came close, making an exaggerated display of his white breast (Fig. 9). Neither the trespassing nor the display

Fig. 8. A male Hairy Woodpecker in combat readiness as he faces an intraspecific opponent.

aroused Male A'. He moved away, pecking at places of no special interest and Male B returned to his own territory unchallenged.

Male A''s lack of interest in territory, whether his own or his neighbor's, was also shown in his trespassing. On both February 7 and 22 he wandered into Pair B's territory. Female B met him on both days. She attacked by

Fig. 9. Male Hairy displaying white breast, a pose basic to the bill-waving dance.

advancing rapidly up the trunk or along the limb where A' happened to be, without displays, but moving directly at him. His response was to fly to another tree. Female B desisted after a few attacks. Her neighbor Male A' was unresponsive. One might assume that he lacked a will to fight. But this was not so. I once saw him exchange blows in defending his roost hole. On another occasion Female B was on a suet feeder in our yard. Male A' drove her away and when a starling attacked, he swung under a limb in a threat display, then attacked and drove the starling away. It would be nice if one could explain all one saw among birds. Male A' remains a puzzle. I have detailed other of his peculiarities in a later section.

Fights of any length among Hairies, as with other woodpeckers, are nearly always male against male or female vs. female. The latter conflicts are rare in spring. I have seen more of them in the summer and fall. On July 24 I watched Females A and B fighting by the same section of boundary, along the dirt road where their mates had fought in late winter. The females were resting a meter apart when first noted. They soon started bill-wavings accompanied by doll-like *queek*s that continued for only a few minutes. Female B then flew to the vicinity of her mate. He was accompanied by a juvenile and showed no interest in the encounter. I saw three other female-female encounters in New Hampshire, all in September and October. I have wondered why the females should have fought in the summer and fall. I think this is because their hormone levels may remain up longer after the breeding season than those of males, leading them to experience a recrudescence of territorial behavior when day length, in the fall, is the same as in the spring.

# HAIRY WOODPECKER

## Sexual and Social Aspects of Male Conflicts

In watching the prolonged conflicts of Males A and B in late winter, ones that repeated themselves for several months along one section of boundary, I wondered whether their function was purely territorial. The males emerged from their roost holes with seemingly abundant energy and aggressiveness. A rival male, each knew, was not far away. Soon joined by their mates, the two made for the known spot. Instead of being ordeals, the conflicts were a way of working off steam. The males seemed to enjoy them. An analogy that came to mind was of a tennis match in which both contestants were satisfied with the boundary (the net) staying where it was. Both then played, spurred on by having their mates on the side lines. If a conflict continued for an hour, both males showed signs of restlessness by pecking here and there. While this might be called displacement activity, it seemed to me a sign that the two were actually becoming hungry. They had, after all, had no chance to feed since emerging from their roost holes at dawn.

A feature of the conflicts was that their effects were not limited to the males. The females were aroused by attending as was shown by one or the other taking a copulation pose, with mates flying to them in lulls of fighting. The display, or dances, therefore, seemed to be something more than territorial. They were a way of synchronizing the development of sexual drives well before the onset of nesting.

## Early Breeding Behavior

### Winter Courtship and Trial Nest Sites

Male and female Hairies pay little attention to each other in the fall when they lead independent lives. They were together in only four of 48 encounters that I had with them in one year from September through November. An early sign of breeding was on December 22 when a female, clinging to a healthy white birch, with head in her shoulders, gave a delicate drum followed by two taps. Her head turned a bit to look at her mate, then she drummed in the same way again.

The main onset of breeding behavior comes in January. On January 10 I found Female A resting below a broken branch of an aspen. Her mate rested 20 m away. When she tapped, he moved closer and drummed for seven minutes. She tapped with renewed enthusiasm when he came even closer. She was taking the lead. She wanted him to come. But he was not ready and the two flew away. The trunk of the aspen where she rested for 30 minutes was too decadent to have made an actual nest site. It was enough like one, however, to serve as a center for courtship early in the year.

Male B, in an extension of the same kind of episode, started drumming at 07:20 on February 8 when his mate flew to him in courtship flight. Although she squatted in a precopulatory pose, he was not interested. A more complete performance took place three weeks later. This time Male B mounted and fell off to the left in what appeared to be a full copulation, two months prior to nesting.

Pair A started an excavation relatively early in 1965 but were in no hurry. They had been mated the year before and were adjusted to each other and to their territory. I was able to locate the male on January 31 by his tapping on a live aspen with a rotten center. He started excavating in late February at the same spot where he had tapped previously. My watching was simplified by his habit of excavating in the middle of the day. He continued to be unhurried, pausing frequently to rest and preen. His mate generally took little interest, but did work for 17 minutes on March 13 with her head in the hole.

The male did not work hard. There was no need to. It was still early in the breeding season and the hole was serving mainly as a center for courtship. With the need of a finished cavity over six weeks away, to have completed one early would have exposed it to the risk of a flying squirrel, or other competitor, taking it over.

## EXCAVATION

The period of midwinter courtship is succeeded by a relatively quiet one in March. It is seldom before mid-April that real excavations begin. A prolonged tapping on April 18 led me to a female resting by a freshly excavated depression. When her mate came, she flew away giving *jeek*s. Males do most of the work, but need this kind of assurance that their mates agree on the nest site. With it, they can work steadily for up to an hour at a time. Although females do but a small part of the total, they may work hard at the entrance at the start of an excavation. Female H was excavating from the outside on May 1. She would swing into the hole with half of her body to peck 12–15 times, then swing out. Each time she came out she looked all about giving *speak*s. She was doing the same on the following day. Her *speak*s may have reflected her nervousness at having her head in the hole, while her body was exposed, on the outside, to possible attack by a predator. I have noticed a similar nervousness with Pileateds at the same stage of excavating. Male Hairies, once they can get inside, can peck at rates of up to 190 pecks a minute, tossing sawdust out from the entrance. Occasionally, as a hole nears completion, a bird will fly to a distance with a billful to shake it loose. This is a symbolic removal of feces, weeks before young are in the nest. A female on May 1 flew from her excavation 10 times in succession to discard sawdust 12 m away.

Courtship flights can reach a peak at times of excavating. This is especially so if the hole is in an open place. A pair was excavating one May, in an old maple that was separated from woods by 30 m of lawn. The female sometimes flew from the woods to the excavation with quivering wings, making *joick, joick, joick*s. Alighting on a limb, she then floated to the excavation on

47

outstretched wings. When her mate came out to change places, he circled the lawn in a fluttering flight as he left.

### Copulatory Behavior

While copulatory behavior may begin as early as January, full copulations, with few exceptions, do not begin until late April when nest excavations are well begun. I followed Pair F for an hour on April 16 as the two moved through woods, foraging in a loose association. Their course brought them back to their nest by 07:00. The female then invited copulation by giving *tewk* notes and assuming an invitation pose.

I found her by the excavation again three days later. After tapping, resting motionless a few minutes, and then flying off in courtship flight, she joined her mate in foraging through the woods. He seemingly took the lead in each of two copulations. One was by approaching her from below as she moved out on a branch and the second was by drumming a few bursts, then flying to her.

Male F was working up to 40 minutes at a stretch excavating by the last of April. He now took the lead in all copulations. As the two woodpeckers were no longer foraging together, due to his spending so much time excavating, he had to drum to get his mate to come. On April 28 he drummed loudly on an oak, looking all around as he did so. I then heard a low answering drum. Minutes of silence followed. Female F then began *tewk* notes and he glided over to copulate with her. I saw two more copulations on May

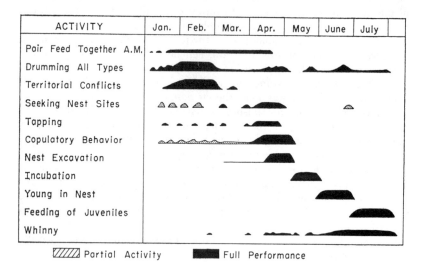

| ACTIVITY | Jan. | Feb. | Mar. | Apr. | May | June | July | |
|---|---|---|---|---|---|---|---|---|
| Pair Feed Together A.M. | | | | | | | | |
| Drumming All Types | | | | | | | | |
| Territorial Conflicts | | | | | | | | |
| Seeking Nest Sites | | | | | | | | |
| Tapping | | | | | | | | |
| Copulatory Behavior | | | | | | | | |
| Nest Excavation | | | | | | | | |
| Incubation | | | | | | | | |
| Young in Nest | | | | | | | | |
| Feeding of Juveniles | | | | | | | | |
| Whinny | | | | | | | | |

▨ Partial Activity ■ Full Performance

Fig. 10. Summary of displays and activities of Hairy Woodpeckers in the breeding season

FIG. 11. Hairy Woodpeckers (male above) in full copulation.

2, each preceded by similar preliminaries. It was on this day that Male F spent his first night in his nearly completed excavation.

Copulations at other nests began as early as the second day of excavation and continued up to the fourth day of incubation (Fig. 10). At times of excavation, they were often initiated by the partner away from the nest returning to it. Female H was excavating on May 3, when her mate flew to the hole. She flew out to a branch and Male H flew to her. After copulating, Male H flew to the hole to excavate. Later on the same morning, Male H was excavating, when his mate flew to the nest making *joick*s, then went to a branch 2 m away. He then came out to copulate. Curiously, in the afternoon, Female H came to a branch near the hole making *tewk, tewk* intimate notes. When Male H came, she pecked him away, even though she had assumed an invitation pose. The same events happened again a half hour later. Her aggressiveness was possibly part of that observable at nest holes at times of egg laying.

In copulations the male, in falling to the left, often ends up with his body parallel to that of his mate (Fig. 11). In a few copulations, however, I have noted males as ending with bodies upside down and at right angles. Although the position seems improbable, I have observed it for sapsuckers and Red-bellied Woodpeckers.

## Nesting

### Incubation

Whereas Hairies of most pairs became silent during incubation, those of Pairs H and J gave *speak*s, *whinny*s and *joick*s, by way of greetings at times of changeovers. Changeovers at the end of a day require special timing. When I entered the woods before dawn on May 20, the first sapsucker drummed at 04:45 and a flicker at 05:10. There was no stir at the Hairy nest, however, until 05:35. This was when Female H arrived with a medley of *joick*s to relieve her mate from his overnight stay.

Events were reversed in the evening. Male H came to relieve his mate at 19:30 which gave her about 30 minutes to feed before roosting. But on May 20 he was late in coming. She emerged from the nest, fed hastily on a birch, reentered, only to emerge again as if restless. Male H finally arrived at 19:45 for the last change of the day.

The Hairies of Pairs H and J were attentive to incubating and shared the task more or less equally. Those of Pair C, on the other hand, were so restless that I wondered how the eggs could hatch. Female C came to the nest on May 23 making *joick*s and her mate left. But instead of taking his place, she flew to a swamp to forage for five minutes. She then returned to sit on the eggs for 15 minutes. In the course of the next hour she emerged six times to idle, preen, and scratch. Only a third of her stay was spent incubating. Her mate's attentiveness, on nine of the 12 days I watched, was not much different. On the last day he spent only 12 of 33 minutes on the eggs. Yet in spite of the casual behavior of the pair, the eggs hatched and two young were subsequently fledged.

Hatching is signaled at most nests by some change in the behavior of parents. Male C, for example, appeared to be disturbed by something when I arrived early on May 21. He not only drummed at a rapid rate, but also preened in the quick, nervous manner characteristic of displacement activity. I soon saw the parents bringing prey to the nest, prey so small as to be hardly detectable.

### Parental Care and Foraging

The members of Pair B were adapted to each other, or so it seemed from their quiet behavior, prolonged courtship, and close cooperation in nesting. The situation of their nest in 1965 was optimal in a number of ways. It was located in an open woodland that did not attract starlings and the hole was 4 m up in the rotten center of a living aspen, the center providing easy excavating and the living walls, tough outer protection. Female B alighted below the entrance at 06:30 on May 22, the day after their eggs hatched. She had food in her bill and, after waiting for Male B to wriggle out, giving low conversational notes as he did so, she entered to remain inside. This close brooding continued for five days. Female B alighted by the entrance on the sixth day, giving a few *tewk* notes, but Male B had left. The brooding was over. Brooding at three other nests lasted from seven to nine days, with duties more or less equally shared.

Parent Hairies entered to feed nestlings until 16 days before their fledging. After that, as the young began to climb to the entrance, parents fed increasingly from the outside. I could then see that the bill of parents and young met at right angles in the transfer of food. Parents, and especially the males, sometimes spent a few moments poking back at their young to aid them in arranging prey. At two nests the males made 39 and 42 percent of the feeding visits and their mates 61 and 58 percent. But these figures do not reflect the amount of food brought. The females, although they made more visits, brought less per visit. This was indicated by their arriving, much of the time, with bills closed and little prey protruding. The males, in contrast, brought large items that could be seen. Three males brought suet. One of them, seemingly as a result, had a matting of feathers at the base of his bill, a situation discussed further by Jackson and Hoover (1975).

Foraging of the sexes differed, the males tending to go to a distance, while females were apt to stay closer to nests where they were within hearing range of the vocalizations of their young. This may have been one reason that they made more feeding visits. A feature of the foraging of females was the amount of time spent on the ground. Female G, for example, whose nest was located in an open beechwood, appeared to be little disturbed by my proximity. She tossed leaves to uncover partially buried limbs of beech and other trees in seeking prey from rotten wood. It took her about five minutes, on an average, to fill her bill with prey. Her activities varied with the weather. The woodland floor was dry by mid-June, but a heavy rain on the sixteenth made logs and branches soft and soggy. Female G was especially active the next morning, making as many as seven visits to her nest in 23 minutes, all to and from an oak log that had been unrewarding in dry weather. Female G appeared to be much at home on the ground. She not only preened, but, as I had observed on May 6, also copulated there.

Two other nests were in a woodland swamp. Here, as in the beechwood, the females were often low, moving over fallen logs, moss-covered old stumps, and pushing among ferns and other ground vegetation. They seemed to be generalized feeders, gleaning, peering, and poking on a variety of trees, dead and alive. Their ability to find prey in such a variety of places enabled them, I thought, to keep within easy hearing distance of their young. A few females have seemed so intent on foraging as to neglect their body feathers which, by the end of the nesting period, appeared disheveled and soiled.

# HAIRY WOODPECKER

## Intrapair Relations and Temperament

The members of pairs do not pay much attention to each other when busy feeding nestlings, other than exchanging a few low notes when they come at all close. Occasionally, however, the two arrive at a nest at the same time. A question always in my mind is which sex will take precedence. Male B was about to enter the nest one morning when Female B alighted close by. She greeted him, then moved to his place and entered as he moved aside. But things have not always worked out the same. When Female C came to the nest with prey, Male C arrived almost immediately afterward, giving *tewks*. Although she was nearer to the hole, she gave way and he entered. A week later, under similar circumstances, Male C flew to an adjacent branch. But when Female C paused, he flew back and entered. Of special interest was another nest where the female, finding the male already in the hole feeding the young, entered on top of him. She came right out to let him leave, then re-entered. From the variety of outcomes in these situations, I have found it impossible to say that either sex is dominant during the nestling period. Sometimes one sex, sometimes the other, takes precedence, without signs of friction.

I have also tried to assess with Hairies whether one sex or the other may be innately more wary. An occasional individual of either sex can be unusually apprehensive. I found it difficult, for example, to get at all close to Nest A in 1965. Male A, if around to see me coming, immediately started an almost uninterrupted series of loud vocalizations as he flew near, then circled away, making ruffle noises with his wings. His excitement was considerable. Aside from *speak*s given in a shrill fashion that made them resemble the *peek, peek* notes of American Robins, he gave sputters of his own. These had a quality of harsh laughter. A common sequence was *speak-chrr-charr-jer-jer-jer, charr-jer-jer*. Male A's excitability seemed to be communicated, to some extent, to both his mate and young. Both made sputters, those of the female being an even *speak-ha-ha-ha-ha*.

## Lone Parents

I followed three nests where a parent had to care for its nestlings alone in the last 5–6 days before fledging. At two of the nests, one attended by a male and the other by a female, I believed that the missing partner had been killed. Each of these nests contained two young. The third nest contained only a single nestling. Although I saw the male daily, he never came to it in the last five days, leaving his mate, as seemingly the more conscientious partner, to carry on. I think that this was because with only one young one, there was simply not enough work for the two of them to do effectively.

All of the lone parents were successful. There were, however, differences in behavior. The lone male doubled the number of visits he had been making to a rate of 8.4 times per hour. But he appeared unhurried, leaving the nest unattended for 30 minutes on one morning and 40 on another. The female with two young also doubled the number of her previous visits, feeding at a rate of 13.8 times per hour. This rate would not have been so high had she not speeded it up to 28 on the last day. The third lone parent, also a female, had, curiously, a rate of 18.6 visits per hour, in spite of her having only a single young one. One feature common to all of these single woodpeckers was that their rates increased on their final day.

## Nest Leaving

What makes young leave a nest where they have spent nearly four weeks? Does it take some final nudging to get them to fly? Nest D was high in the forest canopy in a dead beech. Female D fed a young one at 07:00, then returned to feed it again in five minutes. When she left, the fledgling wriggled from the entrance and flew toward the ground. Both parents fed the remaining young during the next two hours. Male D then fed a nestling leaning from the entrance. When he flew, the young one flew off with him.

There was now a break of 70 minutes before Female D fed the remaining young one. After her second visit, the fledgling flew out after her. Thus three young had left over a period of 3.5 hours. There was little indication at this nest that the parents had done anything special to get their nestlings to fly. They went when they were ready.

Parents at other nests, on the other hand, appeared to entice their young. Neither parent came to Nest C between 06:30 and 07:45. Male C then came with a piece of suet. According to my wife, the fledgling at the entrance seemed so hungry that it tumbled out of the nest as if trying to get more. It then flew off close behind its parent.

At Nest J, in contrast, the parents fed their young 11 times between 05:20 and 06:06. On her next visit, Female J reached toward a fledgling. When it leaned out for the food, she backed away. She did this several times, the fledgling stretching more each time until it was out. Thus there seemed to be two methods of enticing young, viz. to starve them, making them so hungry that they tumbled out, or, holding food just out of reach, forcing them to lean out a little too far.

## Defense of Nest Holes

### Conflicts with a Male Sapsucker

Hairy Woodpeckers do not ordinarily come in conflict with sapsuckers unless one of them happens to come too close to a nest of the other. Then it is simply driven away. Theoretically, however, the two species could compete for nest sites. They have much the same body size and hence need sites of the same diameter. But there are factors that serve to keep them apart. One is that Hairies start breeding earlier than sapsuckers and, another, that sapsuckers will nest in trees containing old holes, whereas Hairies will not do so if they can possibly avoid it. Yet, in spite of these circumstances, I once found a pair of Hairies fighting with a male sapsucker.

The Hairies had been excavating a hole in a hop-hornbeam infected with the tinder fungus, *Fomes igniarius,* when a male sapsucker appeared and inspected it. The female Hairy paid little attention to this initial visit. The sapsucker returned the following day and began an excavation of his own 75 cm above that of the Hairies (Fig. 12). By this time he was more aggressive and was able to drive the female Hairy away. The main conflicts, however, did not come until a few days later.

I had begun watching the female Hairy at 06:30 on April 21, when the sapsucker arrived. He wasted no time. He struck the Hairy and the two fell to the ground. They lay there for a moment. When they had reascended the trunk, the Hairy renewed the conflict, thus precipitating a second episode of grappling in which the female Hairy was beaten. The sapsucker pursued her from tree to tree, then returned to inspect her excavation.

The female Hairy remained at a spot 20 m away for the next 15 minutes. She preened in a quick, ineffective manner and made an unusual number of *jeeks.* Meanwhile her mate, who had been absent, returned. He tapped at the entrance of the excavation as if trying to get her to come. But she remained where she was.

When the sapsucker came back, he swooped at the male Hairy so hard that the two fell to the ground. They remained there for nearly a minute. When they took wing, it was the Hairy that chased the intruder, who never returned as far as I was aware.

An interesting aspect of these conflicts was the relative fighting abilities of the two Hairies. I had never been sure whether the sexes were equal or not. But one could hardly have planned a more decisive demonstration. When attacked and having to fight in an almost identical manner, the female Hairy was beaten and the male won. I think this has implications as to why male woodpeckers spend the night on the nest. If they can strike harder and are more aggressive, they, by natural selection, have become the ones to guard nests at night. Another consideration, in the case of Hairies, is that males have larger and longer bills (Selander, 1965).

## STARLINGS

Whereas Downies are seldom molested by starlings, Hairies are almost certain to be if they attempt to nest along the edges of fields or open situations. Their nest entrances are of just the right size. Starlings keep a close eye on the development of Hairy excavations, but do not try to take one over until it is completed. Then the battle begins. The starlings are tireless and they always win. The effect on the Hairies is one of stress, a stress that sometimes continues to show itself in disturbed behavior later on.

A pair of Hairies in Lyme, New Hampshire was robbed of two successive excavations before making a third, and successful one, deeper in the woods.

FIG. 12. Female Hairy Woodpecker and male Yellow-bellied Sapsucker contend for nest site in a hornbeam infected with the tinder fungus, as indicated by the large fruiting body or conk.

Starlings have search images as to what they like for nest holes. They do not like ones among trees, especially if facing the ground or obscured by branches. The third excavation of the Hairies had all of these protective features, but both of the pair were now excitable and difficult to observe. The male gave many *speaks*, pecked on the bark, or preened in a quick, ineffective manner (both displacement activities) as he moved about the nest tree in the course of frequent changeovers. When he came to the entrance during incubation, he bowed in and out many times before swinging in. His mate was similarly agitated and remained so throughout the nesting period.

I observed much the same signs of stress in another pair. The two made a first excavation in a dead elm arising from a beaver swamp. I watched the two copulate on 22 April but, as seemed inevitable in so open a situation, starlings soon took over. The woodpeckers moved to a wooded slope and nested in a tall paper birch. I now witnessed what I had seen with the pair outside of Lyme. The Hairies, seemingly as a result of their earlier encounters with starlings, became unusually excitable. Whereas I had watched them at close range and without difficulty the year before, I now had to approach with care and remain at a distance. My feeling is that Hairies are highly sensitive birds. Starlings are newcomers, in an evolutionary/historical sense, and fighting with them is a stressful event. One Hairy can defeat a starling at a suet feeder. But once starlings become set on pirating a newly excavated hole, their team work always wins.

Starlings can affect a pair of nesting Hairies even when not intent on taking their nest. Pair B of Hairies nested in a butternut located between two fields in 1964. This placed them in an aerial highway of starlings that stopped to perch when passing. In the few moments of a stay, they often edged over toward the nest, even though it was too hemmed in by branches to be of serious interest. When an especially inquisitive starling approached on June 5, the male Hairy faced it in a threat display, with bill raised and wings outspread. Both birds held frozen poses momentarily. The female Hairy then joined her mate and the two of them drove the starling away. But the most notable feature of the Hairies' behavior was the way they took turns guarding their nest, whether starlings were near or not.

Female B was active and restless when on guard. She stayed close but spent her time moving hurriedly over limbs and trunks of adjacent trees, even though insect prey was scarce on these overworked locations. She occasionally flew to a dying elm 60 m away where she was still within view of the nest. The persistence with which Male B and Female B guarded their nest must, expectedly, have reduced the time they might have spent gathering food for their young.

## SQUIRRELS

If Hairies leave an open situation to nest in woods, it can be a case of exchanging one hazard for another. Flying squirrels, like starlings, find the nest holes of Hairies of the right size and are quick to slip into a hole when they can.

A pair of Hairies nested on a wooded slope of oaks and beeches in 1967. Their first hole was 8 m up in the straight trunk of a beech. The female entered on May 2 and remained inside as if incubating. On later visits, I found the nest occupied by a flying squirrel. The pair excavated a second cavity. Here they nested successfully and I observed no signs that loss of their first nest had led to any stress. The same happened with two other pairs.

Red Squirrels nesting at the same time as Hairies, can keep the woodpeckers on guard. A nest that had an entrance on the underside of a sloping branch, was only 2 m below a squirrels' nest. Two juvenile squirrels began to crawl about on June 5. The female Hairy was too excited to take effective action. She popped into her nest, came out, flew to a neighboring tree, returned, jerked her body in exaggerated swings and made almost incessant *chip* notes. Her mate, in contrast, flew in to alight quietly on one side of the nest cavity. There he clung motionless, surveying the squirrels at close range. He then entered the cavity to rest with bill out. As with other pairs of Hairies I have observed, this male appeared to have a temperament different from that of the female, one that made him, I thought, a more effective, or at least a less excitable guardian.

A second pair of Hairies, that had lost a first nest to starlings, finally nested late in the season in the sloping fork of a dead elm in a wooded swamp. The entrance was on the underside and had a well-beveled edge. This made it easy for whichever of the pair was within to look at the ground. It also made it easier to strike down at intruders coming up, as a pair of red squirrels did in almost daily visits to the elm. This forced the Hairies to take turns guarding. They did so largely in the morning, for the squirrels were less active in the afternoon. On July 1, two days before fledging, the squirrels circled about a fork of the elm making grunting noises as if mating. On this occasion the male Hairy remained in the nest for 46 minutes, during which time his mate did not come to feed the young. Several times, when a squirrel came within 30 cm or so of the hole, the male, with head drawn back inside, darted his bill in and out with lightening speed. While the squirrels were well beyond reach, the demonstration may have served notice that the male was ready for them. Twice, when the squirrels came, the nestlings started wailing, a vocalization that I had not heard previously. It ceased when the squirrels left.

Gray Squirrels can also be a threat. Although Male B was generally away from his nest more than his mate in the nestling period, he remained close when there was any danger. On June 6 I found him giving an uninterrupted series of *speak*s. It took a while to discover a gray squirrel resting at a level with the hole and 7 m away. Although a gray squirrel is too large to enter the nest of a Hairy, I found that one had gnawed and largely destroyed the entrance of a nest within a few days after the young had flown.

## Raccoons

As for all other woodpeckers, raccoons are a serious threat. No other likely predator can chew a nest open more readily. With this in mind, I thought that Pair A had an unusually poor nest stub in 1965. I do not think this represented poor judgement. I had covered the woods of the Hairies' territory for two successive years, both in winter and summer. By 1965 the supply of good stubs or live trees with decayed centers of a suitable diameter, was exhausted. There were none left. The Hairies, in consequence, had to nest in a decayed birch stub or not nest at all. Yet it seemed likely, that, with a nest so low to the ground and in such rotten wood, a raccoon would get it sooner or later.

As I approached the stub on June 10 I feared something had happened. I could tell by the female's vocalizations that she was excited. But great was my surprise, on coming close, to find her hovering not over a raccoon, but a skunk. I stood still as the skunk came almost to me. The Hairy followed closely, giving repeated *chip-ha-ha-ha*s. I now saw that the entrance to the nest in the birch stub had been chewed away. The young Hairies, however, had survived and one of them, looking from the ragged, enlarged entrance, gave a series of sputters. On closer examination I found strands of fur and the wide-spreading claw marks of a raccoon. The skunk, it seemed, was a red herring, there by chance when I came along.

What I found remarkable was that the raccoon had not been able to chew the nest open and devour the young. I believe that the male Hairy, as the one to spend the night on the nest, had been able to defend it. A Hairy is small compared to a raccoon, but its long, sharp bill, operating through a nest entrance, could be effective if aimed at the eyes or sensitive nose of a raccoon. It is doubtful if a Downy or a Yellow-bellied Sapsucker could have survived an attack in a rotten stub.

### Postnesting

#### Recrudescence of Breeding Behavior

Greetings at times of changeovers, which may vary from *tewk*s, to *jeek*s and *joick*s given largely by the female, are an indication that courtship continues throughout the nesting period. It is, seemingly, a lessening of work that leads to an increase of displays toward the end of nesting. On June 19, three days before fledging, Male H flew from his hole in a fluttering flight as his mate arrived nearby giving *tewk*s. She then launched into a spectacular floating flight that brought her to the nest. Male H had meanwhile flown to a stub where he started tapping, the first tapping I had heard since the time of excavating.

Some of the liveliest renewals were in midsummer when juveniles first became independent. I was by a beaver pond on July 14 when a female landed on a dead stub giving *joick*s. After drumming and preening a few minutes, she gave more of the same vocalizations in response to the drumming of her mate. He then flew to her as she left in a courtship flight. A female on July 22 floated down, with wings widespread at a **V**, to the start of an excavation. She tapped 4–5 times, rested, and tapped again. When a male came close, she greeted him again with lively *joick*s.

### BEHAVIOR OF JUVENILES

When I visited Nest B early on the morning of June 12, two fledglings had left. Could I find where they had flown? One gave its position away by making *speak*s in a small pine and a second, I soon found, was following its mother up a dying elm. As fast as she uncovered larvae, she bent over to feed it. The fledgling jerked its body, half-started its wings, and made sputtery *whinny*s.

The female flew back to the nest a few minutes later with prey in her bill. But the third and last fledgling had already left. She bowed in and out looking for it, then flew about giving *speak*s. Where was the last fledgling? I finally spotted it emerging from some ferns as it started up a tree.

I interrupted events by capturing two of the fleglings for handraising. With only a single young one left, which parent would care for it? By the following morning I found the female taking charge. She had been the most attentive in feeding the nestlings and continued to do so with the fledgling. The latter called attention to itself with *speak*s, *whinny*s, and a *quare*, tree froglike note when she approached to feed it. This was in a wood about 200 m from the nest.

Male and female Hairies usually divide the juveniles, some of which follow one parent and one or two the other. The sexual differences in the foraging of Hairies reveal themselves in the way parents feed their young. Female parents, moving rapidly over limbs and trunks, do not like to be followed. One female did a bill-waving dance to make her young one stay behind. She then returned to it after gathering prey. I saw similar behavior at a suet feeder when a female came in alone, then flew back to feed her young one in a tree. Male Hairies, in contrast, tolerate close contact. A male at the same feeder bent over to feed suet to a young one repeatedly. On June 28 another male, digging prey out of a dead maple limb, fed a juvenile in the same way.

Juvenile Hairies can display a variety of behavior. One waiting for its mother moved about haphazardly, pecking ineffectively and remaining quiet except for occassional *whinny*s. The vocalizations may have aided in keeping it in touch with its mother. She made a few *speak*s plus a *whinny* when she came and the young one replied as it flew to her.

Some juveniles make an amazing variety of *quaver*s, intimate notes, *queek*s and even *jer-ha-ha*s as though going over the whole gamut of Hairy vocalizations. Another juvenile that I observed on 17 and 28 July seemed excessively dependent in the way it made almost incessant toy-like *queek*s and half-started its wings. One of my handraised juveniles went through the same clownish performance to me, even after being fed.

I have noted juveniles following parents and being fed until mid-August. Juvenile Hairies may, therefore, be dependent on parents for as much as six weeks. Their bills during this time are shorter and weaker than those of adults.

Young Hairies are like young Downies in playing at dodging passing chickadees and in curiosity. A juvenile flew toward me on June 9 and spent five minutes close by, even moving out on tree limbs to come closer.

Some juveniles of both Hairies and Downies have red on the head and others not. Those with red are not necessarily males as Snyder (1923) has shown. One of my handraised juveniles, with much red, proved to be a female after molting.

## FAILURE TO NEST AND STRESS

A most unusual series of conflicts between two males took place one May in Tamworth, New Hampshire. *Speaks* and sputters first attracted my attention to where Males X and Z were displaying with bill-waving dances by their common border (Fig. 13). The conflict was a mild one that ended with the departure of the intruder, Male Z.

Male X was feeding near his mate on the following morning, May 5, when he suddenly looked alert. Male Z had invaded again. Male X flew to meet him and after a brief encounter, the invader left. Male X now flew back to his mate. As often happens in such situations, copulation followed as if the emotional intensity engendered by the conflict had carried over.

Male X was resting and sunning himself on a dead limb in the center of his territory as I watched for 20 minutes on May 17. His rival, Male Z interrupted these activities by appearing in woods below. I was thus present at the start of a conflict that lasted for an hour. It involved a spectrum of activities ranging from bill-wavings and wing flashing displays, to bodily clashes with loss of feathers, all accompanied by occasional *wick-a-wick-a-wick* vocalizations. The two males appeared to be evenly balanced. It was only by a slight margin that Male X drove his rival back the way he had come (Fig. 13).

Why, I wondered, should an intruder have been able to prevail so long? An answer came on May 25 when Male X in one part of the woods and his mate in another, carried on prolonged duets of drumming. These began at 05:45 and continued, off and on, for 14 hours until 19:45. Female X tapped a number of times at a potential nest stub of poor quality. It appeared as if she were trying to get her mate to come and inspect it. He never came. Efforts of the two to find an adequate site had reached an end point. Neither had been successful and the prolonged drumming was an emotional reaction to their failure.

After this breakdown between Male X and his mate, there was a sharp change in the encounters between the two males. The invading male now drove Male X into the center of his territory which he abandoned to his rival. Without a mate or nest, his will to resist had gone.

## HAIRY WOODPECKER

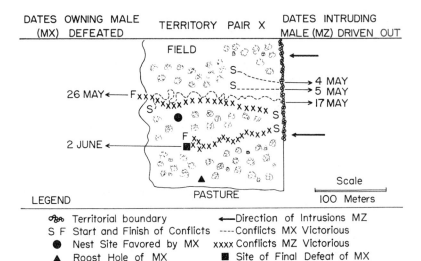

FIG. 13. Five invasions by intruding male Hairy Woodpecker, Male Z, into territory of mated male, Male X, showing manner in which Male X was ultimately defeated on his own territory in May and June 1963.

The debacle came on June 2. It was precipitated when Male X brought Male Z, the invader, to the boundary by drumming. As on May 26, Male Z forced Owner X back to the center of his territory. Much of the fighting was close to the ground. Male X had seemingly had enough after a half hour, for he worked his way to the bottom of a brush pile to hide. But Male Z followed. I could see a spasmodic beating of wings. It was the final clash. Male Z came out after a few minutes, rapped on a dead branch, and flew off. Male X emerged five minutes later. He gave a few *speak*s and sputters, then flew in a direction away from that taken by Male Z.

What was the meaning of the month-long conflict and why should an outsider have been able to defeat an owning male on his own territory? Conceivable answers lie in a combination of circumstances. If Male Z, the invader, had lost his mate, as appeared to be the case, a drive built up in courtship may have found outlet in destructive aggression. The neighbor's territory per se could have been no use to the invader. He fought to work off a thwarted reproductive drive. I did not know how else to explain his persistence.

The failure of Male X to defend his territory rested on a different situation. A feature of the conflicts was that Male X won encounters up until May 25. This was the date he and his mate had the duets of drumming carried on in what, to me, was an agonizing fashion, for over 14 hours. It

61

was the final break. Without a place to nest the woodpeckers separated. After this Male X lacked the will to fight. The psychological advantage passed to the invader.

I might not have appreciated the background of this situation had I not been following the succession of trees in our woods over several decades. A combination of hurricanes and lumbering had provided a supply of stubs in previous years. Woodpeckers throve. I had no trouble in finding nests in those days. In time, however, no larger trees remained. The supply of stubs dwindled and vigorous young trees took over, offering no dead wood of a suitable size for excavating nests.

My first appreciation of this depletion came from observing a pair of Yellow-bellied Sapsuckers. These had nested in the same woods as those fought over by the Hairies. A year finally came when the sapsuckers failed to find a tree for nesting. The result was that the male, with no nest to attend to in May and June, flew the rounds of his territory, seeking to precipitate conflicts with males of neighboring pairs occupied in raising young.

The sapsuckers, like the pair of Hairies, might have been able to nest had they moved elsewhere. Both species, however, remained attached to the locality, an attachment that led eventually to what appeared to be pathological behavior.

## Unusual Fall Courtship of a Female in Maryland

The best way to the best studies, I feel, is by chance. Over and over I have found that recognition of an ideal situation, where the terrain was open and a bird easy to follow, has been the way not only to discover but also to have the best watching. This was true, at least, of a female Hairy Woodpecker followed for over 130 hours in a swamp in Maryland from September 1958 to April 1959.

In those early days of watching I did not realize that the southern race of Hairy Woodpeckers (*P.v. auduboni*) differed in behavior from the northern race (*P.v. villosus*). While the northern Hairy is easy to watch, the southern Hairy is the shiest of eastern woodpeckers.

What wakened my interest was the loud, persistent drumming of a woodpecker in September and October, when other woodpeckers were largely silent. The drummer was a female Hairy that I was to follow until spring. The terrain consisted of a rim of trees, swamp poplars, willows and others surrounding a hectare of open swamp. Since the swamp was dry in the fall and frozen in the winter, I was able to walk about with ease.

Several situations indicated that Female H's territory (Fig. 14) had definite boundaries. One was that she made rounds of drum trees, of which three were visited on many occasions and five others with less frequency. She used particular spots on each where she could get the greatest resonance. The territory, as measured by the greatest distances between drum trees, was 430 m long and 235 m wide.

Further aids to the location of boundaries were the sites of seven conflicts, five with intruding females and two with intruding males. There was a tendency for conflicts to be repeated in definite zones. Two of the female conflicts were in one zone and two in another. Conflicts in a third zone were of a different pattern. On 14 March Male H fought another male and a week later Female H a rival female along a boundary not far from where the two excavated a nest a month later. But this is going ahead of my account.

I heard drumming from Female H's main drum tree during September, but it was October 18 before the swamp was dry enough to start consistent observations. Female H drummed hundreds of times on favorable days. Such a day was November 8. She began drumming at 07:45 on what I called her China Tree because, due to its weathered hardness, it had a tone that I could recognize 800 m away. Her drumming, at a rate of 11 bursts a minute, was at an intense level. The female's eagerness was also reflected in another way. At 08:00 on the same morning I found her feeding among low willows, but pausing here and there to drum one or two bursts on places of no particular resonance. She drummed 19 bursts on eight different places within 10 min-

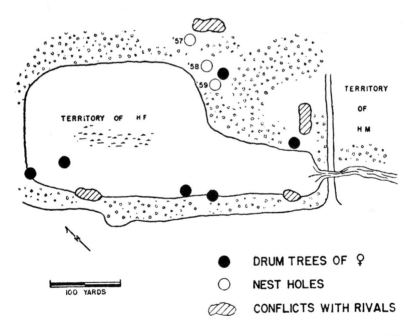

FIG. 14.   Fall and winter territory of the female Hairy Woodpecker, Female H (HF), showing her main drum trees, zones of boundary conflicts, and nest sites in three successive years.

utes, so great was her urge to drum wherever she might happen to be. I could still hear her at close to sunset. Her performance was particularly striking because no other woodpeckers were drumming.

It became clear in November that she was drumming to attract a mate. She had drummed 98 bursts in 20 minutes as she moved from her main China Tree to a dead willow close to the territory of Male H on November 9. Here she stopped the instant Male H flew to join her. The two Hairies were together for 15 minutes. Female H did not always move close to Male H's territory, however, to attract him. She often drummed on a low tree, nearly 430 m away, and he would fly to her there. On December 26 I watched as she drummed, then flew to the top of an adjacent tree as if expectant, before flying to him. Such meetings were always of much the same form. The two rested not far apart as they exchanged a few rapid *jeek*s. Then, after a few moments, they launched themselves into what I called a duet flight. Standing in the center of the swamp, I could watch the two, one rising, one falling (Fig. 15), as they swung in great bounds and loops above the trees, now one, now the other in the lead as if without apparent aim.

Female H also displayed more usual types of courtship flight (Fig. 16). One of these, on November 8, was of special interest. She had done much drumming and participated in a number of duet flights by late afternoon. I was standing in the swamp at 16:30 when Female H, flying toward me in a bounding flight, suddenly broke into a bat-like flutter with alternations of floating with wings motionless, making *tweek tweek* notes as she did so. This flight, one she sometimes performed after a meeting with Male H, was the

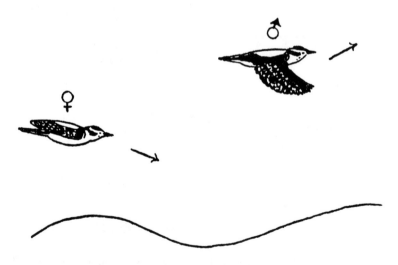

Fɪɢ. 15.   Duet flight of the pair of Hairy Woodpeckers (Female H, Male H) which took place above the treetops, usually over the territory of the female.

"TWEEK, TWEEK"

FIG. 16. Hairy Woodpecker (Female H) in a floating display flight.

climax of her day. After drumming a few more bursts she took a long flight, I presumed to her roost hole.

Female H faced a rival female in each of five conflicts observed between November and March. A conflict on 17 January was representative. Female H alighted on a tree trunk above the intruder and waved her bill. Her rival posed as if frozen. Female H dropped to a lower position, then pursued her adversary up the trunk.

A lane between the territories of Female H and Male H afforded a view of the activities of the male. Female H made only occasional visits to Male H's territory. I heard exchanges of *jeeks*, but never saw her drum nor did I witness duet flights on his side of the lane.

Male H visited his mate's territory far more frequently, usually in response to her drumming. He sometimes, however, took the initiative. I heard him begin to drum on a number of mornings when Female H was silent, moving to trees nearer and nearer to their common boundary. When by the lane on December 7, I heard *jeeks* as he flew across to join her. Within a minute the two were flying into a duet flight. The pair, at times, had duets of drumming, with each remaining in its own domain. Male H's rate was usually only half of hers. He spent increasing lengths of time in Female H's territory as the winter progressed. He occasionally drummed there, but in a weak manner, on indifferent places, and never on her drum trees.

Female H had drummed almost incessantly on the morning of November 22 when, at 11:30, she alighted on a small tree 10 m from me. She now tapped eight to nine times, paused, then tapped eight more series to a total of nearly 80 taps. I heard Female H tap on three other occasions between

November 9 and December 7. Tapping is one of the first indications of interest in a possible nest hole. On February 11, Male H flew to a fresh excavation, one belonging to a pair of Red-bellied Woodpeckers, and tapped three bursts just below it. Female H was close. I do not think Male H had any real interest in the hole. The sight of it had simply stimulated him.

Pair F became less demonstrative in late winter when the breeding activities of Downy and Red-bellied Woodpeckers were becoming increasingly evident. The last extensive drumming I heard from Female H was for 40 minutes on April 7. Female H and Male H now became difficult to locate. I was excited, therefore, to find Female H excavating a hole in a living ash on April 25.

Female H did all of the excavating on the two mornings I watched. Her activities on April 26 were particularly noteworthy. She was working out of sight, but came up at intervals to toss sawdust, sometimes as much as 37 billfulls, from the entrance. In a half hour she came out three times to drum and return. It appeared as if she wanted Male H to come. When he did come, he looked at the excavation, flew to her to exchange a few *jeek*s, then flew away, leaving her to continue.

When a pair of bluebirds came by, Female H flew at them without excitement. Her behavior changed when a starling arrived. Female H now displayed in a bill-waving dance. I never encountered Female H after April 26. Her excavation was complete, as my son found by putting up a ladder and testing with a probe. I never learned what had happened to her.

I have never encountered another female Hairy that took so much the lead in courtship, territory, and nest excavating as Female H. On the other hand, I have had no further opportunities to study southern Hairy Woodpeckers. A second pair of Hairies, located 1,000 m down the swamp, paralleled Female H/Male H in the following respects: (*i*) the female was shy and restless, taking long bounding flights from one end of her territory to another; (*ii*) she drummed at a fast rate of 8–11 bursts a minute and more frequently than her mate; (*iii*) and the male was not only easier to approach, but to locate by his *speak*s. His mate resembled Female H in never making this vocalization under ordinary circumstances. Difficulties of terrain made a detailed study of this second pair impractical.

It is of interest that Shelley (1933) in his studies of banded Hairy Woodpeckers in New Hampshire, witnessed two instances where females took the initiative in selection of nesting territories. In one case the female also selected the nest site and her mate rarely came near while she was excavating. With most pairs I have watched in New Hampshire, however, males have done the most drumming and the larger part of excavating. It would seem therefore, that a range of behavior is possible.

The duet flights that I witnessed with Female H and Male H are ones that I have never observed elsewhere. Pynnönen (1939) has described a similar type of flight for the Great Spotted Woodpecker of Europe.

## Handraising Hairies

My first observations on captive woodpeckers of any kind began with three young Hairies from a nest in Maryland. They differed in stages of development. The feathers of the smallest were only just emerging, while those of the largest were well along. This indicated, as is usual among woodpeckers, that they had hatched on different days. They all sucked vigorously on a small pair of forceps (Fig. 17), when we lowered food into their throats and they produced fecal sacs, when probed at the other end.

We shut the nestlings in a dark cabinet between feedings. They made low peepings as they settled down to sleep. These reminded us of a chorus of frogs in the swamp from which they had come. When I opened the cabinet in the morning, all three heads shot out begging for food.

The young began to preen each other and to stretch their wings as days went by. Their gradation in size remained. At 18 days, the largest was well feathered and twice the size of the smallest that was, nonetheless, healthy and vigorous. All three had ivory white tips to their bills, as well as oral

Fig. 17. Vigorous feeding reaction of young Hairy Woodpecker taking food from forceps at estimated 13 days of age.

flanges at the bases of their lower mandibles. These knobs aid parents in feeding young within darkened nests. They are sensitive and we found that tickling them with a toothpick was an easy way get a nestling to beg.

We placed a young Blue Jay in the cabinet one morning, little thinking the woodpeckers would pay any attention. Their reactions, however, were immediate. With bodies pressed down, they raised their heads, opened their bills and made a harsh, pulsating noise like that of a young starling. They reacted in similar fashion to some suckling rats a few days later. These reactions were a unique performance. We saw nothing like them at other times. At the other extreme were the *perp, perp, perp*s made by the young Hairies after being fed. These had a most contented sound.

It was notable how behavior varied. Our first set of young Hairies was peaceful, a second set was not. We got the latter when they were about halfway through the nestling period and placed them in a section of hollow log. The young woodpeckers were restless if removed, but settled down when replaced.

The female was the larger. She not only seized the food in an aggressive way, but also pecked so hard at her smaller brother that he cowered in fright. I divided the log with a partition, thinking to help him out. But the female climbed over whenever she got a chance to peck at him again. This aggressiveness may have survival value. No harm is done ordinarily. But should parents find less food in cold, wet weather or other unfavorable circumstances, a younger hatchling might not be able to compete. Unable to get its head high enough in the struggle for food, it would weaken and die. Death of the weaker one would then cut the brood to a size the parents could feed.

We kept the young Hairies (Fig. 18) in a large aquarium in the kitchen, where we could feed them readily. The two got along well. They bubbled over with *purr*s when we removed the cover of their container and fed read-

FIG. 18.    Nestlings at estimated 18 days of age still retaining white tip on upper mandible.

ily from our hands. Within a few weeks they were ready to transfer to more spacious quarters.

Once in the aviary, only the female continued to come to me and this she did over the next two years. If I sat in a chair where I could eat lunch and birdwatch at the same time, she alighted on the ground, then started going over my shoes. From here she climbed to my knee, then up my jacket to my dinner plate, exploring buttons and button holes on the way and sometimes pecking hard blows. Most of the exploring, however, was done with her tongue.

The tongues of woodpeckers are remarkable. It is worth having a pet one just to feel its tongue operating. I say feel because the tongue of a Hairy darts in and out with extreme rapidity. The feeling on the skin is like that of a fine electric buzzer or of a jet of air.

Once the tame Hairy reached my dinner plate, all was in the open. I could see that her tongue came out no farther than a half inch. She explored around a bit of tuna before taking it in. But it is one thing to have a Hairy Woodpecker on one's hand, or on one's shoulder exploring an ear and another, I found, to have it take an interest in one's head and scalp. There was little doubt as to what the Hairy felt about my cranium. The scalp was obviously bark and what lay underneath was wood containing larvae.

Sounding things out with preliminary pecks, the Hairy rained blows on what to her, no doubt, were small tunnels. She could sense something pulsating. The pulsating tubes, of course, were arteries. A few sharp pecks from the Hairy were enough to start blood spurting.

Anyone seeing me hastening from the aviary with blood running from my scalp, might think keeping woodpeckers a hazardous occupation. But no serious harm was done. Even my Pileated never struck any really hard blows and she was much larger than the Hairy.

It is always a pleasant experience to have a pet, whether dog or woodpecker, greet one in friendly fashion. My Hairies greeted me by jerking their bodies about, half-starting their wings, and raising their head feathers. They also made chittery and other low notes ranging from sputters to doll-like squeaks. This is the way a dependent juvenile greets its parents. A peculiarity of these greetings was that I had to wear the same clothes. If I put on something new, like a white sweater, they became afraid, and did not come to the wire.

Our female Hairies were the tamest. I had ideas as to why this might be. One was that females take the lead in courtship in the wild. They fly to mates in mid-winter, making low *tewk, tewk* notes, whereas males at this time seem relatively unresponsive. The male's sexual drive is spread over only a few months; that of females over more months of the year. She thus appears the more affectionate over a longer time.

A difficulty in keeping woodpeckers in Maryland was that we drove to New Hampshire each summer. What were we to do with them? One cannot entrust the keeping of birds to others. This is not because friends may not be trustworthy. It is simply because handraised birds are more dependent on those who care for them than one might suppose. Hence we took our woodpeckers with us.

In transferring the woodpeckers from aviary to cages for these journeys, I worked at night. It was easier, for one thing, to catch the birds in the dark. For another, it meant that they could not recognize me. I did not want them to think of me as an enemy that pursued and grabbed. One has to be careful with handraised birds. One false move and hopes of having a tame woodpecker, favorable for study, may be lost.

A near catastrophe happened one year on our return. I was trying to move a bulky cage into the house, when the cage door opened and out flew my favorite Hairy. She flew to a trunk of a pine, then to the top of a tall tree and off. What a loss! Recovery looked hopeless, so I went on with the rest of my birds.

I noticed the Hairy in a neighbor's yard hours later. Could I catch her? I got some of her usual food, including a half orange that woodpeckers like particularly, and set out to try my luck. "Here Woodie," I called, "here Woodie, Woodie." The female made chittery greetings and started to back down toward me. Then she changed her mind and flew to another tree.

Instead of pursuing, I took a position at the foot of still another tree and continued to call. This time she flew over and to my great delight, started to feed from my fingers. Could I catch her? Slowly I let one hand come above, then with a gentle swoop she was mine. Within a few minutes she was back in the aviary, seemingly unaffected by her hours in the open.

## METHODS OF COMMUNICATION

### VOCALIZATIONS

*Speak.*—This is the commonest note of Hairies in all months of the year, expressing excitement from any cause. Some Hairies give shrill *speak*s when an intruder approaches a nest.

*Whinny.*—A series of *haan, haan, jer, jer* or other notes given so rapidly that they almost run together. Whinnies become frequent in spring as nestlings develop. Both juveniles and parents use them to keep in touch with each other.

*Sputters.*—These have elements of whinnies but are louder and more sharply varied. Some versions, *chip-cha-haa-haa* or *chrr-chrr-jer-jer*, are almost like a lilting, sardonic laughter, although expressive of intense alarm, as by a nest.

*Greeting notes.*—These range from *jeek, jeek, chewi, chewi,* and *tewk, tewk,* to loud *joick, joick*s.

*Conflicts.*—Hairies may give shrill *queek, queek, queek*s or occasionally *wick-a-wick-a-wick*s in the excitement of conflicts.

*Vocalizations of nestlings.*—Young Hairies make steady *pee-urp, pee-urp, pee-*

*urp*s in the nest, that rise to a louder *click, click, click* as a parent approaches. These latter notes become harsh at time of feeding. Sudden fright may produce surprisingly harsh, pulsating notes.

## DRUMMING AND TAPPING

The drummings of Hairy Woodpeckers, coming at rates of from four to 16 or more bursts a minute, communicate a range of meanings dependent on intensity. Males usually drum more than females, although females can, at times, drum more than males. Among types discernable are:

*Calling for a mate.*—If members of a pair roost at a distance from each other early in the breeding season, a male will usually drum at dawn to get his mate to come to him.

*Drumming for copulation.*—A male, if at a peak of readiness prior to egg laying, may drum in a prolonged fashion, if need be, to attract his mate. Females may also drum for copulations, especially at the start of a breeding season.

*Location drumming.*—When a female comes at last, in response to the drumming of her mate, she may announce her coming with a single low burst. The male then stops, but may resume his drumming if she comes no closer.

*Duets.*—Hairies form pairs in midwinter, nearly three months before they nest in the last of April. Among activities strengthening the pair bond are duets of drumming, in which a burst from one stimulates a burst from the other. Such duets may continue for 15 or more minutes, with either sex taking the lead. Duets late in the season are often of a different nature. Males may favor one place for a nest site, the female another, but in woods that are inadequate, neither place is really suitable. The result is a tug-of-war that may end in a failure to agree and a breakdown of the pair bond.

*Territorial.*—Although any loud drumming may serve territorial purposes, a male may drum opposite to the boundary with another male, as if in challenge.

*Demonstrative.*—Hairies start drumming wherever they happen to be when an intruder appears. This association of drumming and conflict holds for many species of woodpeckers.

*Contentment.*—A Hairy Woodpecker may rest on a bare limb in the sun alternating a few bursts of drumming with preening for what seems to be the pleasure of doing so.

*Lone male or female.*—Hairies generally drum at rates of four to five bursts a minute. On February 9, Male C drummed for a prolonged period at a rate of eight bursts and three days later, at an extraordinarily fast rate of 26 bursts a minute. He was without a mate and, I believe, trying to attract one.

*Tapping.*—A Hairy Woodpecker searching for a nest site may percuss as it moves up a stub or drum a burst here and there. When it locates a likely place, it taps at an easily countable rate of two to three taps a second as a way of inviting its mate to come and look.

## Displays

*Bill-waving dance.*—A Hairy of either sex points its bill upward and at times even backward (Fig. 9), then swings its bill back and forth like a conductor's baton, while jerking head and body and making half-starting motions with its wings. The bird on the offense does the dancing. These displays are also used in interspecific encounters as against a starling near a nest hole.

*Display of white breast.*—This can occur briefly as an isolated performance (Fig. 9) apart from the bill-waving dance of which it is a main component. I saw it on several occasions when an owning male faced another male who was unresponsive to challenge, possibly due to immaturity. It is conceivable that the white breast of the Hairy serves a signaling purpose, since it shows up well in the bare woods of late winter when agonistic and courtship behaviors are at a peak.

*Combat pose.*—A Hairy Woodpecker ready to strike or to meet blows in a conflict holds itself with bill open, wings held out slightly from the body, and tail fanned (Fig. 5). Outer tail feathers sometimes twitch independently of the rest of the tail.

*Head feathers.*—These are usually pressed down in conflict, giving sharp outline to the head. They may, otherwise, be raised in mild excitement from any cause.

*Defense.*—When threatened or about to be attacked, a Hairy Woodpecker may hold a frozen pose with head and bill pointed straight forward; spread its wings horizontally; or swing around a trunk or branch with wings fully outstretched backward.

*Displacement pecking.*—A woodpecker, in pauses of a conflict, may start pecking on indifferent places.

Hairies can fly silently or make a loud *brr* with their wings, indicating that they are disturbed or excited. The noise can also inform a mate in what direction its partner is flying.

*Resting motionless.*—A sign of close accord between members of a pair in the early breeding season.

*Courtship flights.*—An irregular type of flight, either floating with wings at a **V**, or fluttering and bat-like. The flight is always a sign of emotional intensity.

## Literature Cited

HAARTMAN, L. VON. 1968. The evolution of resident vs. migratory habit in birds. Some considerations. Ornis Feen., **45**: 1–7.

HINDE, R. A. 1952. The behaviour of the Great Tit (*Parus major*) and some other related species. Behaviour, Suppl. 2. 201 p.

# HAIRY WOODPECKER

JACKSON, J. A. AND E. E. HOOVER 1975. A potentially harmful effect of suet on woodpeckers. Bird-banding, **46**: 131–134.

KENDEIGH, S. C. 1961. Energy of birds conserved by roosting in cavities. Wilson Bull., **73**: 140–147.

KILHAM, L. 1959. Head-scratching and wing-stretching of woodpeckers. Auk, **76**: 527–528.

———. 1960. Courtship and territorial behavior of Hairy Woodpeckers. Auk, **77**: 259–270.

———. 1965. Differences in feeding behavior of male and female Hairy Woodpeckers. Wilson Bull., **77**: 134–145.

———. 1966. Reproductive behavior of Hairy Woodpeckers. I. Pair formation and courtship. Wilson Bull., **78**: 251–265.

———. 1968. Reproductive behavior of Hairy Woodpeckers. II. Nesting and Habitat. Wilson Bull., **80**: 286–305.

———. 1969. Reproductive behavior of Hairy Woodpeckers, III. Agonistic behavior in relation to courtship and territory. Wilson Bull., **81**: 169–183.

———. 1973. Dying elms: boon to woodpeckers. American Birds, **27**: 736–738.

LAWRENCE, L. DE K. 1967. A comparative life-history study of four species of woodpeckers. Ornith. Monogr. (Amer. Ornith. Union), no. 5, 156 p.

MAXSON, S. J., AND B. D. MASON 1981. Commensal foraging between Hairy and Pileated Woodpeckers. Wilson Bull., **52**: 62–63.

PYNNÖNEN, A. 1939. Beiträge zur Kenntnis de Biologie finnischer Spechte. Ann. Zool. Soc. Zool.-Bot.-Fenn. Vanamo, **7** (2):1–166.

SELANDER, R. K. 1965. Sexual dimorphism in relation to foraging behavior in the Hairy Woodpecker. Wilson Bull., **77**: 416.

SHELLEY, L. O. 1933. Some notes on the Hairy Woodpecker. Bird-banding, **4**: 204–205.

SNYDER, L. L. 1923. On the crown markings of juvenile Hairy and Downy Woodpeckers. Canadian Field-Nat., **37**: 167–168.

# 4

## BLACK-BACKED WOODPECKER

### NEST ACTIVITIES

These birds nest in northernmost New Hampshire as well as high up in mountains farther south. I observed two pairs in June, 1963, by the Second Connecticut Lake in a strip of coniferous forest left from lumbering.

The nest observed most closely was 2 m above the ground, in the rotten center of a living spruce. It somewhat resembled the hole of a Red-cockaded Woodpecker in the way the Black-backeds had chipped away the bark, leaving an extensive area of bare wood around the hole (Fig. 19), a situation also noted by Short (1974).

The Black-backeds usually flew through woods directly, then glided for the last 10 or more meters to their nest. A parent feeding its young turned its head so that the opened bills of the two met closely in the transfer of food. It soon became apparent, at this and a second nest, that the sexes behaved differently. The females made about three times as many visits as their mates, but came with bills closed and little prey protruding. The males came less often but with bills well-stuffed. The number of visits by either sex varied with circumstances. After a heavy rain, when insect life seemed especially abundant, both members of Pair B visited their nest 12 times in 20 minutes. On the other hand, neither of Pair A visited their nest between 20:00 and 21:00 hours at the end of June 18. It was dusk before Male A arrived for the night, rapping a few times on the side of the nest tree, as if nervous, before entering.

The females were more nervous than their mates at both nests. This was shown not only by the rapid series of *chets*, made when I came close, but also by the flashing of white-edged nictitating membranes that showed up well against their black feathers. An apparent result of this shyness was that when I stood within 4 m of Nest B, Female B refused to come, while her mate, unintimidated, made five visits in 35 minutes. Another difference between the sexes was in nest sanitation. All of the observed instances ($n = 7$) were by the males. On June 19 Female A fed her young five times in seven minutes without entering. Male A came only once in 23 minutes, but after feeding, he entered to emerge with a large mass of feces.

The females not only made more feeding visits but also spent more time by their nests. Female B, in something of a routine, fed her nestlings, then ascended a dead balsam to drum 2–9 bursts in a leisurely fashion, preening and scratching in between. She then, on some visits, flew back to the nest to enter and rest for a few minutes with her head out. She always left off guarding when Male B arrived. It was the persistent drumming of Female B that first led me to her nest in mid-June.

A foreign male that trespassed near Nest B was attacked by whichever

Fig. 19. Nest hole of Black-backed Woodpecker in a living spruce with heart rot. Female by entrance.

parent happened to be present. Female B was resting by her nest on June 19 when the intruder appeared. She flew halfway to him, raising her wings as she gave a shrill *pet-pet-wree-oo*, then chased him through the woods. Male B met the intruder later on. He gave a *wreo* and a threat display, as Female B had done, but then advanced in a bill-waving dance. This greater willingness of males to display rather than to attack is something I have noted with other woodpeckers.

A situation I found confusing was that the partners of Pair B greeted each other in much the same way that they met the intruder. Male B, on seeing Female B within the nest one morning, gave a sharp *ki-ki-wree-oo* while spreading his wings horizontally. She flew off immediately. On another occasion she swung around the nest tree, putting the trunk between herself and him as she raised her wings to give a *wree-oo*. I was only 3 m away on another day when, at close range, I could see Male B's head feathers bristle out like a bottle brush when his mate came in sight. The bottle brush effect is one that I have seen with only one other woodpecker, the Red-headed. With that species, also, it appears to be agonistic.

Other encounters between the two of Pair B were milder. On one occasion the two did no more than peck gently at each other on coming close, and on another, Female B gave low *grr, grr* notes when her mate raised his wings. The members of Pair A paid little attention to each other as they went about caring for their young. It is possible that the difference between the two pairs arose from the fights that Pair B had with the intruder. The excitement aroused in the encounters may have spilled over into intrapair relations.

The Black-backeds collected prey within several hundred meters of their nests. They often moved as if in frantic haste. On June 28 I found Female B scrambling along the underside of a fallen spruce, making *chets* as she paused to extract beetle larvae from under bark. I later found her in a high, isolated spruce. In spite of obstructing branches, she knocked, then seized and tossed away bits of bark. At other times I found Black-backeds moving hurriedly over and among the fallen logs, slash, ferns and other vegetation of the lumbered areas.

The young in both nests made chittery vocalizations that increased when a parent approached with prey, then diminished after the adult had left. The nestlings also made a steady *click-click-click*. I removed two in a pinfeather stage on June 19. They made an almost incessant noise, varying from *chet-chet-chet* to *chet-cha-chaa*. These vocalizations became harsh at the slightest disturbance. A striking feature of the nestlings was the almost ferocious way they attacked their surroundings, including the forceps with which they were fed, their cage, and later themselves, as if each was trying to swallow the other. Red-headeds have been the only other nestlings that I have found comparable.

The young Black-backeds greeted me by flapping their wings while making a steady flow of *chets*. Both of our captives had central yellow patches on their otherwise black heads. A surmise, however, that both were males, turned out to be erroneous. When they molted later on, both turned out to be females.

It is difficult to get an adequate picture of the nesting of Black-backeds on the basis of only a few pairs. Fortunately, Short (1974) has since made more extended observations in Hamilton County, New York. Taking our observations, which are almost entirely confirmative, a few points need special emphasis. One, well-supported by Short, is that female Black-backeds feed young more frequently than males, but carry fewer items of prey per visit. The bills of males, Short noted, were more frequently crammed with insects. He estimated that the males, in spite of making fewer visits, may have brought in a half to two-thirds of the food supplied to the nestlings. From this he makes the interesting speculation (p. 10) that "unless the female changed her mode of feeding, she could not by herself feed the number of young found in this nest, whereas, if she disappeared during the nestling period, the male could successfully feed the young. . . . " While I have not been able to verify this for Black-backeds, it is very much the situation that I have observed for widowed Yellow-bellied Sapsuckers.

Short also noted the aggressiveness of young Black-backeds. "The nestlings," he wrote, "waving and hitting with the bill, so beseiged the adult that it often had to make several attempts before successfully 'running the gauntlet' into the nest."

My observations on nesting Black-backeds ran parallel to those made on Hairies in several respects. The females of both species tended at times to make more visits, with fewer prey, and to stay nearer nests, as if guarding, than their mates. To a human observer the Hairies appeared to have close pairbonds as judged, among other ways, by their exchanges of low notes and exuberant vocalizations made as they approached mate and nest. The Black-backeds, in contrast, especially those of Pair B, appeared as if hostile to each other. But it takes time to know any species well. Male and female Downies greet each other with a harsh *chirr*, that sounds much like the *chrr* used in conflicts. But these notes may sound different to them. With experience, one comes to realize how difficult interpretations can be or, to put it differently, how long it takes to have an inkling of how birds may look and sound to each other.

## METHODS OF COMMUNICATION

*Drumming.*—Most drumming came in bursts of two seconds, at relatively long intervals of 30–40 seconds. The diminution at the end of each burst, as well as the long intervening intervals, were suggestive of the drumming of Pileated Woodpeckers, as was the rapping.

*Rapping.*—Sharp single blows given on a convenient place when nervous, as when about to enter a roost for the night.

## BLACK-BACKED WOODPECKER

*Chet.*—This note is the commonest one of Black-backeds and comparable to the *speaks* of Hairy Woodpeckers. It generally serves as an expression of mild excitement. One female gave *chet*s at a rate of more than 100 per minute when I came close to her nest. The *chet*s sound more like the notes of a sparrow or blackbird than a woodpecker.

*Wreo.*—This is a resounding note, often given singly as a greeting between members of a pair. It is preceded by shorter syllables such as *pet-pet-wreo* when given at greater intensity, as when used against a rival.

*Displays.*—Members of pairs occasionally greeted each other by raising their extended wings horizontally or, when facing rivals, by extending them vertically, the feathers of the head, at times, bristling out in all directions.

### LITERATURE CITED

KILHAM, L. 1966. Nesting activities of Black-backed Woodpeckers. Condor, **68**: 308–310.

SHORT, L. L. 1974. Habits and interactions of North American three-toed woodpeckers (*Picoides arcticus* and *Picoides tridactylus*). Amer. Mus. Novit., no. 2547, 42 p.

# 5

## PILEATED WOODPECKER

The Pileated is our largest woodpecker now that the Ivory-billed is probably extinct. Both birds have (or had) flaming red crests and handsome black
and white plumages. The Pileated is almost entirely black when seen at a
distance, but the first thing I see when stalking it through dimly lit woods

of hemlock or other trees, is the white stripe down its longish neck. I say stalking, because Pileateds in the north are as wary as Ruffed Grouse. They make a low pecking, the blows coming slowly, when excavating in rotting logs and trunks. It is these sounds that I follow in trying for a view of their activities.

They sometimes work on large pines and hemlocks, digging into the heartrot where carpenter ants (*Camponotus* spp.) have their galleries. But the opportunities I have had of watching them in New Hampshire have been few. This is not from lack of effort. Pileated Woodpeckers in the north have large territories and are too thinly scattered to follow successfully. They are more plentiful in the south and it is there that I have learned most about them.

## ROOSTING

### MARYLAND AND GEORGIA

There is a closer association of roost holes and old nest holes with Pileateds than with Hairies and Downies. If there is a stand of large trees in one place, as I found with sycamores growing along the banks of the Potomac in Maryland, Pileateds may build a succession of nest holes in succeeding years, using the old ones for roosting. This represents an economy of effort. I have never seen Pileateds excavating roost holes in the fall as is common among Hairies and Downies. But if something happens to old nest holes, Pileateds may have to shift to other places. Rounds (1958) describes a pair of Pileateds that entered holes in the walls of a barn in Maine to roost under the eaves, the male on one side and the female on the other.

Pileateds, as shown by rapping, are usually nervous if one stands close to where they are about to go to roost. One winter I watched a Pileated enter his roost hole, then knocked on the trunk below. The male flew out to an adjacent tree and rapped. When I walked away, he returned to his hole at once, apparently not overly disturbed by my routing him out.

Female Pileateds, like the females of most woodpeckers, are apt to roost in the less good holes, the males in the better ones. A female by the Potomac roosted in a hole with two entrances. In late February she behaved most strangely. Coming to the lower hole in the late afternoon she looked in, then flew to a nearby branch and hung upside down. She repeated this maneuver three times, then flew away. I found her behaving in the same way on March 22. She hung upside down on the branch five times, once after each look. Two days later I arrived early and saw a female Wood Duck enter the lower hole. The Pileated entered the top hole soon afterward, only to come out and fly off, apparently unwilling to contest the hole any longer.

On Sapelo Island, in Georgia, I recorded the hours kept by a male Pileated in emerging from his roost in the morning and returning to it in the evening. Between January 31 and 8 February, his times of emerging were from three to nine minutes before sunrise. On two days of rain he emerged 16 to 27 minutes after. There was more variation in his times of going to roost. These varied from 20 to 57 minutes before sunset. He thus went to roost at a greater light intensity than he got up in the morning. On a rainy evening he retired 84 minutes before sunset.

## STREAM OF *CUK*S ON FLYING TO ROOST HOLES

Pileated Woodpeckers usually fly to roost holes silently. Sometimes, however, they give loud *cuk*s that make a dramatic performance. *Cuk*s were given on 19 of 27 occasions that I watched a pair roosting in Maryland between October 1958 and February 1959. In a typical instance, the male flew silently to a tree about 50 m from his roost. He waited a few minutes, then at 16:40 (sunset at 16:39), flew to his hole in a sycamore uttering a barrage of *cuk*s. These ceased the moment he reached the hole and popped in. The *cuk*s, given at rates of up to three per second, constituted a vertible stream of sound, audible at a distance. On 16 November both members of the pair had flown to their holes in this manner. The holes were 30 m apart.

The Pileated Woodpeckers in Maryland began to fly to their holes silently on 26 March. This was when the male had started a nest excavation that, by 8 April, was large enough for him to spend the night. I now wondered whether the *cuk*s were a phenomenon limited to the nonbreeding season. In the course of the next 14 years I found eight more Pileated Woodpeckers' nests, mostly on visits to Georgia and Florida. There, as in Maryland, the woodpeckers flew to them silently. Few of these nests, however, were found early in the incubation period.

On 24 March 1973, I found a male finishing a nest in a dead pine in Luray, South Carolina. Incubation began three days later. The male did all the nest attending on the first day. At 09:35, after being away for a while, he returned, making a loud series of *cuk*s from 100 m away until he landed below the hole. Would he do the same on following days? I was watching below the tree not long after dawn on 28 March. The male put his head out at 06:20 to give a high call. This was in response to the *cuk*s his mate gave continuously while flying in from a distance. I continued to watch until the seventh day of incubation. On each day, with the exception of one I missed, either the male or the female flew to the nest at times of changeovers making *cuk*s, the bird on the nest usually answering with a single high call.

A question is why the Pileateds at Luray should have flown to their nest in noisy fashion, while pairs observed at nests elsewhere had not. This may involve the degree of human interference. According to accounts in Bent (1939), Pileated Woodpeckers were at one time hunted as game birds. It may be that an increased wariness has been a factor in their survival. When undisturbed, as at Luray, they fly to both roost and nest holes with loud *cuk*s, whereas, with increasing wariness, the *cuk*s may be reserved for roost holes alone. If roost holes are close to human dwellings, or an observer frightens the bird, *cuk*s may not be heard at all.

A further question is why Pileateds should make vocalizations that seem designed to reveal their whereabouts. The European Blackbird is more circumspect. According to Lorenz (1970), it gives a loud warning, then flies silently to roost elsewhere. Several reasons for a reverse type of behavior are conceivable. One is that Pileateds seeks to startle any competitor that might be lurking in a roost hole, to reveal itself. But this appears unlikely. Although flying squirrels sometimes show themselves if one knocks on a tree, other species, such as gray squirrels, are difficult to arouse.

A more likely hypothesis is that Pileateds address their *cuks* to their own kind. Pileated Woodpeckers maintain close pairbonds the year around and, when conditions are favorable, as by the Potomac, they may roost in holes that are not far apart. When one of a pair goes to a hole, it lets the other know just where it is going. This may serve to prevent both birds going to the same hole and competing. It is also a way of keeping in touch in the final moments of a day. Another aspect of the woods by the Potomac was that an extra male roosted nearby. The calls, therefore, may have also been territorial, a warning to the second male. The habit of giving loud vocalizations may be a feature of the genus *Dryocopus*, to which Pileateds belong. Blume (1964) describes and gives a figure of the large Black Woodpecker of Europe flying to its roost giving *kurr*s all the way, punctuated by a *kijah* on alighting at the hole. He considers the calling territorial. The habit of giving loud vocalizations is not mentioned in Bent (1939), nor by Hoyt (1957) in her excellent account of the roosting of Pileateds. She has since written (pers. comm.), however, that she "could hear the long series of *cuks* as the birds in Sapsucker Woods approached the roosting area in winter and early spring. It was from that that we could ascertain which of several roost holes was being used."

## Conflicts Near Roost Holes

Territorial behavior is not restricted to the breeding season. It can occur around roost holes in fall and winter. A pair of Pileateds had roost holes 80 m apart by the Potomac. An extra male roosted in the vicinity and the two males had at least nine conflicts between September and March. In the late afternoon of 13 December, both flew to the base of a tree near where I stood. They shifted around the trunk as one tried to strike at the other. The male on the defensive raised his wings in a full threat display. The silence of this conflict was interrupted when a female flew to the base of the tree making shrill *g-waick*s. The three Pileateds were now close together. The two of the pair were resting on either side of the intruder, engaging in bill-waving dances accompanied by *woick*s, when the male in the middle suddenly raised his wings in a threat. There was a flurry of wings, the female left, and the males resumed their silent conflict.

A different type of conflict took place at dawn on January 10. Male A flew from his roost at 07:21 giving *woick*s as he headed toward his mate, who was close to the second male. The female now foraged on a stump in seeming indifference while the two males fought for the next 20 minutes. One male alighted below his rival, then chased him up a tree trunk to upper branches. The fleeing male flapped his wings as if to speed his ascent. He then took flight and a pursuit followed, round about through the woods, until the two alighted on another tree. The male being pursued sought a respite, on several of such sequences, by clinging upside down to a terminal branch, a position that made it difficult for his opponent to attack.

A reason that these conflicts persisted through the winter may have been that the owning pair eventually excavated a nest in the vicinity the following spring.

A feature of conflicts among Pileateds, as among the equally large Crimson-crested Woodpeckers studied in Panama, is that they strike at each other directly. This is in contrast to the prolonged bill-waving displays of Hairies and Downies in the early breeding season. It may be that the large picines, at greater risk of predation because of their size, cannot afford to expose themselves in prolonged displays. Brief but fiercer encounters, therefore, could have a selective advantage. On the other hand, woodpeckers with such powerful bills might injure each other. It is of note, therefore, that a contestant can seek safety by hanging upside down.

## WINTER FORAGING AND ASSOCIATED BEHAVIOR

I was interested one winter, on Sapelo, to follow a pair of Pileateds from dawn to dusk, although not all in one day, to find out what events made up their lives.

### RENDEZVOUS AT DAWN

Setting out at dawn for the grove of tall pines where the male roosted, I knew just the spot where, in spite of dim light, I could get the best view of his roost hole, 30 m up in a pine. Minutes passed with nothing happening. The hole remained dark and silent. Then, at 08:05, the Pileated looked out, withdrew, and gave a high call from within. After this he swung out. Once in a good position at the side of his cavity, he gave a rolling drum. The drum as well as the high call were messages to his mate. She had spent the night some distance away and now gave an answering call.

Day after day I found the two getting in touch with each other soon after sunrise. On this morning, the female flew to a dead pine where the two often met. Her mate loitered on the way. A minute later the female took a looping flight among the pine tops to the east and, after a moment, the male followed.

### FEEDING BEHAVIOR

The foraging of the pair was largely confined to pines and live oaks covering the southern end of the island. The pines were large loblollies where the Pileateds worked on dead limbs, digging into one small area for five to 10 minutes before moving on.

The area where the Pileateds worked the longest, was where 40 pines of medium height had died in a circle, as though the agent killing them had spread from a center. Pines at the center had lost terminal twigs and much bark, while those in a midzone still retained their bark, although it was easily peeled away. The outer rings of pines were ones that had died most recently. They retained some needles and their bark was firmly adherent. The pair of Pileateds concentrated on the pines of the midzone. Here they were so occupied that they worked for periods of up to three and a half hours, moving about infrequently and showing little variation in the way they fed. After alighting on the trunk of a pine, a Pileated spent about three minutes knocking away bark with glancing blows, occasionally seizing a piece in its bill to pull it away. It then ran its tongue over the areas of frass, open tunnels, and wood that lay beneath. When I pulled away bark from similar places, I found numbers of termites (*Isoptera*) and no other insects. The termites thus appeared to be the principal prey. After finishing with the bark, the Pileateds spent 10 to 15 minutes digging holes into the wood to a depth of several centimeters. Although I was unable to find pitch tubes of bark beetles on any of the 40 pines, I did find them on a group of five dead pines where the woodpeckers worked for half an hour.

Another feeding place was on small pines, 5–7 cm in diameter, killed as a result of crowding in young stands. These were well decayed. One pine was so undercut by a Pileated that it fell over on top of him.

When foraging on live oaks, the Pileateds ascended trunks and large branches, exploring crevices in bark and knocking away occasional pieces. They dug into small cavities, but rarely for as long as five minutes. They also worked on dead limbs and stubs that had died a long time previously. When feeding in this manner a Pileated might spend 20 minutes in one tree, then move to another close by, as though finding places to feed without difficulty. This was also true of the pines. It seemed that prey was generally available, making it easy for the pair of Pileateds to forage together.

In Florida I watched a pair foraging in a pasture with scattered pines. Quantities of logs and stumps, left from lumbering, had become rotted where they lay water-soaked on marshy ground. During observations that lasted from 15 minutes to an hour or more, I found the Pileateds foraging at ground level on rotting logs, stumps, or fallen pine branches, on 19 of 25 occasions. On the other six the woodpeckers worked higher up at the bases of trees. Other foraging places included a well-rotted maple stub where the male worked for over an hour digging, then turning and twisting his head as he fed. On one occasion the female scaled bark and dug into the dead limb of a living pine.

The Pileated Woodpeckers in both Georgia and Florida fed on fruits of several trees but possibly no more than once a day. On Sapelo they came almost exclusively to camphor trees.

For some reason Pileateds become noisy when feeding on fruit or berries, making the woods resound with their *cuk*s. *Cuk*s from the camphor tree came at the rate of 192 a minute. When the two Pileateds joined in noise making, the cacophony was amazing. It sounded like two hens that had just laid eggs. In order to reach the fruit, as I could see once I had a good view, the birds had to hang upside down at the end of a swaying branch. It was, seemingly, the exposed position that got them excited.

The Pileateds came to these trees at no special time. I found them there early in the day, at noon, and once just before roosting. On February 5 the female fed on a camphor tree for 25 minutes and her mate for 15. These were their longest times. On February 10, in the course of feeding for three and a half hours on recently dead pines, the pair fed for five minutes on the fruit of a greenbriar.

The Pileateds on Sapelo seemed to have little leisure in winter months. I sometimes found the pair resting and preening early in the afternoon. But on the whole, I felt that they took off little time in the course of a winter's day. They were too occupied in finding food.

## TERRITORY AND INTRASPECIFIC CONFLICTS

While Pileateds are usually difficult to follow due to their long flights, the situation on Sapelo was simplified by the salt marshes. The greatest distances at which the pair foraged (Fig. 20) were about 1770 m east to west and about 400 m north to south. These formed an area of roughly 70 ha of which nearly 20 percent was open spaces of little use to the woodpeckers.

I saw four territorial intrusions, all resisted by the owning male. The first I knew of a conflict was one noon when there were *g-waick*s ringing through the live oaks. I hurried over to find Owning Male feeding next to his mate. It took a few minutes to locate a trespassing male, near the ground and 25 m away. The Owning Male did no more than give *g-waick*s every minute or two for the next 10 minutes. Then he flew at the intruder, striking down at him until both birds were facing each other on the ground. The invader soon gave in by turning and spreading his wings. This made it difficult for the Owning Male to strike effectively. He returned to the tree trunk and soon flew away. The second male then resumed feeding.

An encounter on 31 January, also deep within the territory of the pair, was of a different type. When an intruding male came to the top of a dead oak and drummed, the Owning Male alighted three meters away. Instead of attacking, he preened for eight minutes. His opponent rested, then flew away. It seemed possible that the absence of conflict may have been due to the lack of a female to spur on the two.

Two other encounters were alike. On each an intruder flew through an

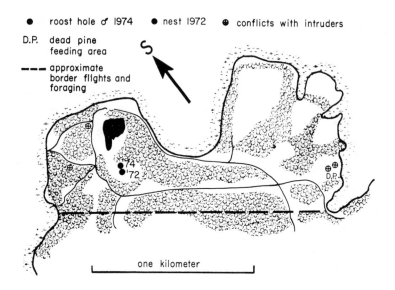

FIG. 20. Midwinter foraging territory of a pair of Pileated Woodpeckers on Sapelo Island, Georgia.

area of dying pines where the pair was feeding. The Owning Male immediately flew in pursuit. After an absence of 10 minutes, he returned to join his mate.

### INTRAPAIR RELATIONS

The members of pairs of Pileateds in both Florida and Georgia, with few exceptions, remained together from shortly after they left roost holes at dawn until they returned to roost in the evening. The two on Sapelo were seldom as much as 30 to 40 m apart as they worked on adjacent or nearly adjacent trees. Every so often one would fly to the other. On seven of 17 occasions the female flew to the male, alighting two meters away, then hitching to within 30 cm. She twice gave *woicks* (i.e., low, intimate vocalizations) and once waved her bill (Fig. 21) as she approached. The response of the male varied. He waved his bill with head thrown back on one of her approaches. When feeding at other times he moved away and she fed where he had been. This behavior was also noted in Florida.

Once, when the female on Sapelo took over a particularly good place, he returned and struck at her. This was the only time I saw him displace her in this manner. On two of the 10 times that the male flew or moved close to his mate, the two simply came close, once almost touching bills, then separated. The eight other occasions were all on the group of 40 dead pines.

Here it seemed that the straight trunks, close together and without foliage,

FIG. 21. Bill-waving dance of female Pileated.

enabled the male to see what his mate was doing. If she happened to have a good feeding place when he was without one, as happened five times in five hours, he flew over and displaced her. This was without display of any kind although she usually raised her crest as she left. He then fed for some time where she had been, turning and twisting his head as though finding prey.

The male displaced his mate three times in three minutes at the end of the afternoon, waving his bill each time. But he showed no particular interest in feeding after she had left. After the last displacing he flew toward his roost hole a kilometer away. I noted in these episodes that when the male displaced his mate from places where he wanted to feed, he never waved his bill. It seemed, therefore, that the bill-waving at the last of the day was probably pairbonding.

The Pileated Woodpeckers in Florida fed closer together than in Georgia. They were often less than eight meters apart and sometimes only 30 to 50 cm. This closeness may have resulted from prey being concentrated in scattered logs and stumps. In these situations I saw the female displace the male five times, but never the reverse. The two occasions when the male did displace her were when she was feeding higher up on a dead pine. This was of interest, for it was the same as the situations noted on Sapelo.

After feeding in one locality for 20 minutes to two hours or more, one or the other of the pair on Sapelo flew off to feed elsewhere. In Florida the male usually left first, soon followed by his mate. On Sapelo either bird might be the first to leave and thus no sexual difference appeared to be involved. This agrees with Tanner's (1942:60 ) remark on Ivory-bills that "In traveling and feeding through the woods, the pair would follow each other, neither sex consistently" taking the lead.

The sun was low over the salt marsh on Sapelo when first the male, then the female left on a long flight toward the pine grove where they had started the day. By the time (18:00) I reached the grove, a male bluebird was peering into the male Pileated's roost hole. The bluebird entered to rest on the rim looking out. After 20 minutes of this, he was sharply driven away by the female Pileated. This was the first time I had seen her come to the male's roost. She swooped at the bluebird, then hitched to the side of the cavity to drum one long, resounding burst. Her mate came right away to alight above her. Both birds tapped. Tapping commonly connotes attachment to a nest site. The pine had, possibly, once been a nest. It was obviously too dilapidated to use again. I believed that the tapping was mainly symbolic, a demonstration of "affection" of one Pileated for the other.

The female left and was soon making *cuks* far to the east. The male hitched to his hole, bowed his head in and out several times, then swung in. He now gave *cuks* for 12 seconds in response to the *cuks* of his mate. After looking out briefly, he withdrew and gave a burst of drumming. These flourishes were the last I saw or heard from him for the day. Following the direction the female had flown, I found her having a last fill of camphor berries before flying to her roost.

## Varied Meanings of *cuks*

*Cuks* are the commonest notes of Pileateds. I have found them being used in a variety of ways. The male or female at Sapelo might give a few in flying from one tree to another, seemingly as location notes. *Cuks* can also express exuberance. I several times saw the female, then the male, take a long flight over the trees, each giving a wild, and to me thrilling, stream of loud *cuks* as it flew. The Pileateds may have been enjoying the morning or just each other's company at the beginning of the breeding season.

There are other occasions when Pileateds give *cuks* in an almost predictable fashion. One of these is when feeding on fruiting trees. The noise made by the pair on the camphor trees at Sapelo was considerable. But I once heard an even greater clamor when four Pileateds, parents and young, were feeding on a grape vine in New Hampshire. Why should these birds, usually so silent, attract attention to themselves? I think the *cuk*s relate to fear of predation. This is from two sets of observations, one on chachalacas, a neotropical game bird. A few were liberated on Sapelo years ago and still remain there. It was in Panama, however, that I first noticed something about these birds that feed on fruiting trees. Whenever a hawk, flying along the edge of a wood, headed toward a group of them, they set up a clamor that was startling to listen to. If hawks prefer to come upon their prey swiftly, silently, and unawares, would not such a barrage have an unnerving effect? Might it not be enough to spoil an attack?

The idea came to me, in watching Pileateds feeding on camphor trees, that their *cuk*s might have a similar effect. Pileateds, being large birds, cannot perch well on small branches laden with fruit. They are, therefore, forced to cling upside down in awkward positions. *Cuk*s might be protective in making a hawk aware that its prey was alert. Pileateds do respond to the presence of hawks with *cuk*s. I was watching a pair in Florida when a Green Heron flew from a swamp, pursued by a Red-shouldered Hawk. Two Pileateds started *cuk*ing immediately and continued to do so for several minutes. I have heard the same response to Sharp-shinned and Cooper's Hawks.

Why should Pileateds travel and feed as a pair? While a number of factors may be involved, including an early start on a breeding season, defense against predation could have something to do with it. When a Pileated is knocking away pieces of bark or excavating into wood, it may not be able to look about effectively. Two pairs of eyes and ears should be better than one. There may thus be a selection pressure for keeping a pair together. One, giving *cuk*s on seeing a hawk, could alert the other.

## Early Breeding Behavior

### Lone Male Seeks a Mate

I followed a lone male Pileated as he made rounds of his drumming trees on 11 mornings between December 25 and March 2. In this time I never saw him in association with any other Pileated and his behavior, in seeking a mate, was different from that of any other male I had encountered. It was not difficult to follow him in Seneca Swamp when trees were bare of leaves. His flights were over treetops and his persistent drumming made him easy to locate. The distance between the extremes of his trees was about 700 m. On January 12 Lone Male drummed continuously for three hours from the time I first heard him at 07:20. At 08:30 he was drumming at his usual rate of one burst every 25 seconds on an oak where an old woodpecker hole gave added resonance. Lone Male ended by taking a long flight to the other end of his territory. He soon returned, giving high calls on the way. From 08:50 to 09:30 he drummed almost without interruption. A neighboring mated male, in contrast, drummed for five minutes at a rate of one burst every 40 to 60 seconds. This was at 08:00 and he was silent thereafter.

The Lone Male gave a number of high calls. These were mostly on flying from one tree to another or on a long flight to the end of his territory. The only other vocalizations were *g-waick*s. These all came from the one place where Lone Male was most likely to have encountered a neighboring pair. What was striking about Lone Male's vocalizations was the absence of *cuk*s. As this was also true of a lone, hand-raised female, I have felt that *cuk*s have their chief functions among members of pairs.

### SEARCH FOR A NEST SITE

A pair of Pileateds may have to try a number of stubs before finding one suitable for nesting. On March 1 and 2 I watched the male and female of a pair excavating in a pine in southern Florida. The stub was 20 m tall and contained 11 holes, of which the top five were obviously old. The most dilapidated of these was the roost of the female. There were six fresh holes, all perfect, in the lower part of the stub. The Pileateds had made six tries, but had been stopped, on each attempt, by the hard inner core of the pine. After copulating , the male flew to an adjacent swamp followed by his mate. I was unable to keep the pair in view. I did, however, hear *hn, hn* vocalizations and drum-tapping. On the following morning I found the male starting a new excavation, 12 m up in a dead stub arising from the swamp. The female arrived making low *hn, hn* notes and the male gave three bursts of drum-taps at the edge of the new hole. Both Pileateds excavated during the day and the hole enlarged rapidly. When the female flew to it making *cuk*s, her mate put his head inside immediately. I could see that he was drum-tapping by the vibration of his crest as well as the peculiar position of his head. She then drum-tapped on the outside. The two were, it seemed, in agreement over their new location.

Each of the birds did a half hour of excavating in the afternoon. The male was able to get one-half of his body into the hole, but there were indications that he was losing enthusiasm. He failed to drum-tap during the afternoon changeovers although his mate continued to do so. This loss of interest became obvious over the next two days. On March 6 the male rested at the hole for 20 minutes but excavated for only 30 seconds. I think the difficulties of the pair arose from the nature of the woods. These had been heavily cut over and few pines or stubs, of a size large enough for Pileateds remained. This led eventually to competition and repeated fighting.

### INTRASPECIFIC CONFLICTS OVER NEST SITES

A juncture of swamp and open pines was the boundary between the territories of Pairs A and B, as was apparent from the location (Fig. 22) of five encounters. All took place in the late afternoon. At these times both pairs approached the border making shrill *g-waick*s which I did not hear at other times of day. On March 4 I had an especially close view. At 17:00 Female A gave a high call in response to one from her mate and flew to him at the

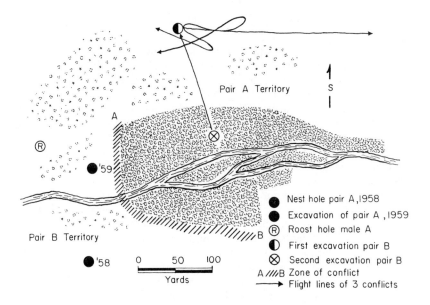

Pair A Territory    S

A

®    ●'59

Pair B Territory

●'58    0    50    100

Yards

● Nest hole pair A,1958
● Excavation of pair A ,1959
® Roost hole male A
◑ First excavation pair B
⊗ Second excavation pair B
A ///B Zone of conflict
⟶ Flight lines of 3 conflicts

FIG. 22.  Territories of two pairs of Pileated Woodpeckers in Florida. Boundaries indicated by zones of conflict.

edge of the swamp. Pair B, possibly hearing these calls, flew to the same area. I now saw one or the other bird of opposite pairs flying toward each other over an open space, alighting on separate trees as they made their *g-waick*s. The calls ceased when Pair A flew back into the swamp.

Intrusions of a third pair of Pileateds, Pair C, indicated that Pair A had to guard a territorial border to the south as well. Conflicts with this pair centered on the many-holed pine stub. Intruding Male C had excavated for 10 minutes on the afternoon of March 2 when Male A swooped and the two grappled in the air. Male A excavated briefly, then flew at Male C who was resting 20 m away. Both members of Pair A were on the pine stub on the following morning when the intruding male gave a high call 250 m to the east. Male A immediately flew in that direction, followed by his mate. One male pursued the other up a dead pine and the two grappled in the air as before. On March 4 all four members of two pairs of Pileateds had a conflict.

The most severe and prolonged conflict I witnessed was on Sapelo when Pair H had nearly completed their nest. When I approached at 06:45 on March 21, Male A was resting on a tree three meters from an intruding Pileated. After a few minutes the intruder flew to the nest tree. Female H was resting inside. She flew out to attack and there was much flapping as the two, male vs. female, circled to strike at each other. When the intruder left, Female H flew at her mate, presumably from an overflow of excitement. He flew off and she followed.

The intruder did not go far. He perched almost motionless for five minutes until Male H returned, then hitched toward him in a bill-waving dance. I heard Female H drumming and the intruder flew toward her. This was the last I saw of him.

The work of excavating in the dead pine continued over the next few days. It now appeared to be close to the time of copulation and egg laying, for Female H entered soon after sunrise and I heard tapping and low *woicks* when her mate looked in at her.

When Male H flew toward the nest at 07:36, the intruding male, I believed the same one, flew toward it also. The two males now circled the trunk in a combination of flying and clinging to the bark. The intruder broke away to ascend to the hole where he met Female H. The two jabbed at each other. After a few moments the intruder backed down to attack Male H as before, then flew back to the hole. The jabbing of bills was more intense this time and the intruder forced his way inside. He emerged immediately, dropping down to attack Male H for a third time. Yet within a minute, he was climbing to attack the nest again. Female H struck so forcefully that breast feathers came loose. But the invader was determined. He forced his way in and on this occasion, after nearly a minute of cackles and scuffles, the female emerged. Her mate had meanwhile flown to another tree. She flew at him and he left on a long flight through the pines, leaving her to preen her ruffled feathers while the invader continued to occupy the nest.

When I came by at 06:25 on the following morning, the Owning Male was preening in the quick, ineffective manner characteristic of displacement activity—an indication that he was still disturbed. He later copulated with the female, however, and nesting progressed, as though the two had recovered.

What was noteworthy in these conflicts was that Female H was more aggressive than her mate, even though she had to fight a male. The fighting was severe. It may have been for this reason that the female, worked up to a high pitch of emotion, twice attacked her mate on disengaging herself.

The conflicts were also unusual because resident birds have a psychological advantage and usually prevail. But, in the Sapelo conflicts, the intruding male was most determined. He fought both members of the pair in succession and succeeded, after evicting the female, in occupying the nest. A possible explanation is that, deprived of his mate at the height of the breeding season, he was driven to aggression by thwarted energies. My first experience with this sort of behavior was with Black-and-White Casqued Hornbills. While watching a pair of these birds in Africa, I saw repeated attacks of an unmated female on a nesting female that was walled into her hole except for a slit by which she was fed. When her fully grown young one finally emerged, the unmated hornbill attacked and broke the juvenile's foot. Why such wanton aggressiveness?

My feeling is that Casqued Hornbills, like Pileated Woodpeckers, have life-long pairbonds. The members of pairs are deeply attached. An individual that has lost its mate at the start of a breeding season, therefore, is much affected. He or she may find outlet by attacking mated pairs that have what the intruder desperately needs, namely a nest and mate.

When I first discovered the excavation of Pair H, I also discovered the remains of a Pileated about five meters from the base of the dead pine. It is conceivable that the intruder was actually the one to start the nest, but, with the loss of his mate, had given it up. This may have been what gave him the persistence, at a later time, to push his way in in spite of the opposition.

## START OF NESTING

### EXCAVATION

As with many woodpeckers, male Pileateds do most of the excavating. At the three nests most studied, this turned out to be close to two-thirds of it, with the females doing one-third and working equally hard. Curiously, we found the same ratios with three pairs of Lineated Woodpeckers. With other species I have studied, females have not only done a lesser amount of the excavating, but the amount has varied considerably from one pair to another. This comparative evenness with which duties were shared among Pileateds was notable. But there was an exception. One male, Male D, was abnormally possessive about the cavity. He refused to come out on most occasions when his mate came to relieve him. As a result he did over 99 percent of the excavating while we were watching. Male D also did far more brooding than other males.

The Pileateds at Sapelo were generally silent while excavating, except at one stage. This was while carving the entrance and able to get their heads inside. Then, whichever partner was at work often gave a prolonged series of *cuk*s on swinging its head out, a phenomenon also noted for Lineated Woodpeckers. The giving of *cuk*s ceased as soon as the Pileateds could get their bodies deeper inside. I wondered if the *cuk*s were not incited by their vulnerability when, with bodies exposed, they were unable to keep an eye out for hawks.

In nearly all changeovers the Pileated at the hole tapped or drum-tapped as its mate alighted by the entrance. Taken altogether, the Pileateds drum-tapped in 81 and tapped on 56 of the changeovers, the two types of greeting being used in the same way by both sexes. An odd situation was that, once when a Wood Duck and once when a Red-bellied Woodpecker came by the hole, the Pileated inside tapped, apparently mistaking the alien for its mate. High calls and single bursts of drumming were means of communicating at a distance. A Pileated at the hole, ready to be relieved, might either call or drum, then after a pause, be answered by its mate in the distance, the returning message seeming to be "I'm coming."

Chips produced in excavating were tossed from entrances, sometimes up to 40 billfuls in succession. On 28 and 29 March, when Pair P had nearly completed its nest, Female P carried sawdust about 12 m away before discarding it. This habit, seemingly common to all woodpeckers, appears to be an awakening of an instinct for nest sanitation before it is needed.

## COPULATIONS AND EGG LAYING

Males were generally silent at times of copulations but females might give *woick*s as the two approached, the female squatting crosswise on a limb near the nest. I heard low *hn, hn* vocalizations only when I was close. On two of 16 copulations, the male pecked gently down on the head of its mate as he mounted, then fell to the left in slewing around to establish cloacal contact. Copulations (n = 16) lasted 6–9 seconds. Male D, aberrant in excavating and brooding, was also aberrant in copulating. He fell consistently to the right and had to mount two to three times in each attempt. Whether his peculiarities reflected inexperience, as Lawrence (1967) has discussed for Downies, or abnormality, I did not know. In three abortive copulations the female squatted, but the male, presumably unready, gave a bill-weaving dance instead of coming closer.

Some regard woodpeckers as birds that maintain an individual distance. But this does not always hold at times of egg laying. I noted both members of pairs of Pileateds entering the nest hole at the same time on six occasions. Male P came to the side of his hole and rested for nine minutes on one day and 16 on the next, while his mate was inside. She tapped a few times from within. Male P ended both of his restings by entering on top of her, but quickly came out.

## INCUBATION AND BROODING

Eggs were unattended for periods of up to 20 minutes in the first few days of incubation. After that Pileateds were close to 100 percent attentive. Seeking more extensive information, my wife and I took turns in two all-day sets of observations. Starting at dawn, before Male F left his nest, we continued watching until he entered for the night. The members of Pair F changed six times on each of the two days. On this schedule Male F did 55 percent of the incubating on the eighth and 43 percent on the eleventh day. This was during daylight hours. As Male F spent nights on the nest (15 hours and 46 minutes on the eighth and 16 hours on the eleventh day on incubation), his total share of the incubating was much the larger.

A question was how long incubation lasted. In a special watch with another pair, I noted that the Pileateds spent little time by their nest in my three and a half hours of watching on March 27. But by the next day, which I took to be the first one of incubation, they were sitting closely. Toward the end of incubation I sought the aid of a tree climbing expert. From him I learned that there were four eggs (one infertile) in the nest on day 14. On the 16th day there were three young. The incubation period, therefore, seemed to be somewhere between 15 and 16 days, a little shorter than the 18 days estimated by Hoyt (1944). The day of hatching is difficult to determine with Pileated Woodpeckers. This is because parents continue to sit while brooding as tightly as in incubation. Furthermore, feeding by regurgitation, they arrive at the nests with nothing visible in their bills. A method I have used in this extremity is counting backward from the day the young first climb to nest entrances, which Hoyt (1944) found to be when 15 days of age. Using this method, I estimated that one pair of Pileateds brooded for 10 and another for eight days in mid-April. In observations totaling 21 hours for one of these pairs, we found that the male did 47 and its mate 53 percent of the brooding. This was during the first five days. The nearly 100 percent attentiveness at this time diminished over the next three days when one partner might leave the nest without waiting for its mate to return.

### DEFENSE OF NESTS

Intruders during nesting can be either intra- or interspecific. A few pairs of Pileateds on Sapelo attracted lone, presumably unmated conspecifics. The Pileated incubating sometimes simply watched or, if the intruder came to the hole, struck out at it before emerging to chase it away. Such encounters were silent and unaccompanied by displays.

Some intruders were more persistent. A foreign female came to one excavation at a time when it was unattended and entered. The owning male arrived shortly afterward. When he alighted, the intruder drummed, then drum-tapped inside. The owning male jabbed into the hole with his bill, then forced his way in. The intruder came out with the male pursuing her up the trunk, both birds flapping with much display of the white of their underwings.

Not all nests had troubles with intruders. Each nest watched was different and many nests, located in quiet woodland, were remarkably free from interference as far as I could tell. The nest of Pair E was of this type—except for one circumstance—a pair of Red-tailed Hawks nested in the vicinity. When a Red-tailed alighted on the nest pine on 28 March, both Pileateds gave high calls, then flew to the pine giving *g-waick* alarm calls. The next day the male Pileated dodged around the trunk giving *cuk*s when a hawk circled overhead. He was in his hole six days later when a Red-tailed flew close by. This time Male E gave five *cuk*s and rapped within the hole. He then flew out to a nearby tree with crest raised and, swaying his body from side to side, gave a high call before flying to another tree to drum. The range of vocalizations and behavior given in response to the hawk by this pair were in contrast to the silence of the encounters with hole-nesting rivals, ranging from gray squirrels, to starlings and pilot black snakes, shown by other pairs.

Gray squirrels are not easily intimidated by Pileated Woodpeckers. A female Pileated was in the vicinity of her nest and young when a squirrel started to climb a pine 5 m away. The pine was covered with vines. The Pileated flew to it with crest raised, pushed her way through the tangle, and pursued the squirrel up the trunk. But this was not for long. The squirrel turned and drove the Pileated from one pine limb to another. She faced the squirrel each time with crest raised and wings outspread. When her mate arrived he attacked, but was driven away. He did not return. His mate was more persistent and attacked the squirrel three more times, facing it on each one with her wings out.

Birds that peered or tried to peer into the holes of Pileated Woodpeckers on Sapelo were Red-bellied Woodpeckers (n = 11), starlings (n = 8), Wood Ducks (n = 3), bluebirds (n = 2), and a Great Crested Flycatcher. None of the birds showed more than a casual interest. The Red-bellies predominated because they shared five of 12 Pileated nest stubs, but with excavations well above those of their larger neighbors. Pileateds reacted to these intruders by coming out, chasing them away, then reentering. These tactics were not too successful against starlings that kept returning.

In a few cases Pileateds reacted more strongly. One female was laying on 27 March, when a pair of Red-bellies came close. She came out with crest raised and wings spread in a threat display. The only other time this display was used was by her mate on March 22. He had flown to his nest hole when he was attacked by a pair of bluebirds. He dodged around the trunk, holding his wings out as he did so. Bluebirds are audacious creatures. It seemed strange, nonetheless, that they should have tried to drive a Pileated from its nest.

A dramatic experience, cited by Hoyt (1957), is that of a photographer who was filming a pair of Pileateds when a pilot black snake climbed the trunk and entered the hole. Photographer Rhein hurried to fetch a ladder. By the time he reached the hole the snake had already swallowed three well-developed young. Having seen Rhein's film, I was startled one May 18, to discover a black snake at the level of a Pileated's nest I had been following in Maryland. The snake disappeared into a crevice behind and above the nest. When its head reappeared in a small hole 10 minutes later, the male woodpecker also had its head out. The two heads were about a meter apart. I now heard *cuk*s as the female Pileated alighted on a nearby tree, flew to the entrance, then entered after her mate flew out. The snake withdrew during the changeover. Its head and neck emerged 15 minutes later, the female woodpecker remained out of sight.

I watched the nest for a half hour on the following day. The snake put its head out for only a few minutes. On May 23, when the sun was first coming out after three days of cold, wet weather, the snake was stretched out on a broken limb. The male Pileated had head and neck well out, as if trying to see the snake about 13 cm away and around the curvature of the stump. Neither appeared excited. The snake moved with great slowness, taking 28 minutes to descend to the ground where it disappeared into the vegetation. One can only conjecture why the snake was in the stump for a total of five days. It may have been laying eggs or simply resting over a period of cold weather. On the other hand it may have been attracted by the buzzing sounds of the young Pileateds in their nest. Constant guarding by the parent Pileateds may have prevented the snake from coming any closer. Parent Pileateds can remain away from a nest for an hour or more. There is, thus, plenty of time at some nests, for a snake to climb a tree and enter, as noted by Rhein and also by Nolan (1959). Nolan came upon a nest in time to see the tail of a black snake disappearing into it. The parent woodpeckers pecked at it without much effect. Once a large snake gets inside, it would seem that there is little a pair of woodpeckers can do about it. Pileateds, like Hairies and Downies, prefer to nest in stubs that are free of old holes. Old holes may shelter anything from black snakes to gray squirrels and screech-owls that could make disturbing neighbors. Better to have a stub of one's own, of which one is the sole occupant. Unfortunately Pileateds are not always able to do this.

## CARE AND FEEDING OF YOUNG

By the time young were about six days of age, as determined in Florida for a nest which I opened at 12 days, parents were feeding them by hanging down into the nest cavity with their tails protruding from the entrance. The tails jiggled vigorously in the process. Young Pileateds climbed to the nest entrance after two weeks and from then on parents feed them from the outside. Two young had their heads and half of their bodies out of a nest hole in Seneca Swamp, when the male arrived. He poked his bill down the throat of one, gave eight to 10 vigorous pumping motions, then repeated the process on the second one. Both of the young sank from sight after being fed. Two days later I noted that the female was making rhythmic motions with her throat as she regurgitated, moving her head rapidly back and forth over the span of 2–3 cm as she did so. An adult may feed a nestling four times in one visit. The food brought to a nest is seldom visible but is not necessarily small for that reason. When one male suddenly pulled his head upward in the midst of poking his bill down the throat of a nestling, I glimpsed a large beetle larva hanging from his bill tip.

Nestlings are usually quiet until an adult approaches. They then begin *chrr, chrr* begging notes as heads and necks stretch up in anticipation. In the excitement of actual feeding, they give a shriller *qua, qua* note just before actively seizing the parent's bill.

There is no regularity to the timing of feedings. While intervals of about 40 minutes are frequent, longer ones may occur in the middle of the day and shorter ones in the late afternoon when, on several occasions, I saw parents feed their young within a few minutes of each other. At two nests on Sapelo the parents made almost exactly the same number of feeding visits: 29 for the male and 26 for the female at one nest, and 36 and 39 at the other.

Nest sanitation is attended to by both parents. When young are small and still remaining at the bottom, a parent may disappear inside, then emerge with a mass of feces. Excreta are carried for a distance before being dropped in the air or knocked off against a tree trunk. Sometimes parents excavate to produce sawdust used in soaking up droppings. Nest sanitation, in nests I followed, continued until within two days of fledging. At one nest the male and female shared the task of nest sanitation equally, while in the other the male removed 12 and the female 29 of the fecal sacs. With no other species of woodpeckers have I seen females doing such a large share of nest cleaning.

## REVIVAL OF COURTSHIP

After the relative silence of incubation and brooding the Pileateds on Sapelo became more lively in their greetings. Whereas the chief greetings of the period of excavation were tappings and drum-tappings, given by both sexes alike, those in the latter part of nesting were lively *woick*s, voiced almost entirely by the females. They gave them not only when coming to change-over with their mates, but also when their mates came to them. I heard both sexes give *woick*s at only one changeover.

There was also an increase in courtship away from the nest. After feeding her nestlings on April 14, Female J flew to a drum stub 30 m away. Here she rested with head drawn into her "shoulders," preened, and drummed nine times in 15 minutes. After 10 minutes her mate flew to a pine 12 m away. Female J flew to him and the two exchanged exuberant *woick, woick*s. The two then remained close to each other (within 40 cm) for 10 minutes. Once when she moved up the pine trunk, he did a bill-waving dance. Female J drummed on the following morning and again male J flew to her, the two exchanging *woick*s. A feature of these meetings was that Female J took the lead.

## NEST LEAVING

On May 25 parents at a nest by the Potomac River started drumming more than they had for some weeks. On May 26 the male drummed a minute just after leaving. The two young pushed their heads way out to look in his direction. On the following day, the male drummed within 10 m of the nest and made low *g-waick*s and *cuk*s when close to it. One of the young gave a peculiar, abbreviated high call. May 28 was the last day in the nest. The young were unusually restless, pulling their heads in and out, investigating the wood around the entrance with their tongues, and looking in all directions. Feeding was on a different pattern than on previous days. One adult fed the young three times in 10 minutes, giving one poke with its bill, flying to a nearby tree, then returning for one more. The performance looked like an effort to get the young to leave.

Both young were still in the nest at 06:45 the next day, but by late afternoon, the nest was empty. I located the fledglings at a distance by their abbreviated high calls. These calls were distinctive and easily recognizable. The two answered each other eight to 10 times in 20 minutes.

Following families of Pileateds after nest leaving is difficult in summer months. One August 4 I was able to watch a pair consisting of an adult male and a juvenal female. The male worked industriously at the rotted center of an aspen while the juvenile rested a short distance away preening in idle fashion. After a time the male reached over, the two bills clasped, and rapid feeding motions followed for 30 seconds. A similar performance was repeated at another tree. The juvenile flew closely behind wherever her parent went and, on one occasion, exchanged low *hn, hn* notes. Family groups may stay together into the fall, the latest date I have seen as many as four Pileateds together, without signs of conflict, was November 24.

## A HANDRAISED BIRD

When I set out to procure nestling Pileateds in Florida, my plan was to secure their dead pine stub with ropes, then, after cutting it off at the bottom, to lower it slowly to the ground. The stub had hardly started down when it broke in two at the nest. When I examined the cavity I found that the walls consisted mostly of bark and rotten wood. A raccoon could easily have destroyed it. It surely would have broken in a strong wind, as Truslow (1967) witnessed for a similar nest. The two nestlings escaped undamaged. I took them to Maryland and the next morning, when my wife and I came to feed them, they flattened down and hissed. We only saw the hissing behavior twice again. Once was when our cleaning woman, whom they had never seen, looked in on them, and once when we uncovered them too abruptly.

The nestlings took food readily. We kept them in a hollow log that made a natural type of nest and within a few days they were clambering up the sides. Once fed at the top, the nestlings dropped to the bottom. Here, with stomachs full, they dozed off, making contented sounding *peep*s. When nearly half grown the male gave a series of *cuk*s and, some days later, began to preen his emerging feathers.

The male nestling died while I was away for a week. His trouble, I think, was a diet of too much dog food. The second nestling, however, a female, survived in good shape. She greeted me with *cuk*s whenever I came to the aviary and flew to eat from my fingers. Afterward, still perching on my arm, she liked to explore the creases and buttons on my jacket. On coming to the left side of my chest, she began to pound vigorously. I think that the pulsations of my heart made her think that larvae of some sort must be there and she wanted to get them out.

# PILEATED WOODPECKERS

By the time "Pilly" was eight weeks old, she played dodgeball every morning when I turned on the aviary lights. The Hairies, Downies, and others of my woodpeckers played the same game, but Pilly remained the most playful of them all, fluttering her wings as she shifted about on the underside of a log, as if facing an imaginary enemy, then circling the aviary (a converted one-car garage), in a wild looping flight.

I enjoyed watching these demonstrations of health and exuberance. Pilly was one of the most affectionate of our woodpeckers, greeting us with *cuk*s as if we were of her own kind. When two months of age she developed a strange attachment. This was to a female Yellow-bellied Sapsucker. Pilly greeted this cagemate many times a day with bill-waving dances, half-starting her wings and giving *woick*s all more or less at the same time. The sapsucker never responded in any way.

Wanting to be sure that the sapsucker was the source of the Pileated's behavior, I removed it from the aviary for several days. The Pileated became subdued immediately. It is said that attachment strengthens with deprivation and this seemed to be true of Pilly. When I reintroduced the sapsucker, Pilly greeted her with the greatest display of bill-wavings and *woick*s we had seen. There was no doubt of the attachment. Of all the woodpeckers in the aviary, Hairy, Downy, and Red-bellied, why should the Pileated have been attracted to the female but not to the male sapsucker? I think it was because the female sapsucker came closest to looking like a male Pileated in having a red crown, white throat, plus black and white bands radiating from the base of the bill. It was these that acted as releasers.

A big event in Pilly's life was adoption of a roost box in the fall. Before this she had spent her nights clinging to wire under the ceiling (Fig. 23). The hollow log was there, but she was hesitant. She kept looking in, but she had never entered a dark hole before. Then finally she entered, came out (Fig. 24) and entered again. The big step had been taken. The box now became her place of refuge. She roosted there at night and kept all of the other woodpeckers away, including the female sapsucker.

One of Pilly's preoccupations was drum-tapping inside her new hole. The drum-tapping sounded so much like our old-fashioned sewing machine, in the way it started up and died down, that our small son was puzzled how the machine got into the aviary.

Another odd sound was the rattle Pilly made with the horny tip of her tongue as she ran it with great in-and-out rapidity over crevices and defects in dry wood. The rattle was not unlike that of a rattlesnake. Pilly's tongue was a versatile organ. She was fond of toast and I found that if I placed a small piece nearly beyond her reach, about 10 cm beyond the wire, I could see how her tongue worked. She would dart it out well beyond her bill and flick it around the crumb in drawing it toward her. It is this kind of thing that one cannot see in the wild. Yet much of the time we watch Pileateds foraging, their tongues are performing wonders deep inside rotten logs and stumps.

FIG. 23.   Female Pileated roosting for night, hanging on wire by one foot (from a photograph).

FIG. 24.  Female Pileated about to enter her roost box (from a photograph).

I put Pilly in a traveling cage each summer and, along with our other
woodpeckers, drove her to New Hampshire. Once there, I transferred her
to a back porch made into an aviary. Pilly almost never gave high calls in
Maryland, but she gave them in New Hampshire. This was in response to
wild Pileateds in the woods. The woods held other creatures as well. We were
awakened one night by piercing screams. I ran to the aviary in time to drive
away a large raccoon. Then I made the mistake of returning to sleep. We
were soon awakened by more screams. This time I found Pilly jabbing at

the raccoon who was trying to pull her through the wire. Feathers littered the floor. Pilly looked like a plucked chicken. She also had one leg dangling. I despaired of her life. My wife, however, was more confident. While I held Pilly on the kitchen table, Jane taped on a metal splint.

Pilly was a model patient through several weeks of near helplessness, allowing us to feed her by hand as if she had reverted to being a nestling. For the first week she clung motionless to the side of her cage. By nine days she began preening and making slight motions with her leg, as well as giving high calls when the wild Pileateds called from the woods. At this time I returned to Maryland for six weeks. When I next saw Pilly the degree of her restoration seemed remarkable. There was nothing to indicate that anything had happened to her. The only real loss, to the raccoon, was the death of her companion, the female sapsucker.

One might ask why the Pileated had flown to the wire and attacked the raccoon. The aviary was 3 m across and nearly as high. There was ample room to keep away. My feeling is that under natural circumstances she would have had a secure roost hole. Then, if a raccoon had attacked, she would have been in a position to jab at its nose and eyes without its being able to reach around and grab her. Pilly's instinct to attack was, therefore, sound enough. It was the artificial situation that led to her downfall.

## CARE OF FEATHERS AND WELL-BEING

Birds have varied ways of maintaining their plumage. Among those noted for Pileateds have been the following:

### PREENING

Pileated Woodpeckers may preen at any time of day. But some times are especially favored. One of the more frequent is within an hour of emerging when sun first strikes the top of some tall dead tree. Pileateds like to preen in the sun in exposed situations. It is difficult to find one preening on a cloudy day. One female I was watching, stopped feeding and began to preen immediately when the sun came out on a dark morning.

If both woodpeckers of a pair are feeding nearby, they may stop to preen at the same time, as though one stimulated the other. Preening often appears in combination with resting. Pileateds, like other woodpeckers, combine preening with drumming, a habit encouraged by their liking to preen in exposed places that may be good places to drum as well. The leisurely way both the drumming and preening are done gives an impression that a Pileated is relaxed and has nothing pressing to do.

Prolonged preening may be stimulated by special occasions. A pair of Pileateds on Sapelo had a severe encounter with an intruding male, as narrated earlier. Although the owning female pecked at him, he forced his way into the nest and had a scuffle with her inside the hole. She came out in a few minutes and flew to a pine not far away. Here she preened steadily for about 20 minutes. One might say that this was displacement preening, a reflection of her being upset by the fray. While this may have been so, what also seemed likely was that her plumage was in disarray and needed attention. I saw much the same thing when a female made repeated attacks on a Gray Squirrel. The squirrel was on a pine trunk heavily covered with vines. The female had to push through to get at the squirrel, but the squirrel was bold and drove her off. After the squirrel had left, the female settled to a prolonged stretch of preening.

Displacement preening is performed when a Pileated is highly disturbed. It is recognizably different from regular preening in that it is done in a quick, nervous fashion that does not seem to be functional. I saw a male Pileated perform in this way after it had been defeated by a rival male.

## Bathing and Behavior in Rain

I have never seen Pileated Woodpeckers bathing in the wild nor have I encountered any descriptions by others. Slessers (1970), in a general account of bathing in birds, thinks that woodpeckers do not bath by wading in water and splashing. From watching hand-raised Pileateds, however, I have no doubt but that these birds have an instinct for bathing. I set some flat stones in the aviary one June, then watered them to wash off the dirt. A Red-bellied Woodpecker of about two months of age and a Pileated of six weeks, neither of which had been exposed to water before, immediately made splashing and bathing motions on the wet stones. They made the same motions when I provided a bird bath a little later. Some weeks afterward a two-month-old Pileated took a soaking bath on a hot July afternoon. In spite of this propensity to bath, even on a wet stone, none of my captives bathed when older, even though the bird bath was cleaned and refilled daily.

Can it be that woodpeckers bathe by exposing themselves to rain as Slessers suggests? I had long supposed that, given a heavy rain, a woodpecker would head for a roost or nest hole. But on Sapelo I had a surprise. It was raining moderately when I started watching by the roost hole of a Pileated early on the morning of February 8. The male did not come out until 08:40 which was 20 minutes later than his usual time. He climbed 2 m above the hole and rested in the lea of the trunk. It now began to rain exceedingly hard. The pine grove where I stood was soon filled with pools of water. It was a veritable cloud burst. Yet the Pileated remained motionless against the pine with his roost hole only a short distance below. The heavy rain ceased after 15 minutes. At the end of 25 minutes the Pileated shook his plumage three times and flew away. At no time had he made motions suggestive of bathing. Skutch (1969) gives account of the behavior of Golden-naped Woodpeckers in the rain in Central America. Sometimes they entered their roost holes, while at others they stayed close by, exposed to the downpour.

## Sunning and Dirt-bathing

Pileated Woodpeckers sun-bathe with wings half spread against a branch, body feathers ruffled and head tilted to one side, but I have seen them do so only a few times. A captive Pileated performed in the same way before a lamp.

There are a few descriptions of woodpeckers dust-bathing. Woolfenden (1975) watched a Red-bellied dusting in a small patch of sandy dirt used by Bobwhite and House Sparrows, and Brackbill (1942) made observations on a flicker. Although I have never read of or seen a Pileated dusting, I witnessed the following performance in South Carolina:

I heard the *cuks* of an approaching Pileated Woodpecker on April 12. The *cuks* continued for three minutes as a male Pileated flew to the base of a tree and paused to look about. He then moved to a mound of clay-like earth, 30 cm high, thrown up where a pit had been dug some years previously. With body feathers fluffed and wings held slightly out, the Pileated settled down like a hen on a nest. He poked his bill into the bank of earth, while continually raising his head to look around. Some dirt landed on his back as he continued to poke about. The Pileated made no effort to tuck dirt into his plumage, as he might have done had he been anting. After three to four minutes he flew to a nearby tree with a small bit of dirt falling from his feathers.

I examined the mound and found it damp except for a thin outer crust. Little sun penetrated through the woods, making it unlikely that the mound could have ever become dry enough to be dusty. The place where the Pileated had settled, hollowed to a depth of about 8 cm, looked as though it had been used many times before. There were no signs of ants or other insects.

It rained hard on the following day. On the day after, at 09:40 and again at 16:32 (almost exactly the time of its afternoon visit on April 12) I heard *cuks* and saw the male come to the dirt pile again. On each occasion he jabbed the earth four to five times, then flew off. The earth was still soaking wet, and I presumed that he no longer found it suitable.

Why should the Pileated have shown so much interest in bathing in dirt? My feeling is that body and feather parasites of woodpeckers, as is true for other birds (Foster, 1969), have breeding cycles that synchronize with those of their hosts. A possible indication of this is the increased amount of preening and scratching done by woodpeckers in the breeding season. It is conceivable that dirt-bathing is also related to an increased activity of parasites. Contact with dirt could act both to alleviate irritation and, if parasites were on the move, remove at least some of them. What seems unusual is that whereas most birds use dry dust on the ground in sunny places, this Pileated used a scoop of damp earth in shady woods by a swamp.

## COMPARISONS WITH LINEATED WOODPECKERS

Lineated Woodpeckers are so much like Pileateds in courtship and breeding that a study of one contributes to an understanding of the other. One is thrown off at first by the differing vocalizations. The alarm call of the

Lineated is a *put-airr* and the high call a series of 8–20 *wic*s diminishing at the end. Otherwise the drummings, tappings, and displays of the two species are identical. Eight of the pairs I studied were at Tikal in Guatemala and one in Panama. A tenth pair was studied in Trinidad by Patricia O'Brien.

*Sharing of the work in excavation.*—The longest times any of the birds were watched excavating were 16 days for one pair and 18 days for another. As both were discovered when already excavating, the actual times must have been longer. Male Lineateds, like male Pileateds, excavated almost exactly twice as much as their mates. The females worked just as hard when they did work. Male A worked an average of 42 minutes in each of his sessions (n = 14) and his mate 55 minutes in hers (n = 6). Comparable figures for another pair were 48 and 44 minutes. Excavations in Guatemala were left unattended for periods of 10–60 minutes, the female being the more apt to leave without being relieved. Once holes approached completion, the males spent the night in them.

*Changeovers.*—Courtship was best seen at times of changeovers. The partner excavating, when ready to be relieved, might give a high call from the entrance and be answered in the distance, either with a high call or a burst of drumming. By the time the other Lineated arrived, the occupying bird was down inside tapping. On two occasions an arriving female drum-tapped. Low vocalizations may have been exchanged more often than we heard them, which was only twice.

*Dominance at the excavation.*—On February 2, a female flew to an empty excavation, then drum-tapped as her mate alighted beside her. He pecked at her and she left, leaving him to enter. Another indication of male possessiveness was that in seven of 30 changeovers, or attempted ones, the male refused to leave when his mate came. I saw the reverse situation only twice. Each of these times was in the egg laying period when females of a number of woodpeckers became dominant temporarily. As with the Pileated, at or close to the period of egg laying is the only time that I have seen one member of a pair enter the nest on top of the other. This happened four instances with one pair of Lineateds between February 11 and 15.

*Copulatory behavior.*—Females initiated copulations by moving out on a limb as the male came out to her. She then assumed an invitation pose, with body compressed crosswise on the limb.

*Failure of a nest hole.*—One pair of Lineateds excavated a hole 8 m up in a dead tree of very hard wood, but at the level of the fruiting body of a fungus. Fungi that soften wood are needed by almost all species of woodpeckers at sites of excavations. The work of the Lineateds progressed from 7 to 23 January. Toward the end of the month the woodpeckers had to work hard to produce even a modicum of sawdust. They seemed to have reached the limit of fungal decay. The cavity was large enough for a Lineated to enter but still not large enough for nesting. The first I knew of this was when the female began drumming on a dead branch at 06:15 on January 24 and continued for 70 minutes. In this time she delivered 108 bursts at intervals of about 50 seconds. Her mate did not come to her or to the excavation. I heard the two drumming on succeeding days as they searched for a new location.

*Scaling of behavior.*—Five of the nine pairs of Lineateds I studied were relatively quiet and did little drumming while excavating. Two pairs, in contrast, that were having difficulties finding a stub, did much drumming and calling. Their disturbed behavior affected their neighbors. Pair C, for example, had a successful excavation but drummed daily in response to the drumming of Pair H who were having difficulties and frequently crossed the territorial border between the pairs. I have noted this heightening of activity under conditions of crowding, or failure of habitat, with other woodpeckers.

*Defense of nest holes.*—Lineated Woodpeckers face an array of hole-nesting competitors. Those such as araçaris, parrots, and tityras that showed only a casual interest were chased away without displays. When a Brown Jay alighted 4 m above one Lineated hole, the female, who had been excavating, came out raising and lowering her crest as she rapped on the tree trunk. She then flew to within 30 cm of the jay, holding her wings out in a threat display and drawing her head back to rap especially hard. The jay paused, then flew. Why this non-hole-nesting species should have received so much attention, I did not know.

The Trinidad pair of Lineateds once left their hole unguarded for 50 minutes. When the female returned she found it occupied by a Ferruginous Pygmy Owl. She clung to the rim of the hole, giving hard raps in between raising her crest and flashing her wings. The male Lineated did the same when he arrived to take her place.

A second owl now appeared and struck the male. He fluttered to the ground, but recovered. The first owl remained in the hole until the Lineateds left. When the female Lineated returned, she entered immediately, but none too soon. The owl flew to the rim but she was able to drive it away. Her mate did not return and she spent the night in the hole, an unusual thing for a female woodpecker to do. The nest was later abandoned.

## METHODS OF COMMUNICATION

### DRUMMING AND TAPPING

*Drumming.*—Pileated Woodpeckers drum in bursts which last for about three seconds and fall off toward the end. Bursts are commonly delivered at intervals of 40 to 60 seconds, four to seven times in a row. Pileateds drummed every month of the year in Maryland, but their drumming, in the late fall, was often no more than a single burst given as a male happened to pass a drum tree. Females drum less than males.

*Tapping and drum-tapping.*—Pileateds tap at a regular, countable rate in changeovers at a nest excavation and less often in actual nesting. They also drum-tap. Drum-tapping is a rapid roll that lasts for about a second, delivered, like the tapping, of which it is a modification, outside or inside a nest cavity and usually close to the entrance. The head of the Pileated vibrates when drum-tapping.

*Rapping.*—Pileateds strike a sharp rap with their bills against any surface they happen to be on when nervous or excited. They frequently rap when approaching a roost hole in the presence of an observer. Rapping is a displacement activity. At times, however, when used along with threat displays in conflicts, it appears to be a redirected attack.

## DISPLAYS

*Threat.*—A Pileated when facing an adversary, whether a conspecific or an intruder of some other hole-nesting species, may extend its wings sideways. The display is used in both offense and defense. Its effect is to make a Pileated look larger than normal and, when facing an adversary, to display the white underwings that contrast so strikingly against the otherwise dark plumage. Threat displays are often accompanied by rapping.

*Bill-waving.*—In this display, as seen from the rear when a Pileated is clinging to an upright trunk, the head and bill are waved back and forth in an arc of 45 degrees. The whole body jerks about, the tail swinging to the same side as the head and bill. When seen with the woodpecker on a horizontal perch, the head and bill are held elevated and well back (Fig. 22). Bill-waving is common among woodpeckers. A source of confusion is that whereas it is used only in conflicts among Hairies and Downies, it is used most often in courtship and less so in conflicts among Pileateds. In whatever situation, it calls attention to the performer. When used in courtship it is usually accompanied by pairbonding *woick* or other intimate vocalizations.

*Raising of crest.*—Pileateds raise the long red feathers of their crests when excited for any reason.

## VOCALIZATIONS

*Cuks.*—These are the most frequent vocalizations of Pileated Woodpeckers. They can be given in rapid succession over a number of minutes, making the woods resound with their clamor. They are usually, however, given in a slower, more irregular manner. Variations make it possible for a single bird to sound like a pair of woodpeckers or even a domestic fowl. *Cuks* appear to have a number of functions. Among them are registering excitement from any cause, as well as location and the pairbond.

*High call.*—This vocalization has a regular pattern of 6 to 8 high pitched *cuks* with a terminal one of lower pitch. It is given singly, the bill being open and the whole body shaking. High calls are a long distance way of communicating. A high call of one partner may be answered by a high call from its mate in the breeding season, or by a single burst of drumming.

*Woick, woick.*—These are intimate, pair-bonding notes given more by fe-

PILEATED WOODPECKERS

males than males. They are used mostly in breeding season, but I have heard them in September. *Woicks* frequently accompany bill-waving and are fairly loud.

*G-waick, g-waick.*—I have heard these loud, shrill vocalizations only in association with conflicts.

*Hn, hn.*—These low, grunting noises are intimate notes made mostly in the breeding season. I am not sure whether these notes are exchanged for it is difficult to determine which bird is making them when two Pileateds are together. The note is identical with begging calls of well-developed young. *Hn, hn*s are sometimes drawn out into a *hn-waan* suggestive of a Gray Squirrel. Low notes can be varied, ranging from *hn, hn*s to *woi*s and *woick*s.

LITERATURE CITED

BENT, A. C. 1939. Life histories of North American woodpeckers. Bull. U.S. Nat'l Mus., **174**: 1–322.

BLUME, D. 1964. Die Jahresperiodik von Aktivitatsbeginn und -ende bei einigen Spechtarten. Vogelwelt, **85**: 11–19.

BRACKBILL, H. 1942. Flickers dusting. Wilson Bull., **54**: 250.

FOSTER, M. S. 1969. Synchronized life cycles in the Orange-crowned Warbler and its Mallophagan parasites. Ecology, **50**: 315–323.

HOYT, J. S. 1944. Preliminary notes on the development of nestling Pileated Woodpeckers. Auk, **61**: 376–384.

HOYT, S. F. 1957. The ecology of the Pileated Woodpecker. Ecology, **38**: 246–256.

KILHAM, L. 1956. Breeding and other habits of Casqued Hornbills (*Bycanistes subcylindricus*) Smith. Misc. Coll., **131** (9): 1–45.

——. 1958. Repeated attacks by a Sharp-shinned Hawk on a Pileated Woodpecker. Condor, **60**: 141–142.

——. 1959a. Behavior and methods of communication of Pileated Woodpeckers. Condor, **61**: 377–387.

——. 1959b. Pilot black snake and nesting Pileated Woodpeckers. Wilson Bull., **71**: 191.

——. 1973. Unusual attack of intruding male on a nesting pair of Pileated Woodpeckers. Condor, **75**: 349–350.

——. 1974. Interspecific actions of sexual signals among hand-raised woodpeckers. Avicult. Mag., **80**: 104–108.

——. 1975. Dirt-bathing by a Pileated Woodpecker. Bird-banding, **46**: 251–252.

——. 1976. Winter foraging and associated behavior of Pileated Woodpeckers in Georgia and Florida. Auk, **96**: 15–24.

——. 1979. Courtship and the pair-bond of Pileated Woodpeckers. Auk, **96**: 587–594.

KILHAM, L., AND P. O. O'BRIEN. 1979. Early breeding behavior of Lineated Woodpeckers. Condor, **81**: 299–303.

LAWRENCE, L. DE K. 1967. A comparative life-history study of four species of woodpeckers. Ornith. Monogr. (Amer. Ornith. Union), no. 5, 156 p.

LORENZ, K. 1970. Studies in Animal and Human Behaviour. Vol. 1. Harvard Univ. Press, Cambridge. 402 p.

NOLAN, V. 1959. Pileated Woodpecker attacks pilot black snake at tree cavity. Wilson Bull., **71**: 381–382.

ROUNDS, W. D. 1958. Pileated Woodpecker roosting in a barn. Maine Field Nat., **13**: 22.

SKUTCH, A. F. 1969. Life histories of Central American Birds. **III**. Pacific Coast Avifauna (Cooper Ornith. Soc.), no. 35, 549 p.

SLESSERS, M. 1970. Bathing behavior of land birds. Auk, **87**: 91–99.

TANNER, J. T. 1942. The Ivory-billed Woodpecker. Res. Rept. no. 1, Nat'l Audubon Soc., New York. 111 p.

TRUSLOW, F. K. 1967. Egg-carrying by the Pileated Woodpecker. Living Bird, **6**: 227–236.

WOOLFENDEN, G. E. 1975. Dusting by a Red-bellied Woodpecker. Florida Field Nat., **3**: 51.

## 6

## RED-HEADED WOODPECKER

I studied all aspects of Red-headed Woodpeckers in Creek Wood, Seneca, Maryland and their breeding behavior in Florida and South Carolina. Their colors, vocalizations, and pugnacity make Red-headeds, at times, the most striking of eastern woodpeckers.

### STORING ACORNS

The 12 Red-headeds I studied came to Creek Wood (area 1.25 ha) in September and remained, living on acorns, until the following May. The woods ran 200 m up from a dirt road, along a small creek. They were surrounded by fields and, with terrain sloping toward the creek, I could look in at the trees at mid-tree level. Still further favoring observations was that, thanks to a pasturage of cattle, the place was open.

The main trees were pin oaks, ash, and black locusts. I made additional observations in bottomlands along the Potomac, but there tangled woods and a flat terrain made recognition of territories virtually impossible.

## HARVESTING

The Red-headeds started collecting acorns in the first part of September and continued to do so through the first week of November. They were energetic in flying to pin oaks, clinging upside down to work an acorn loose, then swooping back to some broken stub to hammer it. Storage in this initial phase consisted of pushing acorns, or pieces of them, into cracks and crevices. Furrows in bark, splintered stubs, dead limbs, and places where vines grew closely against bark, were all used. Competition for the acorns was keen. Common Crows, Blue Jays, and Red-bellied Woodpeckers were also working on the pin oaks. The hastiness of initial storage may have been an effort to gather acorns while the supply lasted. After those on the oaks were exhausted, the Red-headeds went to the ground to gather those that had fallen.

## RE-STORAGE

By the time the leaves had fallen and trees were bare, the Red-headeds were taking acorns from one crevice to another on the same or in another tree. An impression was that they were distributing their stores as widely as possible. This might serve to lessen the amount a competitor could have stolen at any one time. Whole acorns were often split prior to re-storage. This gave opportunity, I thought, to remove acorn-destroying larvae. A high proportion of acorns seemed to be infested. An additional stratagem, in protection of stores, was to hammer acorns into crevices so tightly that they were hard to dislodge. A Blue Jay I watched trying to extract one had a difficult time. The only reason it was not attacked and driven off was that two other jays were distracting the owning Red-headed at the time.

## SEALED WINTER STORES

It became apparent as weekends went by that the Red-headeds, in addition to wide dispersal, firm wedging, and constant guarding, had a still further method of protecting their stores. But I did not discover it all at once. I first noticed something unusual on November 18 when one Red-headed flew back and forth from a rotted stump. Each trip it loosened a sliver 3–4 cm long. Then, arranging it to point forward in its bill, the Red-headed flew to hammer the sliver into a crevice. Although I noticed a few individuals carrying slivers in succeeding weeks, it was not until December 16 that I again noticed numbers doing so. Why should so many be suddenly engaged in the same activity? The answer came when one Red-headed tried to handle an especially long sliver. The two ends hung limply. They were soaking wet for, as in November, there had been a heavy rain the night before. I worked a sliver loose for myself and found that it could be easily molded into a crevice.

Seeking more direct information, I brought my 10-year-old son, Mike, plus a ladder and a saw, on the following weekend. It was soon apparent that acorns, stored in cavities from near the ground to high up in trees, had been sealed in with bits of wood that became hard on drying. Mike and I sawed off smaller trunks for closer looks. Figure 25 shows a cross section. A Red-headed had drilled a round hole into a cylinder-like cavity within the heart wood. The cavity, when filled with acorns, was then hidden from view by sealing the entrance. The acorns in such a cavity could not be removed by the way they went in. It became evident as winter progressed that the Red-headeds had to chisel away wood to remove stores dropped into deep cavities.

Two more drawings (Fig. 26) show a knob sawed from a hackberry tree. The small hole was readily seen because it was plugged with pale splinters. Inside were fragments of a wasp, a cricket, a carabid beetle and two species of moth. I have since found similar caches in Florida. The only previous report of sealing of stores known to me is that of Hay (1887).

### Individual Winter Territories

#### Aggressive Behavior

Red-headed Woodpeckers are agile flyers and those in Creek Wood were swift in attacking territorial intruders. In pauses, or after an intruder had

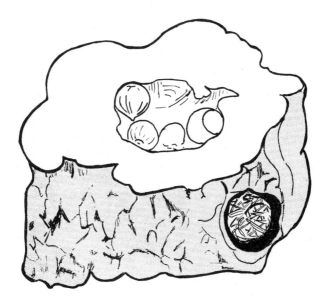

FIG. 25.   Cross section of a dead stub. The natural cavity, used for storing acorns, was reached by a round hole drilled at one side. The entrance was sealed later with splintered wood.

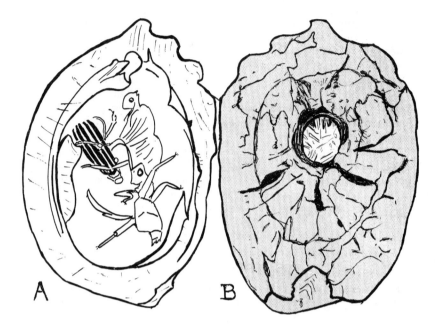

FIG. 26. Reverse (A) and front (B) views of an elevation sawed from the bole of a small tree. A Red-headed Woodpecker filled the natural cavity with insects, then sealed the round entrance shown in B with splintered wood.

left, the Red-headeds did much bowing and calling of rattle-like *quirr*s. When especially excited, as by the trespass of another Red-headed, they spread wings and tails, and their calls became high-pitched. The Red-headeds rarely fought with each other. But when they did, I wondered if all of the Red-headeds of Creek Wood did not join in with excited *quirr*s. On December 16 a flash of black and white was all I saw as a Red-headed suddenly flew the length of the wood, crossing over the territories of three other Red-headeds. Each of these attacked in turn as the intruder passed through its domain.

The Red-headeds attacked and drove away all of the other woodpeckers at one time or another. The Pileated, Hairy, and flicker, however, hardly counted, for they seldom came to the wood. This left the Downy and Red-bellied as the most attacked. Although I had difficulty perceiving that Downies ate acorns, which they do, they nonetheless moved up and down over trunks where acorns were stored. The Red-bellieds were the most clearly competitive. They gathered and stored acorns. The Red-headeds went out of their way to drive them away, more so than any other bird. On January 5 I saw a Red-headed pursue a Red-bellied that had stolen an acorn, way out over the fields. Leaving a territory in this way was unusual.

Sapsuckers were exceptional in being tolerated. They could hardly be classified as competitors, for they did not eat acorns, and they drilled holes from which the Red-headeds took sap. One Red-headed frequently rested within less than a meter of a sapsucker that kept drilling a pin oak within its territory.

Among other birds commonly attacked were Blue Jays, Tufted Titmice, which stole acorns, and starlings. Each Red-headed had one main roost hole and a few alternates. Competition for these began when starlings arrived in January, the males flapping their wings and giving their scratchy songs. But the starlings persisted. Yet, in spite of some severe physical combats, I never saw a starling actually take over a hole. If one did get inside, the owning Red-headed was quick to go in after it.

## LOCATING BOUNDARIES

I needed to be able to recognize individual Red-headeds if I was to learn the boundaries of their territories. Otherwise how could I be sure that the same Red-headed was holding to the same area on successive weekends? With time I found that most of the woodpeckers had markers. Three, for example, were immatures with black bars on their white primaries. The patterns of these bars differed in all three. One of the immatures, furthermore, had a red head and black back, whereas the other two were dull and brownish.

The nine remaining woodpeckers had adult plumage, but each had special traits. Red-headed-5 bowed incessantly and Red-headed-2 swung in and out of its roost hole many times before entering. Of more general value was that each Red-headed had certain resting places to which it returned repeatedly. Each individual flew only short distances in its daily affairs and, by noting the extremes of such flights, I learned much about boundaries. Dividing lines were sharp. Red-headed-9 sometimes flew straight along its northern boundary without disturbing its neighbor, Red-headed-3, who might be only a short distance on the other side.

One of the better ways of delineating boundaries was through observing conflicts between the Red-headed Woodpeckers and titmice. I was standing on the boundary between Red-headed-3 and Red-headed-9 on December 16 when the latter flew to within 7 m of me, in driving titmice from its territory. The titmice now excited Red-headed-3 and that attacked in its turn. When the titmice continuing through the wood, crossed into Red-headed-2's territory, they were attacked for a third time. I was thus able to watch three Red-headed Woodpeckers carrying attacks up to, but not beyond, their respective boundaries.

A fall of snow in January gave me a chance to tramp out what I knew of the boundaries, converting the wood into a giant map. With the Red-headeds flying back and forth in the gamut of their activities, against a background of bare trees and white snow, conditions were ideal and I was able to map out new sectors. As shown in Figure 27, most of the Red-headeds occupied relatively small territories. Larger ones may not have been desirable, for they would have been harder to defend. Another consideration was that the territories had vertical as well as horizontal dimensions. An abundance of dead locust trees with hollow centers for storage may have been of more importance than mere area. The locusts also provided roost holes. From

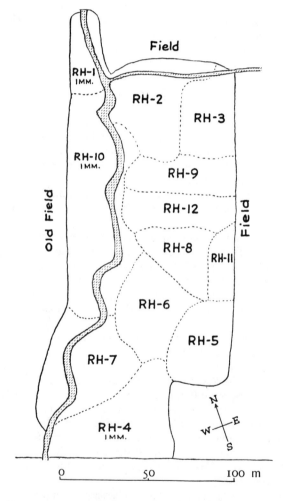

FIG. 27. Map of Creek Wood showing territories of 12 Red-headed Woodpeckers (RH = Red-headed Woodpecker; IMM = immature bird).

these points of view, it was of interest that nearly all of the adult Red-head-eds were bunched in small territories east of the creek where the locusts were located. The remaining five woodpeckers, of which three were immature, occupied less favorable areas to the west.

## COMPARISONS WITH OTHER ANIMALS

The territories in Creek Wood were small and based on storage. I have not read of any similar type of small, well-defended territory among birds, but I have encountered the same phenomenon among two species of mammals. In one case red squirrels harvested pine cones (*Pinus strobus*) in a pine wood clear of undergrowth. Each squirrel, as watched in early September, had a definite territory. One individual often ran around its boundary, possibly to mark it. It carried cones to caches in the center and warned off other squirrels with a loud, sputtery song. In conflicts with neighbors, it was apparent that owning squirrels had a psychological advantage up to their boundaries. In another case pikas, living in a rock slide in Montana, harvested sprigs of vegetation which they built into piles in and under rocks. Each pika ran around its boundaries, marking them by wiping its cheeks. Each also advertised ownership with a loud *caack*, usually uttered from a lookout.

The Red-headed Woodpeckers, red squirrels, and pikas had strategies in common. All had small, readily defensible territories, surrounded by those of others of their own kind and all had warning calls. The pikas differed from the others in storing what could be had in any year. The Red-headed Woodpeckers and the red squirrels, in contrast, were taking advantage of bumper crops, ones likely to be locally absent in a succeeding year. A single Red-headed wintered in Creek Wood in 1958–59. In a near absence of acorns it took long flights to a field to gather kernels of corn. Red-headeds thus appear to be mobile opportunists, migrating to wherever mast can be found, as has also been described by MacRoberts (1975) and Moskovits (1978).

## FEEDING ON SAP

The Red-headed Woodpeckers of Creek Wood took sap from sapsucker holes throughout the winter. It took me some months, however, to discover that they also had their own way of wounding trees. I watched a Red-headed fly to a river birch on December 15 and remain in one place, pecking lightly, and resting intermittently. All I could see was a small patch of indentations. On the following morning the woodpecker worked on another birch and, on December 29, it was again pecking and eating pieces of bark at its original spot. Three other Red-headeds observed in December fed on pin oaks in a similar manner. One flew to an oak on December 22 to nibble bark from an area where feeding had only just begun. The woodpecker was consuming something, for I could not see any bark drifting away. It was feeding at the same place three weeks later but had shifted to a new spot by March. Here sunlight made the exposed area, which had a U-shape, look bright yellow. The arms of the **U**, pecked and nibbled over repeatedly, grew to be 15 to 18 cm long by April. Bark-eating was then at its height. It continued until the woodpeckers departed, for on May 4, I had an excellent view of the last of them feeding at an indented area.

Woodpeckers can obtain sap in several ways. One is to drill holes in the manner of sapsuckers; the other is by wounding an area and consuming inner bark into which sap has permeated and probably become concentrated by the action of wind and sun. Sapsuckers actually use both methods. Beal (1911: 30) writing of Yellow-bellied Sapsuckers, stated that "cambium, or the inner bark of trees, was eaten every month, but most in winter and spring. The greatest consumption is in April." The Great Spotted Woodpecker also eats bark. According to Pynnönen (1939), one in Finland visited a single spot on a birch eight times for this purpose, but the habit did not become regular until March.

Acorn Woodpeckers make holes more or less like those of sapsuckers but, as described by Beal (1911) and by MacRoberts and MacRoberts (1976), they take only sap and not bast or inner bark.

### Sexual Similarity in Plumage

As discussed by Short (1982) the sexes are alike, or nearly so, in only six species of true woodpeckers. In none of them are they more completely monomorphic than among Red-headeds, a challenging problem that has received little attention. I think that it relates to fall territories. Concentrating where acorns are abundant, the woodpeckers are forced, as in Creek Wood, to over-winter within limited areas. Under these conditions the monomorphism, I feel, enables females to hold their own. If males dominated, the females would be crowded into the less favorable areas. This in turn might mean poorer winter survival. If, however, females were selected to resemble males in plumage and hence have the same display colors, they would have a more equal chance in border contests. A parallel is the British Robin (Lack, 1943). These birds form small, individual, fall territories and the sexes are alike in plumage as well as in song.

Lewis' Woodpeckers (Bock, 1970) resemble Red-headeds in being irregularly migratory in relation to fall territories and in being sexually monomorphic. Acorn Woodpeckers which also store acorns are, in contrast, sexually dimorphic. Living in social groups, however, and being largely resident on the same territories the year around (MacRoberts, 1970), they are not exposed to the same selection pressures.

Among sapsuckers, the eastern Yellow-bellied is dimorphic and highly migratory, whereas the western Red-breasted is monomorphic and essentially non-migratory. Are there any parallels to the situation encountered with Red-headed Woodpeckers? In absence of information as to whether Red-breast-eds maintain individual fall and winter territories, I find it difficult to draw conclusions. It seems likely that monomorphism can arise from more than one kind of selection and that what I have described for an acorn-storing species may not apply to other woodpeckers with other habits.

## EARLY BREEDING BEHAVIOR

### SPRING AND DEPARTURE

The Red-headed Woodpeckers of Creek Wood showed few signs of breeding until spring was well advanced. Whereas Red-bellied Woodpeckers were drumming, calling, and forming pairs by the end of January, March 24 was the first day I heard a Red-headed drumming. The drumming came in bursts of a second's duration that was repeated two to three times. Some of the Red-headeds, presumably the females, never drummed, while others did with increasing frequency. On April 20 I heard a new note, a sharp *queearr*. The calling of *queearr*s and the drumming now became common. At the same time I noticed that one woodpecker might fly into a neighbor's territory and be tolerated.

With these developments I began to wonder whether some of the Red-headeds might not stay to nest. Yet in spite of their new activities, the Red-headeds were still spending most of their time within their territories and, even at the end of April, continuing to feed on acorns. Their departure came sooner than I expected. On May 3 I could find only three Red-headeds and on May 5 only one. The woodpeckers had gone elsewhere to breed.

Although I saw some breeding behavior in Florida, it was not until my wife and I visited the Groton Plantation, in Luray, South Carolina that I had a chance to follow it at length.

### IDENTIFICATION OF SEXES

I felt, initially, that it was going to be difficult to study the breeding behavior of Red-headeds. With the sexes looking alike, how could I tell them apart? The problem turned out to be simpler than I had anticipated. I had been studying the related, dimorphic Red-bellied Woodpecker for years and it did not take long to discover that the early breeding behavior of these two species, which takes place close to a nest stub, is practically identical. It was not difficult to distinguish the sexes of Red-headeds by their behavior. One pair gave me a check. This was the only one among 33 pairs, five in Florida and 28 in South Carolina, in which the female was breeding in juvenal plumage. Once I had identified her sex at times of copulation, I had a pair in which the sexes could be identified physically. While this pair was not essential to present studies, it did substantiate that behavioral clues were workable.

## Mutual Tapping

I started in Florida by watching the roost hole of a male Red-headed at dawn on May 1. The male put his head out at 05:20. He stayed within the entrance for the next 10 minutes, calling *queeark*s almost every 2–4 seconds. His mate flew by my head at 05:30. He stopped calling as soon as he saw her coming, dropped from sight, and was tapping inside by the time she arrived. The two now tapped together. I witnessed this dawn ceremony on three successive mornings. But it was evident that her enthusiasm was less than his. After a brief tapping, she ascended the stub to preen, leaving him to continue tapping alone. I noticed that the pair might return every 15–30 minutes, following the male's calling *queeark*. He wanted his mate to accept his roost hole as a nesting site. But the hole was weathered and somewhat decayed. I was not surprised, therefore, to find the male, one morning, starting a fresh excavation. Yet when he and his mate flew from a distance, she did not join him in tapping. The new site was also, it seemed, unacceptable. By afternoon the male was working on yet another excavation. He was here on the following morning when he paused to call *queeark*s. She responded right away and, as she alighted, the two joined in prolonged tapping. Her interest in the stub was now apparent. She replaced him at the site, showing her approval by excavating for a while before flying away.

The attentiveness with which a male may await the arrival of his mate was illustrated, amusingly, by another male. When he was out of sight within his cavity, a mockingbird alighted close by. The male, thinking his mate had come, started tapping immediately. This was the only time that I noted tapping triggered by anything other than the arrival of a mate, the sight of one approaching, or, with advance of the breeding season, the sight of one resting not far away.

## Excavation

Red-headeds often use old holes and, in consequence, excavating was not a prominent activity among the 28 pairs in South Carolina. It was only among eight pairs that were starting new excavations that the differing behaviors of males and females were observed. The males did most of the excavating. Females excavated at three of the holes, but at two in no more than token fashion. It may have been enough to judge whether the sites were workable. Males of all pairs mixed the calling of *queeark*s with their excavating, some more than others. When their mates came, the males tapped, then flew away. This left the stub to the female. She usually paid little attention to the hole. Dropping lower, she worked upward, pecking here and there and inspecting any and all cavities. I have observed similar behavior with other woodpeckers. It stems, I think, from females being more critical than their mates of the entire situation in a stub or tree, rather than just the spot selected for a hole.

The members of one pair tried many locations in one pine over several weeks. None seemed decayed enough to be workable. In this extremity the female excavated almost as much as her mate. At times she even excavated at one site while he worked on another. The pair seemed desperate.

Once an excavation was underway, females seldom joined their mates in tapping. They now indicated acceptance by resting near the male as he worked. One female flew to her mate four times in 40 minutes to rest and preen. Males, in contrast, seldom took time out. It was only when a hole was completed and copulating had begun, that they also became relatively silent and leisurely. One male flew to his hole silently on 26 April to rest for eight minutes, giving occasional low taps. His mate, meanwhile, rested motionless on a pine 30 m away. Their quiet behavior was expressive of a near readiness for nesting. But with conflicts of frequent occurrence on the crowded plantation, no pair had peace for long.

## Agonistic Behavior

Conflicts of Red-headed Woodpeckers were an almost constant distraction at the plantation. Most centered on efforts of invading pairs, or individuals, to win stubs in territories of pairs already established. In mid-April of one year, I located six pairs in an area of five hectares. By the end of the month, 13 pairs had stubs in the same area. Many of the new pairs were now spending much of their time trying to drive still other Red-headeds away. Competition was intense and intruders persistent. A feature of the fighting was the way members of pairs, giving *scree*s, acted together. Their pursuits commonly looped about, only to circle back. On reaching their stub, Red-headeds often alighted close to one another, sometimes attempting copulation in the excitement.

Males did most of the chasing in prolonged conflicts, while their mates remained near the nest. But sometimes the reverse took place. One male was excavating on April 25 when his mate flew the length of a pine grove in silent pursuit of an intruder. From this and other experiences it seemed that the *scree*s, or combat notes, were given mostly when Red-headeds flew as a pair. In spite of the number of conflicts (I took notes on 123), physical clashes were rare.

The drumming of males and their calling of *queeark*s made conflicts on the plantation noisy as well as colorful affairs. One male alighted on a broken branch of his nest stub after chasing intruders. He now drummed for 10 minutes. As noted for other males, he drummed furiously at first, pounding a spike with great vigor. His drumming and calling may, in part, have been a way of working off surplus emotion. But more importantly, it seemed to be an assertion of dominance, a warning to intruders to stay away. His mate, on returning, had drummed only a few low bursts. The dominant role was his. Yet either of a pair might suddenly assume an agonistic pose (Fig. 28) on seeing a rival, even at a distance.

Established pairs did not waste time fighting with each other. Pairs C and

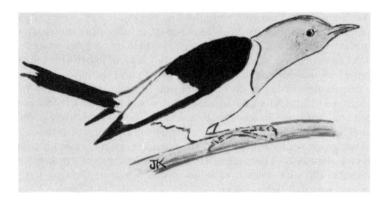

FIG. 28. Red-headed Woodpecker in agonistic pose.

K, that had nest stubs 68 m apart, with pines forming a boundary in between, never paid any attention to each other while I was watching. While such breeding territories seemed small in some directions, the Red-headeds had wide open spaces in others in which to forage.

The Red-headeds I watched in Florida, in contrast to those in South Carolina, were isolated as single pairs, scattered over the scrub. Under these conditions, courtship and breeding proceeded peacefully. The contrast of conditions between Florida and South Carolina is what Wilson (1975: 20) has called a scaling of behavior, "At low . . . densities, all aggressive behavior is suspended. At moderate densities, it takes a mild form such as intermittent territorial defense. At high densities, territorial defense is sharp, while, if densities are too great, there may be a break down into social pathology." I wondered at times, on the Carolina plantation, whether the activities of the Red-headeds did not border on social pathology when some pairs fought for hours without getting on with their nesting.

## Copulatory Behavior

Copulatory behavior, like courtship, is closely associated with nest stubs. Of 125 instances noted, 109 were on a branch within one to two meters of a hole. The behavior began soon after pair formation and developed from token performances to ones with increasing physical contact. At an early stage, males and females assumed sexual poses with bodies in line and pointing in one direction (Fig. 29), then reversing to the opposite direction in an almost military fashion. This behavior was usually seen after tapping by a hole or flying to one suddenly. The positionings appeared strained, as though the two had aversions to physical contact. As a breeding season progressed and the aversion lessened, the female hopped or fluttered on the back of

Fig. 29. Male and female Red-headed Woodpeckers in sexual pose. Female usually occupies the inner position.

the male in reverse mounting. He them moved to mount her, the behavior of the two being almost identical. Full copulations, with the male falling to the left in establishing contact, lasted seven seconds. Occasional performances were aborted when the female, possibly not ready, fell away. Although I did not see the type of copulation noted by Southern (1960), in which the male's final position is on his back, with his body at right angle to hers, I did see it a number of times with a pair of Red-bellied Woodpeckers.

### Nest Site Differences Between Red-Headed and Red-Bellied Woodpeckers

Red-headed and Red-bellied Woodpeckers were both plentiful on the Groton Plantation and I wondered, since the two are of the same body size, whether they might not compete for nest sites. But in this I was mistaken. Each species had its own search image and there was little or no overlap. The Red-bellieds appropriated holes of Red-cockaded Woodpeckers (n = 6) carved in living pines or excavated ones of their own (n = 8) in pines that had recently died. Red-headeds, in contrast, occupied or excavated holes in well-weathered pines (n = 10) or pine stubs (n = 13) that had long since lost their bark and stood more or less in the open. One pine was exceptional in attracting both species. It was easily shared, for the pair of Red-headeds went to the upper part that had been dead for some years and the Red-bellieds to the lower half, that had died more recently.

Trees chosen by the two species differed in another aspect. Those of the

125

Red-headeds, being more ancient, were apt to have collected an assortment of old holes and cavities. These harbored neighbors ranging from starlings and flickers to flying squirrels. One might think that the Red-headeds, being later in starting, might have been forced to put up with less desirable locations. But I was not sure. Red-headed Woodpeckers, like Eastern Kingbirds, due to their superior aggressiveness, can nest in sites that might be hazardous for other birds. Their colors are warning colors. They also resemble Kingbirds in being birds of the open. Both species go after large flying insects and from this point of view, a stub in the open and free of branches could be an asset.

Parameters serving to lessen nest site competition between Red-headed and Red-bellied Woodpeckers have also been described by Reller (1972) for Illinois and by Jackson (1976) for Kansas. The phenomenon thus appears to be widespread.

## METHODS OF COMMUNICATION

### VOCALIZATIONS

*Breeding call.*—A squeal-like *queer* or *quee-ark*. Breeding calls may be repeated many times when a male is seeking to attract a mate to an excavation. It can have territorial functions when given in conflicts with intruders and be an indication of general as well as sexual excitement. Females give *queer*s but less frequently and with less force.

*Attack.*—Males and females often give *scree*s when both are chasing another Red-headed. The *scree* represents a pitch of excitement and reminds one of terns fishing, particularly when Red-headeds are flying.

*Chrr, chrr.*—A harsh, but low intimate note made when members of a pair fly toward or meet at a nest stub, often as preliminary to some form of copulatory behavior. Very similar to the *grr, grr* of Red-bellieds. In both species the notes resemble the begging of well-advanced nestlings. The *chrr*s, like the breeding call and attack notes, are only heard in the breeding season.

*Rattle-like quirr.*—This vocalization was almost the only one heard among wintering Red-headeds and was associated mainly with defense against intruders. I heard it in the breeding season in the first few minutes after a Red-headed emerged from its roost or was preparing to roost at night. *Quirr*s are generally accompanied by bowing, an indication that the bird is disturbed.

### DRUMMING AND TAPPING

*Drumming.*—Given as a single burst or bursts that are well spaced. Drumming is usually associated with the presence of a rival, even if not close by. Red-headeds regularly drum, and with special force, after driving an intruder away. Both the male and female may drum at the same time in such situations, but the drumming of the female is less forceful and of shorter duration. Drumming in low, single bursts mixed with *queers*, are occasionally made by a male seeking to attract his mate.

*Tapping.*—A slow, countable form of drumming that plays a role in pair formation, courtship, and attachment and acceptance of a nest site. Red-headed and Red-bellied Woodpeckers are unique, among other woodpeckers of eastern North America in, at times, tapping together in "mutual tapping."

## DISPLAYS

*Sexual pose.*—As depicted in Fig. 29, the neck is elongated, the plumage sleeked down, and the upper back humped. This pose is observable at the onset of the breeding season as well as later when one partner invites mounting by the other. It is often assumed when the members of a pair fly to a nest after chasing an intruder, an indication of the stimulatory effect of agonistic encounters on sexual behavior.

*Agonistic pose.*—While the neck and body are held as in the sexual pose, the wings are drooped and, at full intensity, the tail is cocked (Fig. 28). This pose can be assumed by both members of a pair simultaneously on the arrival of another Red-headed. It is not to be confused with the threat display, in which the wings are held out sideways. The agonistic pose appears expressive of a sudden flash of anger, as is true of the following display as well.

*Erection of head feathers.*—This display gives the head a bottle-brush appearance and I have seen it only a few times. It is difficult for a Red-headed Woodpecker to assume an agonistic pose unless it is perched on a limb. Erection of the head feathers may be a substitute when a Red-headed is clinging to the bole of a tree, for this is the only situation in which I have noted it.

## LITERATURE CITED

BEAL, F. E. L. 1911. Food of the woodpeckers of the United States. U.S. Dept. Agric. Biol. Surv. Bull., **37**: 1–64.

BOCK, C. E. 1970. The ecology and behavior of the Lewis Woodpecker (*Asyndesmus lewis*). Univ. Calif. Publs. Zool., **92**: 1–100.

HAY, O. P. 1887. The Red-headed Woodpecker a hoarder. Auk, **4**: 193–196.

JACKSON, J. A. 1976. A comparison of some aspects of the breeding ecology of Red-headed and Red-bellied Woodpeckers in Kansas. Condor, **78**: 67–76.

KILHAM, L. 1958. Sealed-in winter stores of Red-headed Woodpeckers. Wilson Bull., **70**: 107–113.

——. 1959a. Territorial behavior of wintering Red-headed Woodpeckers. Wilson Bull., **70**: 347–358.

——. 1959b. Bark-eating of Red-Headed Woodpeckers. Condor, **61**: 371–373.

——. 1959c. Mutual tapping of the Red-headed Woodpecker. Auk, **76**: 235–236.

——. 1977a. Early breeding season behavior of Red-headed Woodpeckers. Auk, **94**: 231–239.

——. 1977b. Nest site differences between Red-headed and Red-bellied Woodpeckers in South Carolina. Wilson Bull., **89**: 164–165.

——. 1978. Sexual similarity of Red-headed Woodpeckers and possible explanations based on fall territorial behavior. Wilson Bull., **90**: 285.

LACK, D. 1943. The life of the Robin. H. F. & G. Witherby ltd, London.

MACROBERTS, M. H. 1970. Notes on the food habits and food defense of the Acorn Woodpecker. Condor, **72**: 196–204.

——. 1975. Food storage and winter territory in Red-headed Woodpeckers in northwestern Louisiana. Auk, **92**: 382–385.

MACROBERTS, M. H., AND B. R. MACROBERTS. 1976. Social organization and behavior of the Acorn Woodpecker in central coastal California. Ornith. Monogr. (Amer. Ornith. Union), no. 21, 115 p.

MOSKOVITS, D. 1978. Winter territorial and foraging behavior of Red-headed Woodpeckers in Florida. Wilson Bull., **90**: 521–535.

PYNNÖNEN, A. 1939. Beiträge zur Kenntnis der Biologie finnischer Spechte. Ann. Zool. Soc. Zool.-Bot.-Fenn. Vanamo, **7**(2): 1–166.

RELLER, A. W. 1972. Aspects of behavioral ecology of Red-headed and Red-bellied Woodpeckers. Amer. Midl. Nat., **88**: 270–290.

SHORT, L. L. 1982. Woodpeckers of the world. Delaware Mus. Nat. Hist., Monogr. Ser., no. 4, 676 p.

SOUTHERN, W. E. 1960. Copulatory behavior of the Red-headed Woodpecker. Auk, **77**: 218–219.

WILSON, E. O. 1975. Sociobiology. The new synthesis. Harvard Univ. Press, Cambridge. 697 p.

# 7

# RED-BELLIED WOODPECKERS

Red-bellieds are generalized and adaptable. They are not only plentiful and widespread but, as members of the group of zebra-backed woodpeckers (formerly *Centurus*), they are widely successful in the neotropics. There are a variety of species, but wherever I went in Panama, Costa Rica, or Guatemala I was sure to hear the *kwirr* breeding call, sounding much the same as that of the Red-bellieds in Maryland. It was, I believe, due to their generalized habits that Red-bellieds were the only woodpeckers that I was able to breed in captivity.

## FALL AND WINTER

### STORAGE OF ACORNS AND BERRIES

Red-bellied Woodpeckers store food in the fall. A female by the Potomac hung upside down to pick poison ivy berries, then flew to a storage place. One of these was among matted rootlets where a vine clung to an old willow. On another day a male reached out to pick berries, then stored them without changing his perch. An occasional *cha-cha* or *cha-aa-a* were all that attracted my notice. The Red-bellieds in Maryland also stored acorns (Fig. 30). A male on October 18 flew against a cluster of pin oak leaves, picked an acorn, then swooped to a hole. Here he hammered it in, only to pull it out to re-store it. Re-storing may aid a Red-bellied in remembering where its stores are hidden. I was standing in an open pasture on December 25, when a Red-bellied flew to a fence post 100 m from the nearest woods. It moved directly to an acorn, pulled it out, then pushed it into another post.

FIG. 30. Two positions of a Red-bellied Woodpecker storing an acorn. The action of the tongue is not apparent under field conditions.

## Territories and Relations with Other Birds

Red-bellieds occupy individual territories after the breakup of families in September. I always found a male in one area in the fall with a female in adjacent areas on either side. The territories were about 1.7 ha in size as judged from the usual flights of the birds. When Red-headeds had occupied the wood, they were continually driving away acorn-eating intruders. The Red-bellieds, in contrast, were tolerant. Blue Jays, Tufted Titmice, and Downies meant little to them. I noticed a jay working on a rotten stump on November 16. A male Red-bellied took over as if the jay were not there, seized a piece of acorn, and flew off. He returned for three other pieces with continuing indifference to the jay who stayed near. I noticed the same indifference to a Downy. Red-bellieds, it would seem, conserve energy by not having to chase other birds away. Instead, they push their stores in so deeply that rivals are unlikely to reach them. This is with the exception of Pileateds. But even with them Red-bellieds do not become excited. A Pileated had been working on a Red-bellied storage place, a depression in a sycamore, when the owning Red-bellied arrived. He perched quietly a quarter meter from the larger bird and waited. I saw the same relations in the aviary where a tame Pileated regularly visited places where a hand-raised Red-bellied stored peanut hearts and other food.

Although the single Red-bellieds along the Potomac were generally unaggressive in the fall, they were attacked by wintering sapsuckers. When a sapsucker tried to drive a Red-bellied from its drill holes on February 22, the two grappled and fell to the ground. The outcome of another conflict was bizarre. A sapsucker attacked, but the Red-bellied, in striking back, was able to seize his oponent in his bill. There the sapsucker hung for a few moments before flying away.

### Handraised Red-bellieds

#### Use of Tongue

The tongues of Red-bellieds can project over 3 cm beyond their bill tips. While not as long as those of Pileateds and flickers, they function adroitly in maneuvering objects at a distance. When I put a bit of breadcrust nearly out of her reach, a female Red-bellied would put her bill through the wire of the aviary. Then, with the tip of her tongue flickering back and forth with lightening speed, she would curl it to the rear of the morsel and set it jiggling toward the wire. Once within reach, she would seize it with her bill. This skill of Red-bellieds worked well in crevices. Our male flew across the aviary one morning to drop a piece of crust down the split top of a post. There I could see the crust dancing, like popcorn in a popper, as he tried to retrieve it (Fig. 31).

Red-bellieds use their tongues continually in locating prey as well as in storage. When I brought home a rotting log from the woods and set it in

FIG. 31. Captive Red-bellied Woodpecker using tongue to recover piece of bread from vertical cleft.

the aviary, it was like presenting cake to children. The Pileated, Hairy, Downy, and flickers were on it immediately. But none seemed as adroit as the Red-bellieds. Turning their heads sideways (Fig. 32) or almost upside down, they sometimes pulled out a fat larva before the others caught anything I could see. The speed of the Red-bellieds was seemingly from not having to peck their way in. They concentrated on natural openings.

## STORAGE OF MISCELLANEOUS OBJECTS

Our handraised Red-bellieds stored not only food, but also miscellaneous objects of no apparent value. When I gave the female a bent nail, she spent

FIG. 32. Red-bellied Woodpecker exploring rotten log with long tongue in search of grubs.

five minutes trying to insert it into various holes. Toothpicks, clips, and even small wads of paper elicited similar behavior. The Red-bellieds also stored objects of their own contriving. Our male sometimes loosened a sliver from a log, arranged it to point forward, then flew in search of a storage place. This behavior, a kind of play, interested me. If the related Red-headed Woodpeckers had done this in times past, might it not have been the origin of their sealing of winter stores?

When hammering an item of food, Red-bellieds hunch their shoulders forward to trap any falling crumbs with their bellies, which they push against the bark. It is then easy to bend down and seize the particle. Most woodpeckers do this, but none more adroitly than Red-bellieds.

## FORAGING AS PAIRS IN FLORIDA

### MALE DOMINANCE

I was watching a male Downy in February as it pulled out numbers of small larvae from the dead branch of a slash pine, when it was supplanted by a female Red-bellied. She then worked the branch in the same manner as the Downy. But it is rare to see Red-bellieds pecking in the manner of Downies or Hairies. During most of the 45 minutes I watched, the female moved along live branches, probing under and flaking bark, staying on top but agile in working around to look underneath. When she started probing an air plant, her mate flew to displace her. Finding nothing of interest, he returned to the spreading pine from which he had come. After a while she flew to his pine. He greeted her with bill forward, head low and a rapid *chaa-aa-aa*—a somewhat hostile greeting. She, paying no attention, moved along live branches as before. Then her mate displaced her again, so fast that it was difficult to see what happened. In spite of the male's seeming hostility, the two fed peacefully, not long afterward, on the berries of a wax myrtle.

I watched another pair in Florida feeding on oranges in midwinter. Orange trees have a dense foliage, but those trees near us had lost their leaves in a sharp freeze. Hearing *cha-cha*s, I looked up to watch a female feeding on an orange on January 31. She was displaced by her mate who did no more than look and move on. During the afternoon I saw him displace her two more times, only once stopping to feed where she had been. She seemed to take the displacings with equanimity. In rests between feedings, the two perched not far apart. This, and their coming and going together, made it evident that they were closely paired.

Male dominance is not always easy to explain. It may function in the fall to space the sexes out in individual territories. It continues into January after pairs have formed or re-formed. Lorenz (1970) argues that male dominance is needed to keep females being females and hence is essential to the pair-bond. But it may have additional values. If a female Red-bellied is displaced, it sets her to looking for new places to feed. A result may be a better use of the resources of a breeding territory.

In asserting dominance, males are aided by their brighter colors. On cloudy days, or at a distance, the sexes of Red-bellieds look only moderately different. But close up, in bright sun, the silky crown and nape of the male is of a more fiery red than that of the female and his cheeks, as well as creamy white underparts are suffused with red which becomes a patch on the belly. This location of a display color is unusual. I think that it stems from Red-bellieds spending a substantial portion of their time, when foraging, clinging upside down.

## ONSET OF BREEDING

### COURTSHIP AND THE NEST STUB

Families of Red-bellied Woodpeckers break up in September. The birds become relatively quiet and it is rare to see a male and female together between September and January. In the fall of 1956 I heard *kwirr*s on only two days. This was when two males were in conflict over a roost hole. I watched several roost holes at dawn. The males left without pausing and flew off with little noise.

Signs of an autumnal recrudescence of breeding behavior were limited.

On a warm day, November 9, a male flew to a dead stub and gave three sets of slow, rhythmical taps. A female appeared, gave a *chrr* note, joined briefly in the tapping, and was gone. The stub where the two met had a small hole owned by a Downy Woodpecker who, after the tapping, drove the male Red-bellied away.

The onset of the breeding season is signaled by the loud *kwirr*s of males ringing out at dawn. At about the same time they start to drum. Changes of weather can have marked effects. During the winter of 1957–58, snow in mid-December broke a period of mild weather. Male Red-bellieds began calling as though stimulated by their whitened world. When I walked into Seneca Swamp in early morning sun, I heard almost frantic *kwirr, kwirr, kwirr*s from many directions. Sounds of mutual tapping came clearly on two occasions. The intensity of this mid-December activity subsided within a week. After a short spell of mild weather, January was unusually cold and windy and I heard almost no *kwirr*s until February.

Wanting to know more of what Red-bellieds were doing, I followed one male on February 3. Just as I arrived below his roost hole, 20 m up in a silver maple, he flew to enter and rest with his head out. *Kwirr, kwirr, kwirr*, he called, then dropped from sight. To my surprise, for I knew little of Red-bellieds at the time, he began giving slow, clear taps from within. His mate arrived immediately. She alighted by the hole and the two tapped together, one inside and one out (Fig. 33). The male reappeared after she left. He called *kwirr* eight times, each time pointing his bill toward the ground, thus displaying the raised red feathers of his crown. He again disappeared as the female came for a second round of tapping.

The hole in the maple was dark and empty when I arrived before dawn on February 7. At 07:00 the male looked out and gave a rapid *chaa-aa-aa*, followed by a few loud *kwirr*s. His mate replied with a flatter *quer* from her roost hole across a creek. Within a few minutes she was flying to him to start a round of tapping that lasted 10 seconds. I had walked around the canal by 07:20 when *chee-wuck, chee-wuck*s drew my attention to the Red-bellied on a dead locust. Possibly the male had seen an intruder. He spread his tail as he ascended the locust to alight on the back of the female in what appeared to be coition. This was two months before the time of egg laying. Thus as with Hairy Woodpeckers, copulatory behavior began early, largely as an aftermath of conflicts.

I watched tapping at the silver maple on February 10 and 13. It was clear that the female accepted the male's roost as a potential nest site, otherwise she would not have flown to him. But by February 16 she had changed her mind. The first I knew of this was that her *quer*s came from a hole she had moved to by the canal. Her mate tried to attract her to the silver maple with *kwirr*s and even by dropping down to tap out of sight, but she did not come. By February 24 the male was excavating a new hole. This was by the canal, the direction the female had moved a week before. With a new excavation and agreement between the two restored, a second round of courtship be-

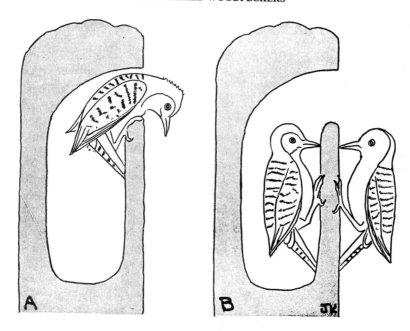

FIG. 33. Mutual tapping of Red-bellied Woodpeckers. (A) Male calls *kwirr* from entrance to his roost hole at dawn, raising crest and pointing bill toward ground. (B) Male starts to tap inside as his mate alights and joins in the tapping.

gan. As with most woodpeckers, Red-bellieds prefer to make a fresh excavation for nesting, rather than use an old one of a year before.

I returned at dawn the next morning. The male put his head out at 06:40 to give a few low *kwirr*s. His mate, once more eager to come, answered immediately with *quer*s, flying to him as he dropped from sight. She tapped but I did not hear him. The new excavation was not deep enough to give him room to maneuver. It was not until March that I heard mutual tapping. The male afterward flew to his dead locust and drummed ten times in five minutes. She came to him there, fluttering on his back in reverse mounting.

## STARLINGS

The newly excavated hole was well established when I left for three weeks. When I returned, starlings had taken it over. The male had moved back to his roost in the silver maple where I had found him on February 3. He *kwirr*ed and tapped alone on March 24. His mate would not come. But, by April 6 breeding activity was on the upswing once more. The male called from his old hole. She did not come, but she replied with *quer*s. I followed them and found her by a new excavation. Her mate met her there and the two tapped side by side (Fig. 34), the first mutual tapping I had heard in weeks. The next morning the female flew, not to her mate, but to the new excavation. He came and started excavating. After a while he called *kwirr*s, she came to tap with him, then stayed on to take his place. In all of these episodes it seemed that it was the female who took the initiative in getting a new excavation started. Her mate, more conservative, tried to stay by the old one. What forced him to leave eventually was that she would no longer come to him. When the second excavation was done, starlings that had been watching its progress, promptly took it. In my first year I wondered how Red-bellieds could ever nest. The starlings were abundant and always successful. But, whether by nesting lower among trees, or at times when starlings were busy nesting themselves, many pairs of Red-bellieds succeeded.

### Behavior of Unmated Males

An unmated male, who had begun an excavation in a sycamore by February 10, became the noisiest Red-bellied in Seneca Swamp, calling *kwirr, kwirr, kwirr* every 10–20 seconds. A female suddenly appeared on February 24. He gave excited *kew, kew*s and flew to meet her in midair. But she left.

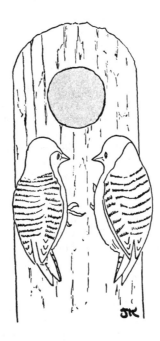

Fig. 34. A pair of Red-bellied Woodpeckers tap together outside of an excavation recently begun.

By March 4 he had still made little progress, either on the excavation or, as I thought, in attracting a mate. That morning he called *kwirr* 60 times in a row. A female then alighted on a neighboring limb and *quered*. He tapped immediately, only to have her fly away. But things were better than they looked. On the following morning I witnessed mutual tapping and after it the female flew to a limb where the two copulated.

A second male called repeatedly from the start of an excavation in a willow stub. On April 20 he got two replies in one morning. The first female came from the east, joined in mutual tapping, then flew back the way she had come. He continued to call. Then a second female flew in from the west. He flew to her, his feathers fluffed out in excitement, but she also left. I suspected that the male had called up two mated females. I had been observing two pairs of Red-bellieds that were his immediate neighbors. Both were being harassed by starlings and the males were relatively subdued. Thus it seemed that, in a disturbed state, the females may have been more attracted by the calls of the unmated male than they might have been otherwise. The male was still alone two weeks later.

## INTRASPECIFIC CONFLICTS

### FEMALE VS. FEMALE

Two females, one an owning female, the other an intruder, fought each other on January 30 and February 6. There were two centers of their fighting. One was the male who called *kwirr, kwirr, kwirr* from various tree tops but appeared indifferent to the fighting; the other center was a nest excavation in an elm. The intruding female might fly either to the male or to the hole. A long circular chase would follow, punctuated by a few *chee-wucks*. The two had body clashes on two occasions and once the owning female, in flying toward her mate and her rival, floated on outstretched wings in a floating threat display. There were few respites in the fighting that, on February 6, went on for two and a half hours.

Another two females fought over a common boundary on April 3. Female A started the fray by flying low over 50 m of swamp at Female B. The two now fought close to the ground. One would fly at the other who would dodge around a trunk. On one occasion the two rose a meter into the air, grappling as they rose. Both withdrew after several minutes. Their conflict, 85 m from the excavation of Pair A and 65 m from that of Pair B, was one of the few witnessed over a territorial boundary. The two had a similar conflict 10 days later at the same place.

A third female conflict bordered on social pathology. I was standing below the nest of Pair E on May 4, when an intruding female (Female X) flew to the entrance 5 m above me. Female E was on the inside. The two females jabbed at each other through the entrance and small feathers floated in the air. The intruder had renewed her bouts of jabbing four times when Male

E arrived. He attacked the intruder from behind while his mate engaged her head-on. The intruder then left with Male E in pursuit. Female X had transferred her attacks to Pair F by the following morning. This pair had a nest 100 m from that of Pair E. Fighting followed the same pattern from 10:15 to 11:40. Male F would chase the intruder through surrounding woods to an accompaniment of *cha*s and *chee-wuck*s, then return to his nest and enter. Female X would return immediately. Male F would then come out to drive her away and another chase would follow. Female F, oddly, took almost no part in the conflict, even when all three woodpeckers were in the same tree. It is possible that the intruding female was attracted by the noise of young, for at one time she arrived with food in her bill. The persistence of the intruding female was possibly due to her having lost her own mate and nest. I witnessed much the same phenomenon in Africa when an unmated female hornbill made attacks for several months on a nesting female.

### CONFLICTS BETWEEN PAIRS

Although Hairy and Downy Woodpeckers have individual markers, I have found none, with one exception, among adults of other woodpeckers. The exception was a male Red-bellied Woodpecker in Seneca Swamp. I had been following Red-headed Woodpeckers all winter and had listened to their *quee-ark* breeding calls before they left in May. After they had gone, I continued to hear *quee-ark*s. Could a Red-headed have remained? I went to look and found, to my surprise, that the woodpecker giving *quee-ark*s was a male Red-bellied. Although his other vocalizations were normal, as I found in following him for three weeks, he never gave the *kwirr* of his species.

I did not hear him again until December 15. This was when the Red-bellieds of the swamp experienced a short outburst of breeding behavior. My next encounter was April 12. On that day the *quee-ark* male and his mate had a prolonged conflict with a second pair of Red-bellieds, 500 m from where I had first met him a year before. The disputed hole was 20 m up in a dead elm. The owning male would bow in and out, his red crest bristling straight backward while the intruding male approached from a distance calling *quee-ark*s. The owning male would then fly at him. The intruding male would then dodge, raising both wings in threat. After being driven back, the intruder male would suddenly dart back toward the hole. The conflict was then renewed. Although all four birds of both pairs were occasionally close, the main conflict was between the two males. Clashes between the females were mild. One female, when pursued, might remain away for 10 minutes. In addition to *quee-ark*s and *kwirr*s, I heard *chee-wuck*s, *chaa-aa-aa*s, and *grr*s, the variety being stimulated, it seemed, by the presence of both sexes. The owning pair retained their hole, for I saw them feeding young there in June.

As discussed in a preceding chapter, increasing population densities may lead to increasing numbers of conflicts (behavioral scaling). This was not the situation in Seneca Swamp. Left alone, the Red-bellieds would have been adequately spaced out. What upset the balance was the number of holes lost to starlings.

## NESTING

### EXCAVATION

There were pairs of Red-bellieds in Seneca Swamp that escaped molesting by starlings. The male of a pair that did so was moving about on the dead stub of a living ash on March 9, calling *kwirrs*. He pecked at random as if percussing the underlying wood. There was no sign of his mate. When I stood directly below a little later, he tapped four bursts of about 15 taps each. She then flew in to join him in mutual tapping. A fresh, shallow excavation appeared on the stub within the next two weeks.

The male did most of the excavating. He often called *kwirr, kwirr* in pauses and his mate, who was usually within 140 m, would answer *cha, cha*, or a flat *quer*. Mutual tapping took place periodically. The nest excavation, however, progressed slowly. It was still early in the year and the female, in an especially cold spring, was in no hurry. She did not participate in the excavating and on April 5, I witnessed two occasions, following bouts of tapping, when both of the pair held their bodies stiffly, as if under tension.

The female sometimes left the nesting territory on a long flight over the tree tops to visit a cornfield in the uplands. Her mate, failing to get any response, then made what, to my ears, were frantic vocalizations. On April 12 he called *kwirr, kwirr, kwirr* every 2–5 seconds for 40 minutes. I then saw the female flying over the leafless tree tops. The male became silent immediately. Within a few moments the two were together.

Egg laying seemingly began within a few days of April 20. On this day both of the pair remained silent and motionless for eight minutes, the male resting inside and his mate on the outside of the nest. She then entered on top of him. When both were inside I heard *grr, grr* intimate notes. The male wriggled out and another silent, motionless period followed. On May 30, I removed two well-feathered young from the nest, located where I had first found the male tapping on March 9.

### INCUBATION

The nest of the *quee-ark* male was only 7 m up in the dead top of a living willow. Both birds were restless during egg laying in mid-May. The female would often put her head out, then withdraw it halfway. Her mate was even more restless. He might somersault out of the hole, call *quee-ark* when he had righted himself, then return inside. There were four eggs by May 18. On May 26 I saw no signs of activity by the nest in 20 minutes of watching. I approached and stood below. At this moment the female flew up close to the entrance and I heard the male tapping inside. She entered after he had flown out. Had I been at a distance, I would not have heard the tapping response to her coming.

## Nestling Stage

I observed 10 pairs of Red-bellieds while they were feeding young. When young were recently hatched, one parent brooded until the other arrived with food to take its place. Parents usually had many insects protruding from their bills on arrival. This prey, while small in the early nestling period, was larger later, when big beetles, long-legged, gauzy-winged insects, and even butterflies, were brought in. The woodpeckers captured most of their prey on tree trunks. A female on May 30 landed low on one tree after another, ascending rapidly. She managed to catch insects even when her bill was well filled. Parents also brought fruits, the size of wild cherries, two or three at a time.

Visits varied with the weather and time of day. They were most frequent early on a warm day. On May 18 the two of one pair fed their young 10 times in 26 minutes. The female made eight of the visits. On June 7, the male and female made two visits each in 18 minutes. The Red-bellieds usually flew directly to their holes in carrying food. One male alighted below the hole and rested. His mate then came out making a slight chatter as she flew off. This was the usual extent of a greeting when the members of a pair met. Hungry young greeted parents with harsh *chrr*s, but I could only hear them when standing close.

Methods of nest sanitation were difficult to observe. Parents, on leaving a nest, were often making motions with their tongues as though they had just swallowed the excreta of their young. I never saw fecal sacs. Of six Red-bellieds taken into captivity as nestlings, none produced them. Two flickers, on the other hand, raised under similar circumstances, produced them frequently. The cavities from which I removed the young were remarkably clean. A further account of breeding behavior is given by Stickel (1965).

### Parents and Juveniles after Nest-Leaving

Thick foliage and the silence of the Red-bellieds made them difficult to follow after their young had left the nest. Creek Wood, however, being open, was favorable for watching. Young were raised there in two succeeding years and, as juveniles, followed their parents about for two and a half months. They were at first relatively inactive, resting while their parents moved up tree trunks or flew into clusters of leaves after insects. Adults dismembered large insects before feeding them to their offspring. The begging cries of the juveniles were of two types. Both were given by my handraised female who would have left her nest in early June. Her begging in June was a high-pitched *psee* or *psee-chew*, but by July this had changed to *grr-ick*. Both vocalizations were of help in locating family groups in Creek Wood.

During the summer the wood was occupied by a male and a juvenile who followed him closely. The female was followed by her juvenile in the same way. These two latter, however, rarely came to the wood, possibly due to the increasing hostility of the male. He was moving about with his attendant juvenile on September 13, when he suddenly flew to the edge of the wood where I saw the female and her young one. The male had his crest raised and there was a burst of vocalizations that included *chee-wuck, chee-wuck; grr, grr;* and *kew, kew, kews*. His mate held a stiff pose, then flew away.

In another summer the family occupying the wood consisted of three juveniles. These had noisy conflicts among themselves. I heard two of them calling *chee-wucks* on July 20 before grappling in the air. All three were on a dead tree a week later. One would perch on the top and the others fly to replace it with *kwirrs* and *chee-wucks*, a game, it seemed, of king-of-the-castle.

## BREEDING IN CAPTIVITY

A pair of Red-bellieds, handraised less than a year before, bred successfully in the aviary, the only two of my handraised woodpeckers to do so. One of the things I wanted to know was how would courtship and other behavior in the aviary compare with what I had seen with Red-bellieds in the wild? That it turned out to be essentially the same was gratifying. Even more gratifying was that I was able to learn more of some phases than I could ever have done in nature.

### EARLY COURTSHIP

On October 22, when about four and a half months old, our female tapped vigorously and called *grr, grr* when the male alighted near her. I had witnessed an almost identical episode with a wild pair five days previously. There was no sustained development of breeding behavior, either in the field or in the aviary, until the beginning of winter.

The aviary female was flying to the male's roost hole at dawn by mid-December. This was a habit that she continued for six months, except for periods when larger young were in the nest. The visits were in the nature of a greeting. She tapped on the outside of the box and by January 3, he was joining her by tapping on the inside. The captive male was slow about emerging. He would rest inside 20–30 minutes after the greeting ceremony, a type of behavior I also observed in nature. The roosting place of the male became the nest box later. His mate developed an almost constant habit of resting in it for an hour or so every late afternoon. I supposed that this was just an individual peculiarity. Fourteen years later, however, while watching Red-bellieds in South Carolina, I found a male excavating inside a hole originally carved by a Red-cockaded Woodpecker. In the late afternoon the male Red-bellied stopped working and flew off. His mate then came to the hole and entered. She remained out of sight until he returned at 18:00, close to his roosting time. As if waiting his arrival, she flew out to a limb, took a copulation pose, and he mounted in a copulation that lasted 3–4 seconds. The male then returned to the hole to enter for the night.

We heard *kwirrs* coming from the aviary on December 28. This was exciting, for we had never heard any previously. The number given at dawn in succeeding weeks varied considerably. On many mornings the male was largely silent. But on others the sound of *kwirrs* coming from the lower part of our house was almost explosive. Such a morning was that of March 3, a day of heavy snow outside. The male gave *kwirrs* in sets of three, over and over before leaving his roost at 06:00. On the following morning, in contrast, we heard only one *kwirr* before 08:00. Whatever meteorological conditions affect bird song, they seemed to operate indoors as well as out. The mornings when cardinals did their most singing in the yard, were the ones when our male called the most *kwirrs* inside our house.

The two Red-bellieds became intimate in the last weeks of March. She was in the nest on March 24 when her mate entered and the pair remained out of sight for several minutes. This togetherness within the nest, more than any I had seen in the wild, was frequent in succeeding weeks, possibly because the male, having no excavating to do, spent much time resting there. If the female came near, he would tap or make *grr, grr* notes. The pair tapped together at other times. On April 30 the female, who had dropped out of sight, tapped when he arrived. This reversal of roles seemed to signal her acceptance of the box, actually a section of hollow log with pieces of board for roof and bottom, as a nest. Later both birds rested silent and motionless, he within and she without.

## COPULATORY BEHAVIOR

The pair was meeting on the top of a tall stub by early April. Here they swung their heads as the male, with crest raised and calling *grr, grr,* kept trying to touch the female's bill with his own. This bill touching became the prelude to copulatory behavior later on. On April 24, the female made repeated attempts to seize his bill in hers.

In early copulation attempts he fluttered on her back or she on his in reverse mounting. Full copulations, which began on April 28, took place when I turned on the aviary lights early in the morning or at most any other time of day. A precipitating event was for the male to fly to the top of the stub where the two had done their bill touching. The female then flew to flutter on his back, the two making *grr, grr* notes. He then mounted her, waving his wings to keep in place as he fell to the left. His final position was on his back, with his body at right angles to hers. Although I never noted this position in the wild, Southern (1960) has described it for Red-headed Woodpeckers. It may depend on the nature of the perch on which the female rests, whether a limb or, as in the aviary, a flattish stub.

## INCUBATION AND CARE OF YOUNG

The first of three eggs was laid on April 29. During the incubation that followed, the male spent nights on the nest, his mate continuing to greet him at dawn. He tapped while sitting on the eggs but she no longer tapped on the outside. Like him, however, she tapped on the inside when he came to relieve her. The pair became increasingly quiet. On May 12, the female, on alighting below the hole, gave *grr-ick, grr-ick*s, the first I had heard of this vocalization since she and other juveniles had given it the summer before.

Hatching was signaled on May 18 by what, to me, was an amazing performance. I had been feeding the woodpeckers such things as peanut hearts, oranges, and suet. The female knew, instinctively no doubt, that such fare was not for rapidly growing young. There were no live insects in the aviary. What was she going to do? She acted promptly when I turned on the lights by alighting on my head and beating my skull. She had never done this before and was never to do it again, except once. This was on July 9 when a second brood hatched. Her message was clear: "I need live prey." I had, fortunately, built up a supply of mealworms. She seized one from my hand, nibbling and crushing it until it was pulp suitable for hatchlings. Once she was in the nest, I could hear *chrr, chrr, chrr*s as the young had their first meal. I think the female displayed intelligence in doing all she could have in an emergency, namely to communicate her need by the most direct means.

The male, seemingly because he was shy, spent an abnormal amount of time inside the nest, both in incubation and during the nestling period. He never took mealworms from our fingers. As a result, it was always the female that took them to the nest. Here she might enter, in spite of his being there, or feed him and let him relay the food to the young.

The nest remained clean. As in the wild, I believed the parents swallowed excreta for they never carried anything away that we could perceive. It is possible that the male's occasional bouts of excavating provided sawdust to soak up any loose matter.

Three young left the nest on 13 June, 26 days after the onset of hatching. They appeared to leave without special encouragement from their parents. All three continued to re-enter the nest for the next few days. Although raised in captivity, they had had no contact with us and were completely wild. On observing copulatory behavior by the parents on June 17, I put up a new nest box. There were four eggs there 11 days after the first brood had been fledged. In 12 more days these eggs hatched.

## DRUMMING AND INTERACTIONS WITH A PILEATED

Of my handraised Red-bellieds, only the male drummed. His drumming was largely next to a window from which he could, at times, see a wild male. This was until his young were 10 days of age. On that day I put our tame female Pileated in an adjacent cage, little thinking anything special would happen. The male's reaction was immediate. He made continuous attempts to attack through the wire, calling *chee-wuck, chee-wuck* and opening his wings in a threat display. The two woodpeckers jabbed at each other. But only briefly. The Pileated had little interest and soon left. The male Red-bellied then drummed for an hour to the neglect of his young.

## RED-BELLIED WOODPECKERS

Of our two female Red-bellieds, one never had a mate. Lacking a male of her own kind, she formed at attachment to the female Pileated. Her attachment lasted for two years. She flew to the Pileated's roost box to tap at dawn and followed it about during the day making *grr, grr* intimate notes or tapping whenever the Pileated came close. The mated female, in contrast, never showed any interest. Nor did the Pileated. All that disturbed her were the attacks of the male Red-bellied. These became so severe that I had to keep the two birds separated and out of sight of each other.

The reactions of the two Red-bellieds, the male and the unmated female, were unique, for neither of them paid any special attention to other woodpeckers in the aviary. These included Hairies, Downies, flickers, and sapsuckers. This was, I think, because the crest of the Pileated was of the same fiery red and silky texture as the feathers on the crown and nape of a male Red-bellied. It acted, therefore, as a releaser of sexual behavior in the female Red-bellied and of agonistic behavior in the male.

### RED-CROWNED WOODPECKER ENTERING ROOST HOLE BACKWARD

I wanted to study some of the zebra-backed woodpeckers in Central America without ever finding a really good opportunity. I thought I had one with Red-crowned Woodpeckers in Panama. The woodpeckers were common in a graveyard near where we lived. It was easy to follow them. But they were the dullest woodpeckers I have ever studied. They fed on the fruits of royal palms, then rested on spikes at their tops. This was about all that I saw of them in hours of watching in January. But it was with a male of these Red-crowneds that I observed something that I had never seen with any other woodpecker.

I was watching the male as he flew to his roost in a narrow stub, peered in several times, then hitched up beyond it and backed down in. By dint of turning as he went in, he was facing out, ready to fly, once settled. The tree involved was a large, spreading one at the edge of woods. It bore a number of other branch stubs with holes. All of these were oval and half as long again as the round holes used by Red-crowneds in nesting. Reconstructions of activities at the two kinds of holes are shown in Figures 35 and 36. The woodpecker in Figure 35 has to back into its narrow roost, for there is no room to turn around once inside. This feat is aided not only by the large, oval entrance and its thin walls, which permit the bird to slip in at a steep angle, but also by the woodpecker's short, maneuverable tail.

The situation is different with a nest stub. Here, as shown in Figure 36, the entrance is thick-walled and just fits the body size of the Red-crowned, both features serving to make the cavity more secure. The Red-crowned can only enter such a hole head first. Once inside, however, it has room to turn around.

Why should Red-crowneds have evolved such a fragile type of roost that demands this special behavior to enter? One reason, I think, is that suitable

FIG. 35. Red-crowned Woodpecker entering roost hole carved in branch stub of small diameter by backing in tail foremost and turning as it does so.

stubs, ones of the right diameter, located high up and sufficiently decayed to excavate, are almost always in short supply. If a woodpecker uses a stub suitable for nesting by carving a roost hole in it in winter, it may not be there in the spring. A good hole can be taken over by a competitor, or, if in damp, warm tropics, rot inside. Any strategy that will conserve stubs should have survival value. One strategem is to use narrow stubs for roosting in the non-nesting season, ones that would be of no use for nesting.

A pair of Red-crowneds was trying to feed on balsa flowers in competition with three marmosets on January 29. The woodpeckers were nervous, as indicated by swings of their heads and bowing. This suggested another reason for their unusual roosting habits. The roost tree of the male was only 30 m away and when he came to it at 18:10, he was still bowing. His hole on this evening was on the underside of a nearly horizontal stub. He was thus clinging upside down when he started to back into it at 18:20. Once inside, he kept looking out. It is difficult to know what may make a wood-

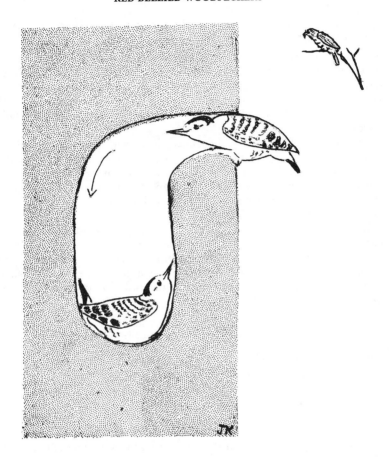

FiG. 36. Red-crowned Woodpecker entering narrow and deep entrance of a nest cavity has to do so head first. This exposes it to the hazard of being temporarily unable to see outward at a time when a predator might attack it from behind. Once inside, it has room to turn around.

pecker apprehensive. The male may have been still concerned about the marmosets or possibly by a Hook-billed Kite, which I believed roosted in or near the same tree. Roosting is an uncertain time for woodpeckes. Individuals of many species may bow in and out repeatedly, looking to one side, then the other. A likely reason, as shown in Figure 36, is that once they start to enter a hole, they are blinded and temporarily defenseless. Red-crowneds have developed a solution by backing in while still looking out.

Skutch (1969) gives further information on Red-crowneds, noting that both males and females may enter their dormitories backward. He does not distinguish whether the holes backed into were of a different diameter than either old or recent nest cavities. His observations, however, were made in a rain forest cleared for planting maize, with only charred stubs remaining. The locality where I watched the Red-crowneds appeared to be a more natural one. While it provided almost no isolated stubs, the woodland border did have large leafy trees with broken branches as well as a variety of wildlife. It may thus have simulated conditions closer to ones under which Red-crowned Woodpeckers evolved their peculiar habits of entering roost holes backward.

An interesting feature of Red-crowneds is the shortness of their tails, an adaptation, it would seem, of use in backing into holes. Selander and Giller (1963) mention two zebra-backed woodpeckers as having short tails. Their statement is that while the tail is supposedly two-thirds as long as the wing in *Centurus* (now *Melanerpes*), it is less than half as long in the Red-crowned as well as in Hoffmann's Woodpecker.

How significant, one may ask, is the association of shortness of tail and backing into holes? Curiously, I was in Costa Rica some years after our visit to Panama when Peter Ward (pers. comm.) told me that while looking out his hotel window in a town on the Pacific side, he watched a Hoffmann's Woodpecker backing into its hole. This is the only woodpecker now known to do so other than the Red-crowned.

## METHODS OF COMMUNICATION

Both sexes of Red-bellied Woodpeckers participate in vocalizations, drummings, and displays, but males are the most active.

### VOCALIZATIONS

*Breeding call.*—A musical *kwirr* repeated twice or a number of times in succession, delivered in sets of three in tense situations. The call of the female is a flatter *quer*. *Kwirr*s are seldom given during the fall but begin, sometimes in explosive fashion, on days of suitable weather in midwinter.

*Territorial call.*—A *cha-aa-ah* shaking the whole body and given the year around, seemingly because Red-bellieds have individual territories in the fall and winter in addition to breeding territories at other seasons. The *cha-aa-ah*, like the *kwirr*, may stimulate response of the same kind from another individual.

*Location and mild excitement.*—An often repeated *cha*. A Red-bellied may give this note when disturbed by an observer.

*Intense excitement.*—Expressed by a triple, high-pitched *kew, kew, kew*.

*Conflict.*—Red-bellieds usually make a loud *chee-wuck, chee-wuck* when engaged in intraspecific conflicts.

*Intimate note.*—A low *grr, grr*, which may be exchanged by the members of a pair from the first days of courtship until the end of the breeding season.

*Begging call of juveniles.*—Young that have recently left the nest, beg with a soft *psee-chew.* The first syllable is high-pitched. They clamor for food in succeeding weeks with a *grr-ick, grr-ick,* which is distinct from, but obviously related to, the *grr, grr* notes of adults.

The vocalizations of nestling Red-bellieds are as varied as among other genera of woodpeckers. A harsh *chrr* usually accompanies feeding.

## DRUMMING AND TAPPING

*Drumming.*—Red-bellied Woodpeckers have two types of drumming. The usual type is an even burst of about a second's duration. A second type is similar except that it is preceded by a few well-spaced taps—*da-da-drrrr.* I have not discovered any difference in meaning between the two. I have heard both types with Red-headed Woodpeckers. Drumming is a far less frequent method of communication with these two melanerpine species than with other genera of woodpeckers. It is heard most commonly in conflicts.

*Tapping.*—Delivered at a regular rate of 2.3 taps per second, with 4–20 taps in each burst. The members of pairs may tap together in mutual tapping. Tapping is closely associated with nest site selection and maintenance of the pair bond.

## DISPLAYS

The feathers of the head and nape are raised when a Red-bellied is excited. This is particularly true of the male, whose red feathers, being somewhat long and silky, give him a striking appearance.

*Threat display.*—Made with wings fully extended at an upward angle of 45 degrees and with tail outspread. In conflicts over holes the wings may be spread out like a moth's against the trunk of a tree. A Red-bellied may also float through the air with wings in, held as in threat display. These woodpeckers do not appear to have any courtship flights.

*Stiff pose.*—This display gives a Red-bellied a rigid, somewhat bowed appearance, the bowing being due to the elevation of feathers covering the upper back.

*Resting motionless.*—Members of a pair may rest near each other or their nest stub for many minutes as the time of actual nesting approaches, a form of behavior common to most genera of woodpeckers. Pynnönen (1939) has aptly described it as *Regungslos-auf-eine-stelle-sitzen.*

## LITERATURE CITED

KILHAM, L. 1956. Breeding and other habits of Casqued Hornbills (*Bycanistes subcylindricus*). Smith. Misc. Coll., **131**(9): 1–45.

———. 1958. Pair formation, mutual tapping and nest hole selection of Red-bellied Woodpeckers. Auk, **75**: 318–329.

——. 1961. Reproductive behavior of Red-bellied Woodpeckers. Wilson Bull., **73**: 237–254.

——. 1963. Food-storing of Red-bellied Woodpeckers. Wilson Bull., **75**: 227–234.

——. 1972. Shortness of tail in Red-crowned Woodpeckers and their habit of entering roost holes backward. Condor, **74**: 202–204.

LORENZ, K. 1970. Companions as factors in the bird's environment, p. 101–258. *In* Studies in Animal and Human Behavior, Vol. 1. Harvard Univ. Press, Cambridge.

PYNNÖNEN, A. 1939. Beiträge zur Kenntnis der Biologie finnischer Spechte. Ann. Zool. Soc. Zool.-Bot.-Fenn. Vanamo, **7**(2): 1–166.

SELANDER, R. K., AND D. R. GILLER. 1963. Species limits in the woodpecker genus *Centurus* (*Aves*). Bull. Amer. Mus. Nat. Hist., **124**: 213–274.

SKUTCH, A. F. 1969. Life histories of Central American birds. **III**. Pacific Coast Avifauna (Cooper Ornith. Soc.), no. 35, 580 p.

SOUTHERN, W. E. 1960. Copulatory behavior of the Red-headed Woodpecker. Auk, **77**: 218–219.

STICKEL, D. W. 1965. Territorial and breeding habits of Red-bellied Woodpeckers. Amer. Midl. Nat., **74**: 110–118.

# 8

# YELLOW-BELLIED SAPSUCKERS

# YELLOW-BELLIED SAPSUCKERS

## WINTER ACTIVITIES

### MARYLAND TO COSTA RICA

Yellow-bellied Sapsuckers, with females moving farther south than males (Howell, 1953), are the most migratory of woodpeckers. The contrast between their winter and spring/summer activities is considerable. I have watched them in winter from Maryland to the Panama Canal. But wherever located, it would be difficult to take a census of numbers. Solitary and motionless much of the time, their mottled plumage makes them blend with bark wherever they rest. I have found this as true in Costa Rica as in Maryland. But there are differences. Sapsuckers in the north take sap from leafless trees and in the deeper south and neotropics, from evergreens. One thing I tried to discover in Maryland was how they survived cold spells. I could not because I never could find them. Their camouflage was too effective. But, given freezing nights and thawing days, they came to life.

After a night of freezing temperatures, official readings (Washington, D.C.) on January 31 were $-2°$ C at 11:00, $-1°$ C at noon, $0°$ C at 13:00 and $2°$ C at 14:00, at 11:30 a sapsucker was drilling holes in a black walnut at the edge of Seneca Swamp. The holes were in horizontal rows, well spaced up the trunk. For the first half hour the sapsucker continued drilling on the sunny side of the tree. Less time was spent drilling after midday, when the bird began feeding. A trip from the bottom to the top of the drilled areas took the sapsucker five minutes or less. Once at the top, it dropped through the air or hitched down backward to begin over again. The volume of excreta shot out was considerable. In a 25 minute period one sapsucker voided 11 times, or once every two minutes. I did not find sapsuckers feeding on three subsequent weekends of warmer weather. What made sap run was freezing nights.

Sap taken in late spring and summer is sap elaborated in leaves and coming down the bole. A sapsucker in summer, therefore, can take sap while resting in one place. Sap stored in trunks in winter is more stationary and rows of holes, well separated, may yield the most. Commensals coming to take sap in Maryland included Tufted Titmice, White-breasted Nuthatches, and Red-bellied Woodpeckers.

I watched a female sapsucker from December 31 to January 3 at Monte Verde in the highlands of Costa Rica. She stuck closely to aggregations of holes where a large tree branched below the canopy, turing her head to one side, then the other in striking glancing blows. Although I could see no glisten of sap, the sapsucker voided as often as three times in 15 minutes. In four hours of watching I did not notice any insects or other commensals coming to the holes. A large weasel with a black head and neck suddenly appeared one morning, but did no more than glance at the sapsucker and move on.

# YELLOW-BELLIED SAPSUCKERS

## Taking Sap in the Breeding Season

### Relation to Wounded Trees

Sapsuckers feed on a wide variety of trees (McAtee, 1911). Regardless of the tree utilized, it is not always clear why they concentrate on a few, leaving others untouched. In the summers of 1962 and 1963, I found three places in Lyme that seemed to provide answers. One centered on a row of paper birches bordering a dirt road and badly bruised by snow plows. Practically all of the birches with sapsucker holes were ones with scars. Other birches of similar size and adjacent to them, but unwounded, had none. Two feeding trees stood back from the road. Although untouched by the plow, they had extensive injuries of unknown origin below their bands of drill holes. Two additional birches, the largest used by Pair A when feeding young, were disfigured by black, clinker-like lesions of the fungus *Poria obliqua*. One had over 900 drill holes. Weakening by lumbering operations may have given the fungus infections a start.

In addition to the birches that had sustained prior injury, I found sapsuckers making small bands on healthy birches nearby. These bands were at the same height as the main feeding holes, but drilling was casual, as if no more than a displacement activity. This drilling of satellites, however, may be significant. By laying down a series of small wounds, the sapsuckers are creating a locus for sap feeding in another year. In 1963 four of the six main feeding trees for one pair of birds arose from satellites started the summer before.

When sapsuckers arrive in April, they take sap mainly from hemlocks and the outermost branches of aspens where buds and catkins are unfolding. I saw no sapsuckers on birches in May. A few drill holes appeared above the snow plow injuries on June 3. I marked them with a pencil. No more appeared until June 25, when the sapsuckers returned to collect sap as steadily as the summer before. An explanation of why they delayed activities is that phloem transport (nutrients coming down from leaves) begins when leaves are fully developed, a stage reached in the last days of June (Zimmerman, 1961).

Three young sapsuckers, fledged from Nest A on July 6 and 7, were able to take sap right away. An ability to make their own holes did not come until August. In the interim they practiced on a dead birch, dead limbs of aspen, and on sumacs, trees that were of no interest to their parents.

In addition to the area of paper birches, I watched sapsuckers where hundreds of unwanted or weed trees had been girdled by foresters. Most of the trees in one area, not much affected by being girdled the previous winter, still had canopies. Trees in another region, in contrast, in a second summer after girdling, were either dead or dying by August. The dying trees were the ones that attracted the sapsuckers, which drilled just above the girdles (Fig. 37a). My observations were on four families of parents and young that were taking sap from birches within or adjacent to their regular territories. A considerable amount of sap appeared to be flowing. This was indicated not only by the staining below the holes, but also by a steady succession of visitors that included paper wasps, Ruby-throated Humming-birds, Black-throated Blue Warblers, Downy Woodpeckers, and chipmunks, as well as the sapsuckers. The chipmunks only had to climb a meter or less to reach the holes. More than eighty trees, dying as a result of girdling, were being attacked. In the first area, where the trees had been girdled the winter before and had not had time to be much affected, I could only find three that had sizeable bands of holes. In the summer after girdling (Fig. 37c), the sapsuckers made a compact band of holes above the wounds in hop-hornbeams. In a second summer, when hornbeams were dying, they made hundreds of holes extending up the trunk (Fig. 37d). Both of these patterns differed from the short linear ones made on ungirdled hornbeams (Fig. 37d). The three patterns, encountered on a single species, show that the drilling of sapsuckers is related to the underlying physiology of the tree.

Sap from trees in leaf is food for varied forms of life. While aphids obtain phloem sap by inserting their stylets into individual sieve tubes (Zimmerman,

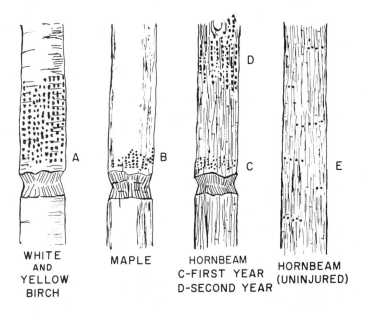

WHITE AND YELLOW BIRCH

MAPLE

HORNBEAM C-FIRST YEAR D-SECOND YEAR

HORNBEAM (UNINJURED)

FIG. 37. Patterns of drill holes made by sapsuckers above girdles cut on different species of trees.

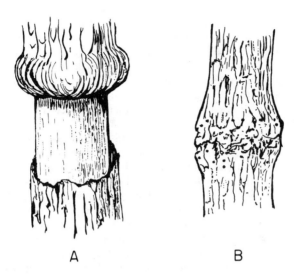

A                                    B

FIG. 38. Excessive growth of wood, representing an increased flow of nutrients to the area above a wound: (A) above girdle (after Hales, 1727); (B) at site of former sapsucker holes on a red oak.

1961), sapsuckers obtain theirs by repeated wounding. This leads to an increased flow of nutrients, an effort of the tree to repair the injury. It has been known since the time of Hales (1727) that nutrients will accumulate above a girdle, as indicated by a layer of thickened wood (Fig. 38a). Sapsucker feeding prevents formation of this extra wood under usual conditions. But when sapsuckers discontinue a series of holes, swellings may appear (Fig. 38b). Southwick and Southwick (1980) have made measurements for sucrose at sapsucker holes in relation to the feeding of hummingbirds. They found that in the summer the phloem sap had a sugar concentration of 16g per 100g solution (0.47 M sucrose equivalent), which is sufficient to support hummingbirds without other sources of nutrients.

## ARRIVAL ON BREEDING GROUNDS

Males arrive in New Hampshire in early April. Seven watched at Tamworth occupied areas much the same as territories of the previous year. Male A flew the same circuit of drum trees. He resembled other males in doing a considerable amount of drumming, with bursts coming at intervals of 40–60 seconds. His behavior toward neighboring Male B, who occasionally came into his territory, was tolerant at first. But on April 16, when Male B was drumming, Male A started drumming 5m above, then swooped to drive him away. He then drummed in the place vacated by his rival. The lone males also did bobbing dances when they met at the same level on a tree. In mid-

April, I watched four males, all within 60 cm of each other, doing bobbing dances more or less at the same time.

Features of the dances between lone males were noteworthy. One was their mild nature and another, that one or the other male might fly off in winnow or courtship flight. It was as though the newly arrived males had a drive for courtship but, in the absence of females, found outlet in performing to another male. Much the same phenomenon has been described by von Haartman (1956) for male Pied Flycatchers.

Of the seven males in Tamworth, six had no mates between April 16 and 20. The first female I noted was on April 24. Male D was drumming on a dead pine, when she, in response, joined by drumming on a branch of no particular resonance. The duet continued for several minutes. She then flew to him and the two had a bobbing dance with *quirk* greetings. Male E flew off in a winnow flight, as I like to call it, because of the noise made by the wings. His flight was to the start of an excavation. He worked there a few minutes before his mate flew to join him. Seeing her coming, he started tapping just within the entrance and kept it up for two minutes. He then flew downhill, exposing the white of his lower back and rump, as well as the white on his wings, in fluttering flight. It was evident from this and other episodes that males try to interest their mates in a site almost as soon as they arrive. A site or a potential one is, from the beginning, a center of pair-bonding activities.

## CROWDING AND CONFLICTS

A lively place to watch sapsuckers, or any other woodpeckers, is where a local population is crowded and nest stubs are few. The resultant scaling of behavior is what I encountered at Tamworth in the late 1950's. Logging, hurricanes, and the nature of trees that grew up on abandoned farmlands, created favorable conditions. Sapsuckers throve. I could find nests without difficulty. Then, as stubs became few, conditions deteriorated. Members of pairs had to put up with decayed, inadequate stubs or, as in the case of Pair A, fail to nest.

Male A, unable to find a new site within his territory, kept returning to his hole of the year before. He attracted attention on May 5 by flying to it in a winnow flight and popping inside. He then looked out to call *kwee-urks*. Female A flew to him in normal flight, looked in, then did a bobbing dance. Another meeting at the old hole took place later. Female A had first drummed, then she and her mate flew to the hole together to dance, pulling their heads up and down in lively fashion. There were further variations on May 6. Male A frequently tapped out of sight and on two occasions, Female A alighted to tap within the entrance. Things looked promising. For a short time I thought that they might use the old nest after all. But I have never known sapsuckers to nest in a hole of a previous year. Male A finally gave up when his mate ceased to come. With nothing else to occupy him, he now spent much of his time fighting or trying to fight with his neighbors. Day after day he flew the circuit of his territory, drumming whenever he found himself opposite to a rival male. Having four other pairs as neighbors, he was often well occupied.

Males A and B were drumming on either side of a wood road that formed their mutual boundary, when their duet was broken by the arrival of Female A. All three sapsuckers now gathered on one tree. Female A was seemingly disinterested as Male A bobbed in a dance with tail fanned and crest raised, close to his rival. When Female A flew to another tree, Male A, then Male B followed. The spectacle of the brilliant yellows, reds, and blacks of the sapsuckers in display repeated itself in a succession of trees. Intense, scratchy *quirks* made the conflits easy to locate. Sometimes one male flew after the other in swift pursuit through the treetops. Many of these pursuits originated at a large paper birch that formed the juncture of three territories. Thus the woods, that should have become quiet as nesting began, resounded with the noise of drumming and breeding calls due to the inability of Pair A to find a place to nest.

## EXCAVATION

### SHARE DONE BY MALES AND FEMALES

Sapsuckers carve a fresh hole each year, having a seeming inhibition against reusing a previous one. A selection pressure may be avoidance of parasites. But an occasional pair, like Pair H in Lyme one year, may give an old nest a try. Male H entered his old hole in late April, called *kwee-urks* from the entrance, and flew off in winnow flights in efforts to get his mate to come. He entered twice on April 29, emerging each time with black, tar-like fecal matter in his bill. It appeared to be a distasteful job for he wiped his bill many times. After the young had fledged the year before, I had measured the accumulation, left in the last days of nesting, as being 6 cm deep. The old feces seemed to act as a deterrent. After a few tries, Male H gave up his efforts. He and mate were later able to excavate a new hole elsewhere.

Sapsuckers generally have to make a number of trials before finding a suitable nest site. The members of Pair D worked on a shallow excavation on May 6, with pecks coming at rates of up to nearly a hundred a minute. The sapsucker excavating might work for a half hour before being relieved. Male D was excavating when his mate alighted and started a *quirk* dance. He tapped vigorously within the entrance (Fig. 39), then flew away in courtship flight. The excavation was abandoned the following day, however, seemingly due to the hardness of the wood.

Pair C had more luck with its excavation. Male C was able to get half of his body into the hole by May 14. He was excavating out of sight three days later, when his steady, fast pecking sounded like a small motor within the tree. His mate came to relieve him every 10–15 minutes. But she did not do much work. She might enter, toss out 20–30 billfuls of sawdust, then come

QUIRK, QUIRK

TAP-TAP-TAP

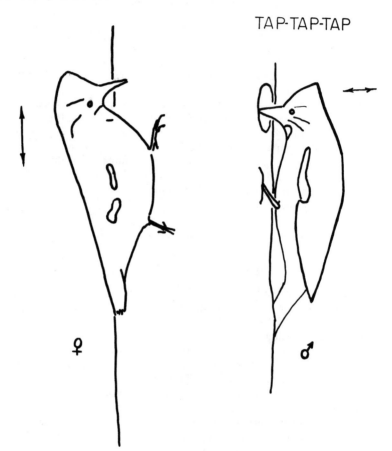

♀            ♂

FIG. 39. Changeover at excavating: male sapsucker taps as female alights and does bobbing dance accompanied by *quirk* notes.

out to rest. Scratching and preening took much of her time. This interested me, for my pair of handraised sapsuckers, the offspring of Pair C in a previous year, also did much preening as their excavation neared completion. It is conceivable that ectoparasites are stirred into activity at this time, a strategic one in terms of transfer to a succeeding generation of their hosts.

Male C roosted in his excavation on May 17. I was by his stub before dawn on the following morning. Female C called *kwee-urk* from a distance at 05:00.

He gave six loud *kwee-urk*s in reply. He had already started excavating before she called.

The way the two of a pair share the work of excavating can vary. At five nests, that were all first excavations, I found that males did nearly all of the work. When they worked, they worked continuously for 15–30 minutes at a stretch. When females changed places with them, in contrast, their excavating was often token in character, with little sawdust removed. But female sapsuckers can work hard under special circumstances. When Pair F abandoned one excavation and began a second one, Female C did 68 percent of the excavating in the first four days. This was excavating of the hardest type, for she dug through 6.5 cm of living sapwood. The heart of the aspen was easier due to infection with the tinder fungus. When this easier digging was reached, the male took over and did 75 percent of the work in the last five days.

Female A worked so continuously in her first four days that she took no time for resting. On a number of occasions she refused to leave when her mate came to relieve her. Why should she have worked so hard? I think it was because females, under usual circumstances, conserve energy needed for egg laying, by leaving the hard work to their mates. But when a first excavation fails, a female that has been becoming physiologically and psychologically ready for egg laying, finds herself with no place to do so. Her need is great. Spurred to get another hole underway, she may then do as much or more than her mate.

## NARROW ENTRANCES

A curious feature of some entrances is that, when carved by males, they make a snug fit for their bodies. But females are not always of the same size. In laying up reserves and developing eggs, they may become larger, too large to get into an entrance just fitting a slimmer mate. This is of no consequence at first, for females usually do not enter when males are doing most of the work. But later on it creates difficulties. The first time I saw Female C enter her nest was on May 20. She had to wriggle to force her way in. After remaining inside for five minutes, she had difficulties getting out. She put her head out, moving it up and down violently. It took five hard struggles before, in a fifth one, she was able to force herself through. Even when feeding young weeks later, she still had to pump up and down to get out. Lawrence (1967) describes a female that lost the feathers of her crown from pushing herself in and out of her nest. Female F, who had carved her own entrance, had no such difficulty.

## START OF NESTING

### COPULATIONS

The first copulation I saw with Pair C was on May 17. Female C had been excavating when she flew to a maple where her mate greeted her with *quirk*s as she moved out on a limb. He followed, beating his wings in a slow, exaggerated manner. She was crosswise to the limb when he mounted, then fell to the left and backward. His final position was upside down, with his body at a right angle to hers, the tails of the two overlapping. Of five copulations witnessed, four were on the same limb. The last one was on the day the first egg was laid.

Features of copulations with other pairs were that females often flew from the nest hole to the copulation perch, as though reinforcing the bond between mate and nest, and that they lasted from 7–8 seconds.

## EGG LAYING

Female J was in her nest for an hour early on the morning of June 2, a long time for her. When her mate came to the entrance, as if to change places, she remained out of sight and, when he returned at 06:21, she struck out sharply, driving him away. I witnessed similar behavior with Female G on May 24, when she had four eggs. Dominance of the female at the nest at time of egg laying is not limited to sapsuckers, for I have also noted it with flickers.

The time between the completion of an excavation and the start of egg laying can be brief or even nonexistent. I found an egg half-buried in sawdust in one nest when the male was still excavating. Circumstances, however, vary. Pairs H and I had finished their excavations by the middle of May in 1976. Egg laying was then delayed, seemingly, by nine days of cold, wet weather. At the end of the cold spell, on May 24, I found one egg and on May 28, four eggs in Nest H. Only two of these hatched. The history of Nest I was more complicated. There were three eggs on May 23, and four on the 24th. Neither the male nor the female had appeared disturbed when I had put up a ladder to look. I was, therefore, surprised on the following day to see the male carry three eggs from his nest. Only a single egg remained. After a wait of six days, four more eggs were laid between June 1 and 4. Of the total of five, three hatched. There were thus high rates of egg failure in both nests, 50 percent in Nest H and 40 percent in Nest I. All five of the unhatched eggs were removed by the parents within a day of the hatching of the others. Whether irregularities in laying and failures of eggs to hatch were related to the long cold spell, directly or indirectly, I had no way of knowing. It was interesting that Male H should have removed three eggs from his nest, ones that, due to the cold spell, might not have hatched.

## INCUBATION

In following nesting woodpeckers, I have distinguished between sessions at the nest and attentiveness. Sessions are the times between changeovers. As the sessions of males at the sapsucker nests were a third to a half longer than those of the females, they did the greatest part of the incubating by day, in addition to all of it by night. The actual times spent incubating eggs during sessions varied. I found most sapsuckers restless during incubation, often looking or coming out. These interruptions added up to apreciable amounts of time. In nearly 31 hours of watching at Nests C, D, and J, eggs were left uncovered for a total of five hours or nearly 16 percent of the time. Females C and D were slow about entering their nests after change-overs in the first five days of incubation, often loitering outside for a time before doing so. But as incubation progressed, they became more attentive and did 60 and 86 percent, respectively, of the incubating in the last 6–7 days. Females H and I, in contrast, were 93 to 97 percent attentive from the start.

Heat had some effect on attentiveness. When temperatures were 36° C in the shade on June 10, and possibly hotter inside their nest that was exposed to the sun, the members of Pair J left their eggs unguarded for 34 of 60 minutes. In the previous three days, the two had incubated close to 100 percent of the time.

There was little ceremony when members of pairs changed places during incubation. Tapping ceased and a female might do no more than give a low *waan* when arriving near the nest. This generally quiet behavior was broken for one pair at the time of hatching, when both sapsuckers greeted each other with *quirk*s and called *c-waan*s. These manifestations of excitement subsided by the following day when both parents carried insects to the young.

## Nestling Period

### Brooding

In three nests, watched for over 25 hours, the parents brooded the young almost equally, keeping them covered for 70 to 90 percent of the time. This was for the first 8–10 days after hatching. Cessation of brooding was more irregular with two other pairs. Pair J, after stopping on June 24, began brooding again on June 26 with the onset of cold, wet weather and Pair I, after brooding regularly for four days, did so irregularly over the next three.

In one year, I had nests with one, two, three, and four young. The two young of Nest J were brooded 82 percent of the time I watched, the three young of Nest I 67 and the four young of Nest A 73 percent. While the differences were not great, the nest with the fewest young received the most brooding. Royoma (1966), writing of the Great Tit, emphasized that heat loss was greater in small broods, where young were less efficient at keeping each other warm.

### Feeding Young

Males and females fed young almost equally (Fig. 40), with the males making 6–10 percent more visits than their partners. I visited Nest J for an hour or more every day from hatching, on June 15, to the fledging of the four young 28 days later. After a low average (Fig. 41) of 10.5 visits per hour

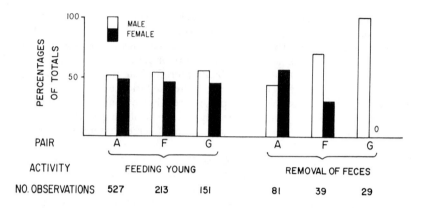

FIG. 40. Observations on three pairs of nesting sapsuckers showing that the task of feeding the young was shared by both sexes to a nearly equal extent in all pairs, but that of nest sanitation varied.

during the time of brooding, the rate jumped to 24 per hour in the mid-nesting period. This rate continued until within four days of fledging when it fell to 16 per hour.

It is important to know how many young are in a nest. I was fortunate to have encountered four nests that contained one, two, three, and four young in 1976. As might be expected, the number of feeding visits increased with the number of young. But this was not proportionate. It seemed that the fewer the young, the more each one got fed. A possible result of this was that the single young one, the survivor of an original two in Nest H, left at 26 days, while the four of Nest J did not leave until 28 days after hatching.

INSECT FOOD

Sapsuckers are versatile insect catchers. They glean by hitching rapidly up trunks, flying against clusters of leaves, and, on warmer days, they catch prey on the wing. They also go to the ground. Only a small portion of their prey is caught by drill holes. When their bills are full of prey, they frequently stop at the holes to take sap before flying to their young. Some prey can be large. I watched a male fly to the ground one morning to catch a luna-sized moth which it carried to a cleft in rough bark to dismember. He then fed the body to a nestling four days from fledging. The nestling had a hard time. But, with helpful pokes from the male, it finally got the moth down. On another day I watched a male sapsucker battle a willow sawfly (*Cimbex* spp.) for two minutes before giving up. I then picked up the sawfly and measured it as being 3.4 cm in length.

Ants are possibly the most common of small prey. One male carried feces plus sawdust to the same small hornbeam in two successive years. I cleared

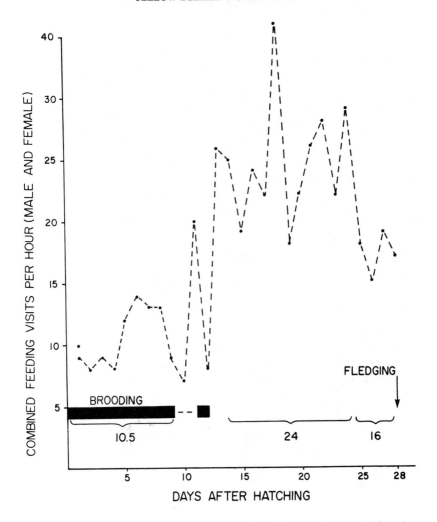

FIG. 41.   Curve of combined male plus female feeding rates for a pair of nesting sapsuckers, showing sharp increase of rate at termination of brooding and decline as the time of fledging approached.

the ground below and, for a time, collected the fecal remains. These consisted mainly of carpenter ants (*Camponotus* spp.). In spite of this, I think that soft-bodied insects, such as crane flies that one can see from the long legs and gauzy wings projecting from bills of parents, form the bulk of prey fed to nestlings. The hard parts of ants, in surviving digestion, show up well in feces and can thus be misleading.

## Vocalizations of Nestlings

Nestling sapsuckers give *check-check-check*s that carry like a broadcast from the nest. I have found the vocalizations helpful in locating nests; predators might do the same. There must be compensating advantages. I think that the message is to "hurry, hurry, hurry." Parents at the height of a nestling period look, at times, almost frantic in their rush to collect insects. The *check-check-check*s may be the stimulus. Von Haartman (1956), using a double nest with some of the young hidden, found that the hunger calls of nestling Pied Flycatchers, which are hole-nesters, definitely stimulated the number of feeding visits made by their parents.

I have heard nestlings give an alarm call only once. This was at a nest on the day before fledging, when an unmated female ascended to the entrance and poked in at the young. She was greeted by an immediate wailing. The young kept it up to 30 seconds after the intruder had left.

## Nest Sanitation

Male sapsuckers do most of the work of cleaning nests. Of seven nests followed at length, I found the females doing none of the work in three, and 2, 22, 30, and 56 percent of it in the others. Hearing a steady pecking coming from a nest one morning, I watched as the male emerged with a bill full of feces and flew to a maple to shake the excreta loose. He then returned to carry out three more loads, all mixed with sawdust. I have never seen sapsuckers carrying fecal sacs and it is doubtful if their young produce them. None of six handraised captives did so. Two of them voided as I took them from the nest. One produced a puddle, the other a wet mash, the wetness of the excreta being, I presumed, due to the sap they had consumed.

Parents vary in how long they continue to clean nests. They ceased their efforts between four and eight days before their young left at three nests. Some males, however, continued to carry out feces until almost the very end. Male G removed seven large billfuls in 30 minutes on the day before nest leaving. Several nests that I examined after the young had left had black, tarry, fecal matter at the bottom.

## Intrapair Relations

Members of pairs rarely arrive at a nest at the same time. When they have done so, I have wondered which sex would enter first. Female B was about to enter with prey on June 13, when her mate arrived with crest raised and giving scratchy *quirk*s. She flew off, swallowing the insects she was carrying as she did so. He then entered. When the two arrived near the nest four days later, I heard the loudest *quirk*s I had heard for some time. She left, but this time she returned as he was leaving. Her mate on both days was the most assertive male that I have encountered. At another nest, the two of the pair paused, as if hesitant, on arriving together. The female was a little closer and entered first, while he waited. Taken all together, I have never found one sex or the other dominant at a nest. The only exception is the dominance of females, for brief periods, during egg laying.

## Lone Parents

When one of a pair is killed during the nestling period, the other one carries on. But the behavior of the sexes differ. Lone females are apt to feed their young at an exaggerated rate of 20–28 times an hour, bringing little prey on each visit. Of three nests tended by such females, the young died. Their begging was feeble and I think that they died of starvation. Two lone males, in contrast, continued to feed their nestlings as though nothing had happened. One of the males lost his nest to predation, but the other fed his young one for nine days when it fledged successfully.

Female C was unusual in attracting a second mate. Her first one was killed by a raccoon, as I learned by finding a pile of his feathers below the hole. The entrance was well chewed, but intact. Female C fed her young one at a rapid rate of 28 times an hour. Her behavior, however, had taken a new turn by the following morning when I found her calling *kwee-urks*. Was she trying to attract a mate? I soon found that she already had. The new male flew to the nest, but instead of feeding the young, he merely percussed, as though trying out a new nest site. When Female C approached, he tapped, then flew off in a courtship flight.

I arrived soon after dawn on the next morning, which was two days after the death of the first male. His replacement drummed soon after dawn. He then flew to the female, who responded by flying off in a courtship flight, similar to his of the day before. The nestlings were now begging loudly and, at 05:40, the new male was feeding them. It seemed remarkable that he had been able to adapt to the role of being a parent so rapidly. This role, however, was short-lived. The raccoon returned that night, killing both him and the nestlings.

## Nest Leaving and After

### Recrudescence of Breeding Behavior

Sapsuckers are generally quiet while nesting. When the male starts drumming, or the members of a pair exchange *quirks* four to five days before nest leaving, the behavior comes as a change. Loud *kwee-urks* may come on the day the young fledge. Such recrudescences of breeding behavior generally last only a few days. But where several pairs have nested not far apart, as in some lumbered or other areas, one pair may stimulate the other. This was true of a pair in Lyme whose young left their nest on June 29. By July 3 the male was working on a new one, in between fights with a rival. There was much drumming and calling of *kwee-urks*, as well as pursuits and bobbing dances. On 16 July, 17 days after nest leaving, the male excavated briefly, then flew off in a courtship flight. This was the longest recrudescence that I witnessed.

## Behavior of Juveniles

At 07:10 on June 30, about 30 seconds after being fed, a fledgling flew from its nest on a circular, downward flight that carried it to a stub 6 m away. The young one had been looking about, with its head out of the hole, for the previous hour. Neither at this or any other nest have I seen parent sapsuckers make special efforts to induce their young to leave.

The fledglings of Pair A were at drill holes soon after their emergence. If a parent was busy taking sap, it gave way as a fledgling approached, the fledgling then trying the same holes. The parents continued to feed their young insects for some weeks. Parent-young interactions were often accompanied by low *week-week* vocalizations. I found it of interest to compare the young sapsuckers of Pair A with young Hairy Woodpeckers in the same neighborhood. The fledgling Hairies were completely dependent on their parents. They followed them about, flying where they flew, and making loud vocalizations along with half-starting their wings. The juvenile sapsuckers, with their weak begging and absence of display, were the reverse. Possibly, being able to allay their hunger, to some extent, by taking sap on their own, they had less urgency about being fed by their parents.

Families of sapsuckers, bound to their territories by their sap trees, stay together throughout the summer. But the parents are the ones staying closest. The juveniles come to associate mostly with each other, exchanging low *woi, woi* or *week, week* greetings, exploring old holes and crevices, flying after insects, and occasionally drumming in a feeble, irregular way. I have watched these activities to best advantage on the bare trees and stubs of beaver ponds. The juveniles were curious, sometimes hitching close to a flicker, a Rusty Blackbird, or a Hermit Thrush, only to be driven away. A few, on encountering a chickadee, dodged about in play, with wings out, as if facing an enemy. They continued to beg when near a parent, even in late summer. Their begging is almost inaudible, a slight up-and-down motion of the lower mandible often being the only indication that it is going on.

I have found juveniles drilling holes as early as mid-August. But they do not do so in earnest until the very end of summer, a few weeks before they leave. Something I have noted repeatedly is that their bills look too long, longer than those of their parents. I think this is because they do not do enough hard pecking in late August and early September. Bills grow continuously and need wear.

I heard steady *quare, quare, quare*s on September 20, then found a juvenile pestering an adult male, presumably its parent. The male kept trying to leave, but the juvenile kept coming close. I saw several other such encounters, where males ended by driving their offspring away.

Family conflicts can continue on migration. Sapsuckers do not nest in Maryland, but in October I found a family of them in Creek Wood. A juvenile, marked by an asymmetrical white patch, joined a second juvenile and an adult female at a band of drill holes. One of the juveniles then flew to join an adult on a neighboring tree. The marked juvenile and another one were at the same spot a week later. But the peaceful state of affairs did not last. On October 22 and 23 I watched four conflicts, all dramatic. The marked juvenile, in a first of these, flew to an oak making *quares*, then hitched over to an adult male at some drill holes. The male kept shifting away. In another moment the two fell to the ground, locked in conflict and making *quares*. The juvenile flew away. The male ascended an oak with a mass of contour feathers sticking to his bill, which he had difficulty wiping off. He then flew after the juvenile in a long circular pursuit over a field. The conflict was possibly territorial for I noticed, over several winters, that Creek Wood was occupied by a single male.

## Sapsuckers in Captivity

I had two pairs of handraised sapsuckers, one in 1958 and another in 1960. Both carried on bobbing dances, tapping, excavating, and copulated. Neither, however, laid eggs. They did not have room enough to carry on courtship flights, in spite of efforts to do so, and I think that they needed a larger cage for nesting success. I was still, however, able to learn much from them.

The first signs of breeding were in late December when the sapsuckers began calling *c-waan* and flying about in an alert, restless manner. Drumming started in January. One of the females tapped every morning in the corner where she roosted, and males and females touched bills in February. By this time they had lost much of their juvenal plumage.

I had one male and three females in 1960. The females formed a series with No. 1 having a bright yellow belly and red crest, and No. 2 the same, but with a duller cast. No. 3 was practically indistinguishable from a juvenile. She was drab and was dominated by the other two. But when it came to choosing a mate, she was the one chosen by the male. In an effort to prove this, I took all three females away and left the male alone for three days. He did a great deal of drumming each day, especially between 06:00 and 08:00. Then I introduced the brightest female. He attacked immediately. Following many *quares*, the conflict note of sapsuckers, and much pursuing back and forth, the female finally crawled behind logs where I had to rescue her. I then replaced her with female No. 2. She was greeted, at first, with a bobbing dance and *quirks*, but the male was soon flying about restlessly without further interest. His treatment of the drab female was very different from that of the other two. He accepted her immediately, and both courtship and excavation of a nest were resumed.

YELLOW-BELLIED SAPSUCKERS

## PREFERENCE FOR NESTING IN *FOMES*-INFECTED ASPENS

Woodpeckers have search images of what makes an optimal nest tree. This, for sapsuckers in New Hampshire, is a mature aspen bearing conks of the false tinder fungus, *Fomes igniarius* (Fig. 42). The fungus renders aspens favorable in several ways. One is by inducing decay in the heartwood which makes it easy to excavate and another, in sparing the sapwood, which remains as a tough outer shell protecting the nest. The tinder fungus infects a variety of trees. Among those used occasionally by sapsuckers are butternuts and beeches. But a number of attributes such as the type of decay, the straightness of the bole, and the usual diameter when mature (20–25 cm) make aspens especially attractive. The following are accounts of *Fomes*-aspens that I followed for most of a decade.

*Territory A.*—I located the first nest hole in Aspen A in 1963. From the time the young hatched on June 12, until they left on July 6, they made a persistent and increasing volume of harsh vocalizations. Whether these were instrumental in attracting a predator, I do not know, but on July 1, I found a rosette of tooth marks around the entrance. These rosettes, as indicated by the claw marks and wisps of hair, appeared to be the work of raccoons. The attack on July 1 had no apparent effect, for the young fledged successfully five days later. A nesting in the aspen the following year, was equally successful. In a third year, 1965, the sapsuckers started an excavation in late April, but had abandoned it by May 2. My guess was that the fungus had not advanced sufficiently to provide room for another nest. Decay of heartwood takes time. After a year away, sapsuckers returned to nest in 1966, 1967, and 1968, but failed to return in 1969 when the aspen was still alive. With five old holes in addition to an equal number of trial ones, the aspen resembled a much used tenement. There was no space left for an additional cavity.

I was not sure how many individuals had been involved in the pairs nesting in Aspen A between 1963 an 1968. Certain pecularities in 1967, however, marked the individuals as the ones that returned in 1968. The female of both years was a black morph, having a black instead of red crown, and her mate, in both years, used the bark of the same small hornbeam as a place to discard feces.

*Territory B.*—The sapsuckers in Territory B nested in a butternut in 1963 and an aspen in 1964, both trees having conks of the tinder fungus. The aspen died in 1965 and was not reused. I had come to feel, by this time, that sapsuckers nested only in aspens that were still alive, even if barely so, as was true of the aspen used by the pair in 1967. This tree had died by 1968. To my surprise, the sapsuckers made fresh excavations, and nested in it successfully in the following two years.

The efforts sapsuckers can make to nest in a *Fomes*-infected aspen were exemplified in 1965. Female B was working on a small, funnel-shaped excavation on a healthy aspen on April 24. This seemed unusual, for I could

Fig. 42. Longitudinal cross section of an aspen (age 75 years and 22 cm dbh) showing extensive heart rot (discolored areas) as well as conks of the tinder fungus *Fomes igniarius*. Tunnels above and below are due to carpenter ants.

see no conks. Closer inspection, however, revealed three small ones where the female was working. The smoothness of the bark made it difficult for her to cling and she slipped several times. I found later that she had roughened the bark to keep herself from doing so. Although now able to hang on, she made little headway.

The pair was working on a second aspen in May. This tree had many conks but, with a diameter of only 12 cm and a crooked bole, it was obviously unsuitable for nesting. Yet the sapsuckers continued and were able to enter on May 7. For the next three weeks I was never sure of just what they were doing. They visited their aspen repeatedly, performing displays, but showed no signs of nesting. Finally, in early June, they moved away. Curious about what the aspen might look like inside, I cut it down. With a diameter of 8.6 cm and a length of 51.4 cm, the cavity had a surprising shape. It was narrower as well as twice as deep as a usual nest. The excessive depth, I presumed, was due to the slope of the hole, which allowed light to slant in. Why should the sapsuckers have worked so long on a site so obviously inadequate? I think that it was the only way they had of expending their breeding energy. Their territory had become exhausted of adequate sites and the two *Fomes*-aspens, inadequate as they were, were all they had to work on.

## PREDATORS

I had come to feel by 1966 that nests in aspens had good chances of success. Only one in ten had failed. In 1967, however, I encountered three, all in aspens, that were destroyed by raccoons.

Female W had already lost her mate when I found her nest on June 24. She was still caring for her young a week later. On the following day I discovered gnawings around the entrance. Looking to the ground, I found two piles of feathers, an old matted one of the male and a fresh one of the female. It is often difficult to know why a predator succeeds. In this case, I wondered if the cavity, 10 m up, had been too shallow. Some sapsuckers are limited, in excavating, by the extent of fungal decay. If a cavity is not deep enough, a raccoon can reach in and pull the sapsucker through the hole.

Another nest had been attacked by June 5. It had further tooth marks two days later. But the sapsuckers continued feeding their young until the raccoon attacked on June 27. So much bark was chewed away by this time, that I could see the sapwood from a distance. I was not surprised to find the remains of the male on the ground. The entrance remained intact. As already described, the female attracted a new mate. In another two days, the raccoon, after a lot more chewing around the entrance, caught him as well as all of the nestlings. Why should the raccoon have succeeded? The nest was, seemingly, in an ideal aspen. It provided ample decay for a cavity 25 cm deep, which is the usual depth of a sapsucker nest. Its chief hazard was in being too low. At only 2 m above the ground, it was the lowest of more than 50 nests that I have found. A raccoon may feel bolder if it has less far to climb. It may also find a nest more readily.

Weasels could be one of the more effective predators of hole-nesting birds. A nest may also be at greater risk if by a stone wall, for weasels often use walls as highways. I had these thoughts as I watched a weasel on a wall that ran within a meter of Nest I. Female I was making *quares* as the weasel stood up to look at me. I found the remains of a nestling below the nest a few days later, and that of a second one at the bottom of the cavity. There were no tooth marks this time, such as are left by raccoons. By looking closely at spots of rough bark, I was able to collect about thirty short, whitish hairs on the bole of the aspen. When I compared these with those on the belly of a weasel, represented by a museum skin, they looked much the same. Although a snake might have entered the hole, there are few tree-climbing snakes in northern New Hampshire. A snake, furthermore, would have swallowed the nestlings whole. It seemed likely that a weasel was the predator. Johnson (1947) gives an interesting account of a male sapsucker attacking a weasel that was trying to enter its nest.

Abandonment of one nest in a *Fomes*-aspen was a puzzle. Its entrance was 8 m above swampy ground. The sapsuckers had been feeding their young for a week when I found that a raccoon had gnawed the hole. But this made no difference, for the male sapsucker was feeding his young as before on the following morning. I was perplexed, therefore, to find the nest deserted a week later. Seeking an answer, I cut the tree down. What I found was a cavity partly filled with frass and penetrated by tunnels of carpenter ants (Fig. 42). While carpenter ants are not predators, their activities by day and night may have been enough to drive the sapsuckers away. But this is hard to say. Conner and Lucid (1976) found tunnels of carpenter ants leading into the cavity of a family of flickers, opened after the young had fledged. Even though the tunnels were teeming with ants, the nestlings seemed to have escaped unscathed.

## REACTIONS TO BARRED OWLS

The only reactions of sapsuckers to actual predators that I observed, were to Barred Owls. A feature of these was the way they were graded according to the stage of nestling. I scared an owl from a perch only 3 m from a nest in 1963, and, in 1967, only a little farther away from the same tree. The young in the first nest were just hatching and in the second were a few weeks older. All I heard from the sapsuckers, in both years, were a few *waan*s of mild alarm. I was surprised, on approaching the aspen in 1968, to find the male much excited by a Barred Owl perched in a grove well away from the nest. The owl flew off but the male continued his shrill *quarr*s. I followed as he flew to the nest, then back to the grove four times, with crest raised and tail spread. Ten minutes after the owl had left, the male sapsucker was still giving *quarr*s at rates of up to 36 a minute. All of this time, the nestlings were leaning out of the hole and begging steadily. They were well grown and ready to fledge. The male fed them a few times, but this did not interfere with his returning to the grove and calling *quarrs*. These continued for a half hour. The size of the young and their vulnerability to predation when about to fledge, may have been what led to the male's concern. His mate, oddly, had continued feeding the young during the whole episode, as if nothing were wrong.

## INTERACTIONS WITH FLYING AND OTHER SQUIRRELS

Sapsuckers keep returning to a *Fomes*-aspen in successive years, as long as they can find room to excavate holes. The old holes, meanwhile, are almost invariably occupied by flying or other squirrels. I found a flying squirrel occupying the 1964 nest of a pair of sapsuckers, in the spring of 1965. When the sapsuckers returned, they made a new hole only 30 cm below that of the squirrel. A low afternoon sun, on June 5, induced the male sapsucker to stop incubating, at least temporarily, to catch insects by the nest. The sun also led the squirrel to look out. I now watched as the sapsuker swooped at the squirrel six times, then clung to peck it as the squirrel withdrew. The squirrel seemed unfazed, reappearing as soon as the sapsucker left.

The sapsuckers of Pair C nested in a *Fomes*-aspen for seven years, with flying squirrels almost always occupying one or another of the old holes. Observing that the sapsuckers were taking turns guarding their nest on June 13, I wondered what the flying squirrels might be doing. But they were not involved. After 10 minutes of watching, I saw a gray squirrel raise its head from a well-gnawed hole, only several meters above that of the sapsuckers. Each sapsucker, as it arrived with prey for its young, turned its head to eye the squirrel.

The two were behaving in the same way on the following noon. But this time, instead of a gray, I saw a red squirrel. It ran past the sapsuckers' nest to squeeze into an old hole not far below. After looking out for five minutes, it ran up the trunk to leap onto another tree and disappear. The sapsuckers gave up their guarding immediately.

Hairy Woodpeckers use the same kind of *Fomes*-aspen as sapsuckers when they can, which is not very often. A pair nested in a *Fomes*-aspen in 1965. Flying squirrels took over their old hole in succeeding weeks. As often happens, the squirrels enlarged the entrance to such an extent that four of them looked out simultaneously when I knocked the next spring. The Hairies made no attempt to use the aspen a second year. Sapsuckers excavated a hole in it in 1966, not far below the gnawed hole of the flying squirrels. I think that this tolerance of sapsuckers for flying and other squirrels as neighbors has advantages in forstalling competition. Being of the same body size as sapsuckers and nesting, at times, in *Fomes*-aspens, Hairies could be severe competitors. But I have never known Hairies to nest in aspens or another tree that already had holes. I think that this is to avoid having squirrels or other animals as neighbors. By using aspens over a number of years, sapsuckers secure them for their own use. That is, by tolerating the presence of flying or other squirrels.

It should be emphasized that although sapsuckers prefer to nest in *Fomes*-aspens, they are often forced to nest elsewhere. Trembling aspens are common, but ones with just the right kind of *Fomes*-infections are rare. Twenty-one of 50 nests that I discovered were in other trees, that included paper birches, beeches, elms, and maples. Three of the nests were destroyed by raccoons. With only dead wood enclosing the cavities, they chewed through walls wherever they were weakest.

## METHODS OF COMMUNICATION

### VOCALIZATIONS

*Breeding call.*—A loud, squeal-like *kwee-urk, kwee-urk* that, at full intensity, is delivered in sets of six or more. Breeding calls are used by a male to attract a mate or, if already paired, to attract her to a nest site. The calls are also territorial.

*Quirks.*—Members of pairs and at times, at the start of a breeding season, two males, give scratchy *quirks* on meeting. *Quirks* are nearly always accompanied by bobbing. The vocalizations plus dances serve to strengthen the pairbond, if between the sexes, or to emphasize a conflict, if between males.

*Intimate notes.*—*Week, week*; *wurp, wurp*, and similar low notes are often exchanged when the pair, or later parent and juvenile, or two juveniles, meet at a sap tree or other place.

*Disturbed notes.*—Sapsuckers give a mewing *c-waan* when mildly excited for any reason, whether a flow of sap in January or the presence of an observer by a nest. When greatly disturbed, as by the presence of a predator or a severe conflict, they give repeated, shrill *quares* or *quarrs*.

### DRUMMING AND TAPPING

*Drumming.*—The drumming of sapsuckers begins rapidly, then becomes drawn out like a slow, telegraphic code—*drr-a, da, da-da, da, da*. It may sound loud and explosive when delivered on a piece of metal, the hard, warped bark of a dead maple, or other place of special resonance. Drumming serves to express territorial dominance and nearly always accompanies conflicts. It can also serve, along with *kwee-urk* breeding calls, to attract a mate.

*Tapping.*—Yellow-bellied Sapsuckers tap at rates of 4–5 taps a second, in bursts of 30 or more taps when at full intensity. A male may tap for several minutes, even when out of sight at the bottom of a cavity, in trying to win his mate into acceptance. Females tap less exhaustively, their tapping serving to register acceptance of a nest site. Tapping ceases toward the end of excavation, but may be resumed, transiently, at the end of nesting. Sapsuckers, when tapping at greatest intensity, spread the "shoulders" of their closed wings (Lawrence, 1967).

## Displays

*Wing noises.*—Sapsuckers, like other woodpeckers, can fly silently, but make a ruffle with their wings when mildly excited. Courtship flights are accompanied by a snipe-like winnow that can be heard for a considerable distance.

*Courtship flights.*—These flights, made with crests raised and short, fluttering wing beats, are usually away from a partner, and either to or from a nest excavation. The performer, in swinging low, displays the black and white of wings and the white of the lower back. Taken with the winnow noise, the flights are dramatic and build attachment to nest and mate.

*Bobbing dance.*—There is something military about two sapsuckers as, with crests raised showing the red frontal shields, and bodies vertical, they pump up and down, giving scratchy *quirks*. Their postures show off the red of the elongated neck (or white in the case of the female), the jet black jugulum, and bright yellow of the belly. The dances are always brief. They may be done singly, as when one partner, already by an excavation, taps, as its partner arrives to do a bobbing dance (Fig. 43). Bobbing dances can occur between males, especially in the early breeding season before the females arrive.

*Elongation of neck.*—A male sapsucker, on seeing his mate fly to a limb to take a copulation pose, may raise his crest and elongate his neck, the red feathers of his throat bristling outward, then fly to her. The performance is much like the sexual-readiness-pose of the male Red-headed Woodpecker. Either a male or female sapsucker may elongate its neck, on suddenly hearing a partner call or tap.

*Touching bills.*—Sapsucker occasionally touch bills in courtship.

*Threat.*—Sapsuckers may extend and raise their wings to look larger than they are in conflicts.

## Literature Cited

Conner, R. N., and V. J. Lucid. 1976. Interactions between nesting birds and carpenter ants. Bird-banding, **47**: 161–162.

Hales, S. 1727. Vegetable statiks. W. and J. Innys, London. 376 p.

Haartman, L. von. 1956. Territory in the Pied Flycatcher (*Muscicapa hypoleuca*). Ibis, **98**: 460–475.

———. 1965. Was reizt den Trauerfliegenschnäpper (*Muscicapa hypoleuca*) zu füttern? Vogelwarte, **16**: 157–164.

Howell, T. R. 1953. Racial and sexual differences in migration in *Sphyrapicus varius*. Auk, **70**: 118–126.

Johnson, R. A. 1947. Role of male Yellow-bellied Sapsucker in the care of the young. Auk, **64**: 621–623.

Kilham, L. 1953. Warblers, hummingbird, and sapsucker feeding on sap of yellow birch. Wilson Bull., **65**: 198.

———. 1956. Winter feeding on sap by sapsucker. Auk, **73**: 451–452.

——. 1962a. Breeding behavior of Yellow-bellied Sapsuckers. Auk, **79**: 31–43.

——. 1962b. Nest sanitation of Yellow-bellied Sapsuckers. Wilson Bull., **74**: 96–97.

——. 1964. The relations of breeding Yellow-bellied Sapsuckers to wounded birches and other trees. Auk, **81**: 520–527.

——. 1971. Reproductive behavior of Yellow-bellied Sapsuckers. I. Preference for nesting in *Fomes*-infected aspens and nest hole interrelations with flying squirrels, raccoons and other animals. Wilson Bull., **83**: 159–171.

——. 1977a. Nesting behavior of Yellow-bellied Sapsuckers. Wilson Bull., **89**: 310–324.

——. 1977b. Altruism in nesting Yellow-bellied Sapsucker. Auk, **94**: 613–614.

LAWRENCE, L. DE K. 1967. A comparative life-history study of four species of woodpeckers. Ornith. Monogr. (Amer. Ornith. Union), no. 5, 156 p.

McATEE, W. L. 1911. Woodpeckers in relation to trees and wood products. U.S. Dept. Agric. Biol. Surv. Bull., **39**: 1–99.

ROYAMA, T. 1966. Factors governing feeding rate, food requirement and brood size of nestling Great Tits (*Parus major*). Ibis, **108**: 313–347.

SHIGO, A. L., AND L. KILHAM. 1968. Sapsuckers and *Fomes igniarius* var. *populinus*. U.S. Forest Serv. Res. Note NE-84. N.E. Forest Exp. Sta., Upper Darby, Pennsylvania. 2 p.

SOUTHWICK, E. E. AND A. K. SOUTHWICK. 1980. Energetics of feeding on tree sap by Ruby-throated Hummingbirds in Michigan. Amer. Midl. Nat., **104**: 328–334.

ZIMMERMAN, M. H. 1961. Movement of organic substances in trees. Science, **133**: 73–79.

## FALL AND WINTER

### MARYLAND

Flickers wintered in Seneca Swamp where, on some fall mornings, their drummings, high calls, bill-wavings and *we-cup*s made them the most conspicuous of woodpeckers. Poison ivy berries were a main attraction. These, plus the fruits of dogwoods, black gum, woodbine, hackberry, and small wild grapes kept them busy from October until January, in groups of three or four to a dozen. To some extent they were like the robins that fed on fruit and made the woods noisy with their pipings. But in winter I was more apt to see the flickers on the ground. What they found there was not always apparent. On February 14, I noted about 20 hopping about in a cornfield lightly covered with snow. From their tracks, I could see where they had pecked at ears of corn. On other days I found them tossing leaves aside where pin oak acorns were rotting or probing damp earth by the swamp, I supposed for earthworms.

It is hard to know how many ants flickers find as far north as Maryland in winter. I noted repeatedly that considerable areas of swamp were empty of flickers on some mornings. It was only when I located a pair of Pileateds, that I found flickers. Both species worked on much the same kind of rotting logs and stumps as though looking for the same kinds of prey.

## Southern Florida

The lawn close to a cottage we occupied at the Archbold Biological Station was a good place to watch flickers in winter in southern Florida. The pair foraged 1–3 m apart. They probed into ant tunnels, holding their bills in a second or two, or tossed sand aside, then flicked up the ants they had disturbed. The male, on February 24, seemed bothered by ants getting among feathers at the front of his head. He stopped every few seconds to scratch with one foot, then with the other. Then I noticed that his mate was doing the same. As the flickers had not done this at other times, I wondered if ants in some places were more aggressive and irritating than others.

It is impossible, for the most part, to see what flickers are feeding on when seeking prey in old stumps or on the ground. I got some idea, however, by watching my handraised flickers. They liked to feed on half oranges. When these had been finished, I added a little dog food and set them out in the yard. They were soon swarming with ants. It was then amazing to see the way the flickers, whipping their tongues in and out as much of 4 cm beyond their bill tips, cleaned up the ants in no time.

The male in Florida, if close, was quick to see whenever his mate found a particularly good spot. He then moved in and took over. The female appeared to be tolerant of these displays of male dominance. On January 14 I noticed something curious when a male was working in a cleft at the base of a live oak. A female landed 2 m away. She moved directly to him, drove him away, and worked where he had been. This was the only time that I ever saw a female flicker displace a male.

One can watch woodpeckers for a long time without ever seeing them drink, as Hoyt (1957) has noted for Pileateds and Sherman (1910) for flickers. This is because these two species, I think, are shy when coming to the ground. While watching the flickers in Florida, I saw one drink at a leaky faucet where Blue Jays were coming. What aroused my curiosity, however, was the way both flickers and Pileateds came to the flat bend of a big oak limb above our cottage door. The limb had a natural cleft that filled with rain water. I kept it filled with a hose when it ran dry and found that both flickers and Pileateds came to it fairly often, whereas I had never seen them come to a permanent pool not far away.

## EARLY BREEDING BEHAVIOR IN FLORIDA

### CONFLICTS

A male alit on a pine tree on the morning of February 2. He called *we-cup*, gave an abbreviated high call, then rested a moment before flying to the ground. A second male, equally unhurried, alit in the same grassy opening and the two faced each other. They pointed their bills up about every 15 seconds to wave them about, thus exposing their throats and black malar stripes (Fig. 43). The dances went on in silence for six to seven minutes. The males then hopped to a new opening for another few minutes of the same performance. Wings and tails were kept closed. Both finally flew to different trees, and the dances, which were for domination of one section of a pasture, ended without physical conflict.

Frost lay on the ground three days later when, at 07:30, I heard a medley of *we-cups* coming from the corner of the pasture where the males had displayed. There were now three flickers, a male and two females. They were all clinging to the trunk of a pine and would occasionally join in bursts of bill-waving to the accompaniment of low *we-cups*. The male was the least interested. He finally flew to a dead stub where he drummed and gave a

FIG. 43.   Silent dance of two male flickers, Florida pasture, February 2.

high call. The two females quieted down as soon as he had left. Their vocalizations were now *chewki, chewki* and their bill-waving became mild. They soon flew away. The trio reassembled shortly afterward on a dead pine where the male was perched on a limb with the females on either side. Dances lasting 4–5 seconds alternated with periods of quiescence lasting 30 seconds. Their dances, unlike those of the two males, were at full intensity. All three birds waved their bills, called shrill *we-cup, we-cups*, raised their red crests and displayed much yellow by partly spreading their wings while fanning and uptilting their tails. The male tried to drum between dances. The females, however, gave him no respite, for they would start a new dance which, to all appearances, he seemed compelled to join. Affairs continued in this fashion for five minutes. The tempo was gradually decreasing when one of the females suddenly flew at the male, driving him from his perch. The attack roused excitement all around. The *we-cup*s were again shrill, and one of the females drummed briefly. A second attack maintained the excitement. This time the aggressive female struck the male as if attempting to alight on his back and the two fell grappling to the ground. The male then flew away. In his absence the females reverted to a mild bill-waving, accompanied by low *chewki*s and *we-cup*s. Variations of these performances went on for one and a quarter hours.

What Cloudsley-Thompson (1965:88) wrote about the Eurasian Blackbird applies well to these two sets of conflicts observed in a Florida pasture. "In general male birds fight mainly for territories, females mainly over mates. Thus, although female Blackbirds fight less often than males in the spring, they probably fight more violently." Triangular conflicts, of two females over a male, with the females fighting intensely, have been commoner among flickers than with other woodpeckers I have studied.

## Search for a Nest Site

Nearly three months later, on April 30, I found a pair of flickers on the dead pine where the two females and a male had fought on February 5. The male was doing full bill-waving dances while she swung and bowed only mildly. She was less excited and soon flew away. He remained on the dead pine, drumming about once a minute and giving occasional high calls. His mate, in spite of being 240 m away, joined in with high calls and drummings of her own, as if communicating with him. He made two moves in her direction (Fig. 44), continuing his part of the duet all the while. What appeared to be an impasse was broken when I chanced to see her returning, first to a pine 20 m away, then to one adjacent to her mate. He stopped calling. There were no more vocalizations from either bird for 30 minutes. During this time he drummed alone until she broke a 20-minute silence by drumming with him. The duet had no synchronization. Each flicker drummed, more or less haphazardly, about once every 40 seconds. A man piling boards finally frightened the pair away. Events which took place two days later suggested

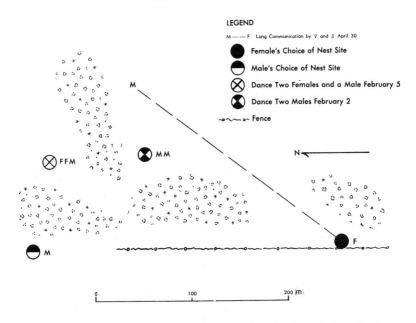

FIG. 44. The Florida pasture. Diagram of the events in the early breeding behavior of a pair of flickers, including conflicts associated with pair formation and a distant communication between the male and female over the site of a nest hole.

that the long communication, followed by the duet, involved possible sites for a nest hole.

## AGREEMENT ON FEMALE'S CHOICE

On May 2 I heard tapping near the tree where the male had drummed in the long communication of two days previously. I then spotted the male as he tapped 12 bursts of 8 to 12 taps each, just above a weathered excavation. His mate was on a limb above. When he left, she flew down and inspected the site. She did not tap, an indication that the stub was not acceptable. At 06:45, a half hour later, I found her calling once more from her pine stub down along the fence (Fig. 44). She now entered a hole in the stub, turned around and looked out for five minutes. Then she withdrew and tapped just inside the entrance, where I could see her bill as she gave two bursts of four taps each. The male reached the entrance by the second burst, his crest raised and tail spread as he made soft *chewki* notes. She slipped out, brushing past his neck. He now entered and appeared to tap inside. By the intensity with which he excavated the hole, already hollowed in a previous year, and by a coition that took place later, it was evident that the male had accepted the female's choice of a nest site.

In the midst of tossing sawdust, the male emerged with a piece of debris. Instead of dropping it out of the entrance, he flew off with it, holding his head high in an awkward fashion. He dropped the debris by an adjacent tree, then wiped his bill. The whole process, soon repeated, was a symbolic removal of a fecal sac, well before nestlings were due.

## Development of Breeding Behavior in Captivity

As with other woodpeckers, my plan was to combine studies in the field with those made in the aviary with handraised individuals. The latter mated and incubated five fertile egg in the spring after I acquired them. I thus had opportunities for observing details of courtship and mating that I would not have had through field studies alone.

### Juvenile Development

I removed two well-developed young from a nest in our backyard in Bethesda on July 7 and considered them fledged on July 11. On this day the female waved her head and body, called *we-cup*, then seized her brother's bill in her own. I was to witness no further bill-touching until December. The flickers were comparatively quiet during July and August but, when approaching each other, they might dance like mechanical puppets and call *we-cup*. They did a little drumming in August and the male gave his first high call at the end of the month. A postjuvenal molt was now underway. The female had lost her black moustache (malar) stripes by September 9. Both flickers now had bright yellow under wings and tails and their reactions to each other became of increasing interest.

### Association and Dominance

The male gave occasional high calls during fall months and often danced and called *chewki* when coming near the female, whose behavior remained subdued. Both flickers drummed. The bursts might start in a slow way before reaching the intensity that became habitual later on. It was evident that the two birds liked to be together, for, if he flew to the ground, she might follow and both would toss leaves and soil within a short distance of each other. His dominance was manifest at feeding places. If he found a good spot, and she approached, he would dance and give *we-cup*s in protest and she would leave. If she turned up something of interest, such as an earthworm, he might displace her quietly. These situations continued throughout the breeding season.

There was one event that lead, on two occasions, to a reversal of the male's dominance. This was when I used a hose to water logs and plants. The male, unlike his mate, was much alarmed by this procedure. On September 17 and again on October 6, he ran about the bottom of the aviary in a furtive manner for some hours. During this time the female assumed a dominant behavior, dancing at full intensity and calling *we-cup*s. She appeared to be stimulated by his submissiveness. This fortuitous experiment suggested that the male's usual activity in dances and vocalizations was a way of maintaining dominance. As soon as he stopped, she took over. It thus seemed, as Lorenz (1970) has described, that male dominance is needed for the female to behave like a female.

## PAIR FORMATION

Wild flickers in Seneca Swamp behaved much like my captives in displaying fragments of breeding behavior in the fall. The swamp flickers were migrants. When winter led to a cessation of their incipient breeding activities, my captives, living indoors, continued to develop. I suspected that something approaching pair formation took place in early December. The female became more assertive and this seemed to stimulate her mate. By December 10 she was taking much of the initiative. After one *chewki* dance at full intensity, the two birds seized each other's bills. The female then drummed. She had done little drumming in previous months. The male drummed regularly on an upright log, and on January 2, his mate settled .5 m below him for an alternating duet. They had many such duets in following months.

## DISPLAYS AGAINST TERRITORIAL RIVALS

I put the pair into a large cage outdoors on February 22. A pair of wild flickers was soon displaying on the outside of the wire. The yard now resounded with high calls and drummings. Both wild birds would fly to the wire with wings and tails outspread, displaying their full yellow, as male displayed against male and female against female. This sex alignment was invariable. The displays continued vigorously throughout the next day, in spite of rain and, with some lessening, for several weeks. The wild female was the most persistent. She would run around the edge of the wire, tilting way over in constant *we-cup* and *chewki* dances, following the tame female wherever the latter moved. The tame female responded with similar dances. The wild female sometimes drummed loudly on a metal gutter above the cage, or gave high calls from adjacent trees. The wild male carried on in the same manner as his mate. He was less interested, however, and would fly away after a shorter time. The tame male did not pay much attention to him.

I found it of interest, in this experiment with an outdoor cage, that the wild flickers were paired and ready to defend a territory in winter and that the displays, vocalizations, and drummings used in the conflicts were the same as those observable in courtship. Also of note was the greater intensity and persistence of the females in conflict, something that I had also noted in Florida.

## BEHAVIOR ASSOCIATED WITH A NEST BOX

New types of behavior appeared when I placed a nest box in the aviary on March 9. The male kept putting his head and shoulders in to inspect the hole and did the first tapping that we had heard.

There was never doubt that he took the lead. His efforts to win over the female now went through a series of phases. A first was to enter the box completely from the day it was installed, while his mate did no more than cling to the outside. Either bird might hang from the entrance by one foot to sound the outside with a few pecks or to explore it with its long tongue. He did most of the early tapping and was the first to tap from the inside. The female responded in a variety of ways. Her more common responses were to drum or give a high call; answer him with soft notes such as *what, what* and, sometimes, to fly to the roof of the box for a *chewki* dance. Although the male took the lead at the nest, she showed her drive in following him about, joining him wherever he might alight, and often initiating dancing.

Other activities included duets of drumming, occasional bill-touching and shrill *we-cup*s. In spite of these activities, it became evident that the first box was too small and that I would have to replace it with a larger one.

Two weeks after I had installed a larger box, the female entered. Both flickers were soon going in together. She usually came out first. If she happened to be inside and he looked in, she might squeeze out past his neck.

As soon as she started taking this greater interest, he began removing the sawdust that I had placed in the bottom. But, instead of tossing all of it out of the entrance, as is customary, he sometimes carried up to five billfuls across the aviary and deposited them. His manner of holding head high in flight was suggestive of a parent flicker flying off with a fecal sac.

If the male tapped while on the outside of the nest, the female might alight on the roof and bend downward in a *chewki* dance. The male would then raise his red nuchal patch and swell upward toward her without moving his feet from the lower rim of the hole (Fig. 45). At a later time, when she began tapping more frequently, she would swell upward toward him in similar fashion or, if he only came near the box, she might swell sideways with her breast toward him, the "swelling" being a slight elevation of the contour feathers. This behavior was a sign of increasing closeness of the pairbond. The female made low *what, what* and *woi, woi* notes as drumming declined and the aviary became quieter. Quiet, with woodpeckers, comes at a peak of courtship. Signs of an increasing assertiveness of the female were bill-touching (Fig. 45) and occasional swoops at the male, whether he was at the nest entrance or on the ground.

Just as everything seemed to be going well, she lost interest. Like all woodpeckers I have studied, the female is the final arbiter of whether a site or cavity is really suitable. The female's loss of interest meant that I must do something. A third and successful cycle began on May 4 when I set the box away from the wall on a pole.

FIG. 45. Some events characterizing the early reproductive behavior of flickers. (Above) Bill-touching. (Left) Male at entrance to nest box "swells" upward toward mate who is doing a *chewki* dance on roof. (Right) Male removing large piece of debris from nest box.

## Full Acceptance

The female's acceptance of the box in its new position was indicated, on May 5, when she tapped 10 bursts of six to eight taps each when just inside. She later tapped out of sight at the bottom, thus recapitulating the behavior of the male earlier in the season. In another change she spent increasing amounts of time clinging to the entrance or quietly disappearing inside. Her mate might look in briefly, then leave. The pair was usually on the ground feeding when she flew up making soft *oik*s to crouch on a limb. Full copulation took place on some occasions and pseudo-copulation on others. In full copulation, the male flew to his mate when she had assumed the inviting pose, mounted her back and took time to get well established. He then pecked down at her bill while falling to the left and somewhat backward as cloacal contact took place. We observed copulations three or four times a day, but there were undoubtedly more of them than we saw. They might take place at any hour.

An aggressiveness, or temporary reversal of dominance by the female, came as a marked change from her earlier manner. When she was in the box, she might draw back and strike at her mate when he came to the entrance.

## Egg Laying

The two exchanged soft, low notes, but drummings and high calls were infrequent as the time of egg laying approached. It was evident when the female was about to lay her first egg by the way she puffed out her breast, thus filling the nest entrance, and drawing her head back as if to strike. She struck at my hand savagely when in the same pose a few days later. This was unusual boldness, for she had always been shy. When a hen's eggshell was placed in the aviary on May 27, the male immediately explored the fragments with his tongue, and left. His mate then flew down and ate the pieces eagerly.

On May 29, the female came to the entrance at 07:00 making soft notes. Her mate tapped briefly from the bottom of the nest, then slipped out and she entered. A similar episode took place the following day, only this time the male remained inside incubating. He did not spend nights in the hole until the next day, May 29, when the fifth and last egg was laid.

In summary, the final breeding attempt began on May 4, copulation was first observed on May 7, the first egg was laid on May 23, and full copulation was last observed on May 27, 20 days after the first one. A fifth egg was laid on May 29.

## Final Collapse

I decided, ultimately, not to allow any full nesting of the flickers in the aviary. This was a hard decision to make but we were about to go on leave with our five children; early breeding behavior, I consoled myself, had been the principal object of the study. The female flicker lost all interest in nesting when I reintroduced the male sapsucker. He was very territorial about the aviary. He attacked the female flicker early on the morning of May 30 and she became too frightened to return to the nest. Her mate waited a long time. He finally came out and began a relentless attack, driving her back and forth across the aviary to the point of exhaustion. He then alit on her body and pecked at her head. She only escaped by crawling into a hollow log from which I rescued her some hours later. I removed the male sapsucker to give her a respite. Amazingly, she recovered sufficiently to resume incubation late in the afternoon.

Both flickers had lost interest by June 5. They were feeding in the afternoon when the male suddenly went wild. There was no immediate cause of his explosive behavior that I could perceive. He gave high calls, drummed, and did bill-waving dances, interspersed with frantic flying to and fro. She followed him about but remained calm. The male now went to the nest and emerged with an egg which he deposited on the ground. He then carried out three more, all of which oozed blood from punctures and contained embryos. The fifth egg was punctured but not removed. After this episode, the male quieted down and the two were as peaceful as before.

## Nesting in New Hampshire

### Excavation

Hairies, Downies, Pileateds and sapsuckers all carve fresh nest holes each year. Flickers do so as well but are often given to using a nest box or old cavity, tossing out former squirrel nests or other debris, if need be, in order to do so. Pair B did this in the hollow top of a willow stub one year. With little excavating to do, Male B spent much of his time resting and preening by the hole, or drumming against the side of it and giving high calls. I could tell when Female B came to trees nearby by the sound of soft *oik*s. Starlings hung around and sometimes looked into the hole. The flickers copulated over a number of days and, just when I thought they might be able to hold the cavity, the starlings took it over. Starlings did this so regularly when I tried to study flickers in farmlands near the village of Lyme, that I gave up and took to studying the nesting of flickers at a beaver pond. This, being well surrounded by woods, was free of starlings.

Pair A started an excavation at the beaver pond on May 16. It was 18 m up in a tall stub arising from the middle of the pond. With no leafy trees to interfere, I had fine views, but I found little to record. The male, working steadily for 60 to 80 minutes at a stretch, did 81 and his mate 19 percent of the excavating in the five days that it took them. This was in a total of 10 hours that I watched. The two did little communicating. A minimum of tapping and a few *oik*s and *chewki*s were all I heard. I could see many small conks where the flickers worked. These, indicators of fungal decay, explained, I thought, why the flickers were able to complete their cavity with such speed.

Although males do most of the work of excavating under usual circumstances, I watched one pair at the pond in which the female did essentially all of it. The male, when he came to the hole, did no more than look in, excavate a minute or two, and leave. His mate, working steadily for periods of up to 85 minutes, finished the cavity in five days. Following copulations, she appeared to lay eggs and incubate, still with little assistance from her mate. I think that this situation resulted from the pair starting their excavation in the second week of July. This was the latest that I have ever seen a pair start to nest in New Hampshire. It seemed that, with the normal breeding season drawing to a close, the male had lost much of his breeding urge while she still retained hers.

## COPULATIONS

I witnessed seven copulations by the pair at the beaver pond in the latter part of May. The first was on May 21, the day the nest excavation was completed and the last, nine days later, on the second day of incubation. Female flickers squat belly flat and crosswise on a limb, with wings drooping, when ready for the male. When close I have heard *woi, woi* and medleys of other low notes that reminded me of Blue Jays. The copulations at the beaver pond lasted 7–10 seconds. About three-fifths of this time was needed for the male to become established, and the rest, for him to fall to the left as the female moved her spread tail and cloacal contact was established. The male pecked down at the female as he started to fall. In most of the copulations of Pair A, Female A was by the hole when Male A first flew to her making *oik*s. She then flew across the pond to a dead spruce and he followed. After copulating, he flew back to the hole and entered.

The behavior of Female A, after copulations two and three, was curious. She continued to rest where she was, with feathers ruffed and eyes blinking, as if falling asleep. This was for nine minutes on May 21 and eight on May 23. Lethargy at time of egg laying is something I have noted in Downy Woodpeckers and in a variety of other species ranging from Common Grackles and White-breasted Nuthatches, to Red-shouldered Hawks. Since it occurs in individuals, rather than being a general rule, I think that it is probably due to egg binding. In all later copulations, Female A flew away right afterward in seemingly excellent condition.

## EGG LAYING, INCUBATION, AND BROODING

Male A drummed and gave high calls once his excavation was complete. Being under pressure no longer, he had time to rest, preen, and seek the attention of his mate in a period when copulations were still going on. He excavated for a few brief spells, but I saw no sawdust produced.

I witnessed an odd incident during the egg laying period with flickers in our yard in Bethesda. The female, after entering her nest hole very slowly, reappeared with an egg in her bill and flew off with it. I saw a gray squirrel enter the nest later, as if taking shelter from the rain. Possibly the squirrel had disturbed the female earlier. The flickers went on to nest successfully, in spite of the intrusion.

There was little with Pair A, at the beaver pond, to indicate when egg laying ceased and incubation began. The pair was restless during both periods, entering, only to look out as if on guard. By the third day of incubation, however, both of the pair were 80 percent, and in the last nine days, close to 100 percent attentive. The actual length of their sessions were hard to determine. Although I spent up to two and one-half hours a day watching, I was never able to see the whole of any one session, i.e., the time between changeovers. I was, however, able to time a session at another nest at two hours and 20 minutes.

The nest hole at the beaver pond appeared deserted most of the time. Unless a Hairy Woodpecker on other intruder landed on the stub, leading the flicker to look out, I had few ways of telling whether the nest was still occupied. On several days I had to throw a log in the water to make the incubating partner look out.

I have found it difficult to tell when eggs hatch in flicker nests because parents, feeding by regurgitation, do not carry food in their bills. They continue to sit, furthermore, as tightly when brooding as when incubating. In this dilemma, I have estimated the days of hatching as being 28 days before the day of fledging. On this basis, Pair A brooded for a little over six days, with Female A doing 79 percent of the work.

## FEEDING NESTLINGS

Once brooding was over and the young large enough, the parents hung down within the entrance to feed them. This left their tails and the tips of their wings protruding and jiggling. The motion was due to the pumping of food. Later, when the young were old enough, I could see the way the opened bills of parent and young interlocked at right angles as food was transferred. Female A pumped four times, on June 18, in feeding her three young. Before several of the pumpings, I could see her making slight gagging motions, as if bringing up food from her stomach. After a feeding, some of this, a pasty, white material, had to be reswallowed to prevent its escaping.

The nestlings showed their bill tips at the entrance at 16 and their heads at 21 days after hatching. Usually only a single nestling looked out at a time. But when a parent came, three heads, all clamoring for food, shot out simultaneously. The parents were cautious about coming. Female A flew to a dead tree 30 m away to watch for 2–3 minutes, as if to see that all was safe, before taking a final swoop to the nest. The male also paused, but closer to and for a briefer time. The feeding visits of the two, as combined, were at a rate of three to four per hour early in the nestling period and two per hour in the final week.

Flicker nests vary in how close one can sit in watching without disturbing the occupants. At one, where I was able to sit close due to thick vegetation, I heard the steady *chrr, chrr* notes of the young and a *twirr* note made repeatedly by the female in coming to feed them. The *chrr*s became *qua qua* by the time a parent arrived. Once nestlings become large enough, they make loud *kee-yous* as they look out over the landscape. The females at three nests were more responsive to the young than their mates, making low *wicka*s and *kee-you*s in the last few days before fledging, as if to entice them. Nestlings were aggressive by this stage. I saw ones occupying the hole strike down at their siblings on a number of occasions, as well as at parents coming with food.

The parents, after feeding from the outside, sometimes entered to emerge with a white fecal sac. Male A flew off with his on a regular course of 100 m or more before being lost from sight. Only once did I see him deposit the sac on a perch, then wipe his bill many times. A kingbird attacked him on some flights. I was by the shore one morning when the male came flying straight toward me, a sac in his bill and the kingbird nearly on his back. The two alighted 5 m away, with the flicker still retaining his load. In a few seconds he flew on with the sac, seemingly undisturbed. At nine days before fledging, he carried away brownish excreta and two days later ceased cleaning the nest. Sanitation ceased at 10 days before fledging at two other nests.

### Sharing Parental Duties

Although both sexes participate, males generally do the greater part of the work in caring for the young. At three nests I watched, they made 64, 58, and 45 percent of the feeding visits as well as removing 90, 75, and 63 percent of the fecal sacs. At a fourth nest, in contrast, roles were reversed with the female doing 79 percent of the feeding and 82 percent of the nest cleaning. This was in a late nesting, with young fledged on July 30. I wondered again, as with the female that did essentially all of the excavating at another nest, whether the male had not lost his drive toward the end of the breeding season. Unlike other males, he spent much time resting by the hole and preening. For a period of three days I did not see him at all. Yet this is not the inevitable result of a late nesting. Another male, whose young were fledged even later, on August 3, still did 58 percent of the feeding. A feature of the sharing of duties among woodpeckers is the role of the female. If a male for any reason does less, she does more.

### Fledging

In four of five nests in which my wife or I saw young leave, it was the female that was most concerned in getting them to do so. The concern began several days before with the making of low notes from a distance. Female

A had been giving *wicka*s to her young for two days when, on July 3, she fed a fledgling briefly, then flew off 30 m and gave a high call. Her young one flew in her direction immediately, followed by his nest mate 10 seconds later. The first fledgling to leave at three other nests left under much the same circumstances. Only a low call from the female seemed needed. The fledglings flew well on their first flights, with no loss of altitude. Once in the woods, they gave occasional *kee-you*s, answered by siblings still looking from the entrance.

The young of Nest A left at 08:35. When the male came to feed them he was nonplused to find them gone. He bowed in and out of the hole, gave high calls, and made gagging motions as if regurgitating food. He then hitched to the top of the stub for more high calls. After another visit to the hole and more bowing in, he flew off, still not knowing where the young had gone.

At a fifth nest, a fledgling, assisted by neither parent, flew when a red squirrel ran up the nest stub, looked in, then returned for a second look.

### Recrudescence of Breeding Behavior

The young of a nest at the beaver pond, in 1977, fledged on June 20 and 21. Two weeks later the male of the pair flew to his mate making low *oik*s and she started to take a copulatory pose. The two then rested and preened. On the following morning, July 3, I found the female giving soft high calls from a stub in the pond. She moved down it, percussing, then spent 15 minutes excavating. When her mate flew to her, she again moved out on a limb, as if to copulate, and the two touched bills. At one time they had a lively dance, with a tilting of tails and *chewki*s. The male was giving high calls when I found him on July 6. When his mate gave a low answering call, he dropped down to an old yellow birch stub and started tapping. After a few minutes of silence, his mate gave a few soft *oik*s. He tapped again. The two now rested motionless for nearly 20 minutes. She finally swooped to the birch stub and he tapped for a third time. Both left when a second female appeared. Although I was by the pond on other mornings, I saw no more of the pair. Their recrudescence of breeding behavior seemed to be over.

### Colonial-type Nesting

Flickers are territorially aggressive in the early breeding season. Their nests, as a result, are apt to be hundreds of meters apart. By the time of egg laying and incubation, the wide territoriality of early weeks is replaced by one restricted to a nest stub and its vicinity. If a second pair attempts to nest close to a pair already established, it may then be able to do so without conflict. This, at least, was my experience in June and July of one year by a beaver pond.

Three pairs of flickers (A, B, and C; Fig. 46) were nesting in stubs arising from the water in late June. Although amicable with each other, they were

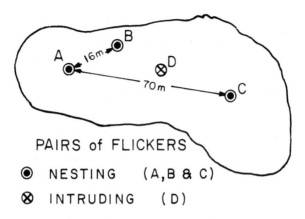

PAIRS of FLICKERS

⊙ NESTING (A,B & C)

⊗ INTRUDING (D)

FIG. 46. Location of nesting stubs of three pairs of flickers (A, B, and C) that nested, and of Pair D that tried to nest, in a beaver pond.

aggressive toward a fourth pair, D, that tried to nest between two of them. My wife and I spent from 40 minutes to three hours a day watching. This was from June 23, when the situation was discovered, until July 18.

Pairs A, B, and C all raised their young to the fledging stage. The nest stub of Pair A, however, fell into the water following a heavy rain on June 29, the day that I had expected the young to leave. Assuming that they would have done so, then the days of fledging for the three pairs were June 29, July 9, and July 18. It is clear from these dates that the onset of the nestings must have been close to 10 days apart. This would have permitted Pair B to establish itself when Pair A, 16 m away, was incubating and, in similar fashion, for Pair C to have excavated a hole when Pair B was incubating.

A staggering of nest times, allowing nests to be closer than might have seemed possible otherwise, is not limited to flickers. Meyerriecks (1960), for example, has described a similar situation for Green Herons. Dennis (1969), in a study of flickers on Nantucket, noted a density of 19.5 pairs per 40 ha. At the beaver pond three pairs nested in an area of less than .5 ha. An ability to nest under such conditions would seem to have survival value. Suitable stubs, if one can judge from the efforts flickers make to find them, are generally in short supply. This shortage is aggravated by starlings. A result is a breaking up of nesting seasons and a staggering of breeding times. This, in the end, may enable flickers to make greater use of stubs where such are concentrated due to beaver or other agencies.

Once flickers are feeding older nestlings and are freed from the tight schedules of incubation and brooding, males become more aggressive. This was seen at the beaver pond where Males B and C, tolerant of each other, persistently attacked Male D. Although most of the conflicts were confrontations with bill-waving dances, Male C, on one occasion, knocked Malè D from the stub where he and his mate were trying to nest.

## METHODS OF COMMUNICATION

Flickers communicate by dancing, drumming, tapping, and varied vocalizations, as well as, at times, by resting motionless. These methods of expression, with the exception of the latter, are used with varying intensity and in assorted combinations, depending upon the situations involved.

### VOCALIZATIONS

*High call.*—A loud *kick, kick, kick* of great carrying power, which, at less intensity, sounds like *wick-a-wick-a-wick.*

*Dance calls.*—The dances of flickers may be accompanied by *we-cup*s or soft *chewki*s, the latter appearing to be the more intimate.

*Intimate notes.*—Notes exchanged by mated flickers are numerous, particularly near the time of coition. Common varieties are *oik, oik, oi-eek, oi-eek;* and *werp, werp;* or *what, what,* all of which suggest the low, conversational notes of Blue Jays.

*Alarm call.*—*Ki-u,* or *kee-you,* usually expressive of only mild excitement.

### DRUMMING AND TAPPING

*Drumming.*—The drumming and high calls of flickers, like those of Pileated Woodpeckers, are often used interchangeably, or in alternation, in an effort by one partner to get the other to come. They are given predominantly by the male. Male and female may drum together, first one, then the other, in an alternating duet. The drumming of flickers is like a miniature pneumatic drill, the individual blows coming at a rapid, even rate from start to finish. Each burst lasts for about a second. Pauses between may be anywhere from 10 to 40 seconds or longer.

*Tapping.*—Flickers tap at a slow, countable rate of two to three taps a second and in bursts of two to 20 or more. There is usually a slight pause between bursts. One can learn to recognize tapping, which is associated with selection of a nest site, at a distance of several hundred meters. Male and female flickers tap separately.

### DISPLAYS

*Wing noise.*—Flickers may make a *wurrp* noise with their wings when flying, even for a few meters. This noise is one of alarm and is not infrequently associated with *kee-you*s. Many species of woodpeckers can make ruffle noises with their wings, but the *wurrp* of flickers is unusual in being somewhat musical.

*Bill-touching.*—My handraised flickers occasionally touched or seized each others' bills, often protruding their tongues at the same time. I have also noted bill-touching in the field.

*Bill-waving dance.*—Flickers dance at full intensity by spreading and tilting their tails, thus displaying the yellow underside; by raising their red nuchal patches and, concomitantly, swinging and bowing their bodies from side to side as their bills jerk up and down in a **W** or a figure-8-shaped course. Many forms are possible in a range between these extremes. The dances are used between rivals of the same sex, male or female, as well as between members of pairs in courtship.

*Resting motionless.*—When a nest site has been decided upon and is on its way to completion, either member of a pair, or both together, may rest motionless for minutes at a time.

*Leisurely preening.*—This and resting motionless are much the same in appearing to communicate an inner harmony.

## Literature Cited

Cloudsley-Thompson, J. L. 1965. Animal conflict and adaptation. Dufour Editions, Chester Springs, Pennsylvania. 160 p.

Dennis, J. V. 1969. The Yellow-shafted Flicker (*Colaptes auratus*) on Nantucket Island, Massachusetts. Bird-banding, **40**: 290–308.

Hoyt, S. F. 1957. The ecology of the Pileated Woodpecker. Ecology, **38**: 246–256.

Lorenz, K. 1970. Companions as factors in the bird's environment, p. 101–258. *In* Studies in Animal and Human Behavior. Vol. 1. Harvard Univ. Press, Cambridge.

Kilham, L. 1959. Early reproductive behavior of flickers. Wilson Bull., **71**: 323–336.

———. 1973. Colonial-type nesting in Yellow-shafted Flicker as related to staggering of nesting times. Bird-banding, **44**: 317–318.

Meyerriecks, A. J. 1960. Comparative breeding behavior of four species of North American herons. Publ. Nuttall Ornith. Club, no. 2, 158 p.

Sherman, A. R. 1910. At the sign of the Northern Flicker. Wilson Bull., **22**: 135–171.

# 10

## CRIMSON-CRESTED AND PALE-BILLED WOODPECKERS, CENTRAL AMERICAN COUNTERPARTS OF THE IVORY-BILLED WOODPECKER

An account of the woodpeckers of eastern North America should include the extinct, or near-extinct, Ivory-billed Woodpecker. I have not, however, studied this species, but Central American Crimson-crested and Pale-billed Woodpeckers seem to be counterparts of the Ivory-billed, and I include them in this study. I have treated these two species together because, behaviorally, they appear to be identical. The two are allopatric. My experience with the Crimson-cresteds was in Panama, and with the Pale-billeds in Costa Rica and Guatemala.

## FEEDING BEHAVIOR

### A PAIR IN THE DRY SEASON

Crimson-cresteds, like Pileateds, have a close pairbond and feed together. A pair, followed for 140 minutes on Barro Colorado, demonstrated various aspects of feeding when the trees were somewhat bare of leaves. The woodpeckers were usually within 15 m and often less of each other as they moved through the mature forest. Most of their feeding was at mid-tree levels. An almost constant feature was the greater activity of the female. She was not only the first to fly (n = 6) when the two flew from one part of the woods to another, but also moved along a greater extent on limbs and trunks than her mate. At one time both flew to a dead limb 4 m long. While she hitched along its whole length, knocking off bark, he did much probing in a limited area, continuing after she had left. This tendency of the male to work one place was shown later when he clung to a spot on a smooth bole where numbers of grubs lay under a strip of bark. He fed on them for 15 minutes, pushing his belly against the bole to recover those that fell. The feeding of the Crimson-cresteds was easy to observe because they usually moved from tree to tree without flying far and, if high up, were apt to move along the undersides of limbs where I could still see them.

## FORAGING IN THE RAINY SEASON

On 4 January I found a male 3–4 m above the ground on a semi-dead tree where, being up on a slope, I could watch him at eye level. He moved out onto small branches, several centimeters in diameter. Clinging securely with two of his forward directed toes on one side, and two on the other, he pecked steadily on the still adherent bark as if finding considerable prey. On one occasion he uncovered a grub nearly 3 cm long. On another tree, he clung to the underside of a slightly larger branch. Here I could see that he delivered three or four powerful pecks in one place, then moved to another without penetrating deeply. Had I been at home, I would have thought the branches more suitable for a Hairy or a Downy.

As pointed out by Bock and Miller (1959), *Campephilus* woodpeckers have remarkable adaptations for clinging. These include a forward direction of all their toes, as well as having their legs directed away from the center of the body. With tarsi pressed against trunks and branches, the woodpecker is stabilized for delivering blows.

## COMPARISONS WITH LINEATEDS

Crimson-crested and Lineated Woodpeckers are so alike in size, shape, and general coloration that it may take one a few days to tell them apart. Cody's (1969) theory is that the two look alike because they hold interspecific territories, each one excluding the other. This is because they have "similar ecologies" and would otherwise compete. What I found on Barro Colorado, however, was completely the reverse. Instead of being intolerant, the two fed together peacefully. I was going up a trail when I heard both the *kwirr-as* of Crimson-cresteds and the *wer-wer-wers* of Lineateds. Sounds of digging then led me to a male Lineated. He pecked briefly, then began probing, turning and twisting his head for five minutes in the manner of a Pileated. It seemed that he was foraging for ants. A male Crimson-crested now alighted a meter below. What would happen? As the slightly larger Crimson-crested hitched up, neither he nor the Lineated raised its crest or showed other indication of excitement. When the two were 30 cm apart, the Lineated moved away. The Crimson-crested inspected the spot briefly, then flew. The Lineated returned to feed for another 10 minutes. What impressed me was the light thrown on the habits of the two species. Where the Lineated found much to feed upon, the Crimson-crested found nothing. On the other hand, the tree itself provided decaying limbs attractive to Crimson-cresteds, for I had watched a pair of them foraging on them a few weeks before. While the feeding habits of the two do overlap to some extent, as Tanner (1942) showed for the Pileated and Ivory-billed, the overlap was not enough to prevent the two from sharing the same tree. That Lineated Woodpeckers are specialized is most clearly seen in their attacks on *Cecropias*, the rapidly growing trees that harbor *Azteca* ants.

## EARLY BREEDING BEHAVIOR

### EXCAVATION

When staying at La Selva, in Costa Rica, I found a male Pale-billed excavating a stub, somewhat in the open and 10 m tall. The stub had fungal decay and was easy to excavate. I watched him excavating for 115 minutes in the morning of January 14 and the female for 57 minutes in the afternoon. On the next day the male excavated for 73 minutes. Thus in four hours of watching, the male did two-thirds and the female one-third of the excavating, the same proportion between the sexes as I have found with Pileateds and Lineateds.

In my hours of watching I had noted a number of Collared Araçaris in the background. Like starlings in the north, these pirates wait until an excavation is done, then take over. This they did, while I watched. The woodpeckers simply left, with no show of resistance. Possibly they realized that contending with adversaries having such large bills (Fig. 47) would be hopeless.

A number of pairs of Crimson-cresteds followed in Panama had difficulties finding suitable stubs. I was pleased, therefore, when my wife found a male excavating on Barro Colorado Island. When his mate flew to change places on December 26, he drum-tapped, made low notes, then drum-tapped again. She tossed some sawdust after he left, but spent most of her time looking out. When he returned in 15 minutes, she disappeared inside to drum-tap at the bottom of the cavity. He peered in before she came out, squeezing past his shoulder. Although the male tossed sawdust, he was soon, like his mate before him, looking out idly. It appeared that the cavity was largely done by the end of December.

Another pair of Crimson-cresteds did not begin excavating until late January. Their hesitancy was probably due to the mass of epiphytes at the top

FIG. 47. Collared Araçaris after appropriating newly finished nest cavity of Crimson-crested Woodpecker.

of their stub that, together with lianas, might have encouraged arboreal mammals or other unwanted visitors. The pair had, nonetheless, carved an entrance by January 22. Changeovers at the nest were as with our earlier pair, with one exception. This was on 31 January when the male was excavating. Instead of dropping out of sight to drum-tap when his mate flew to him, he met her at the entrance and the two touched bills a number of times before he flew away.

## TERRITORIAL CONFLICTS

The stub had been the center of a conflict a month before. I was first led to it by drumming, then heavy sounding flights as one male pursued another. In a conflict that lasted five minutes, one male clung almost upside down below a limb while the other, perched on top, half opened his wings each time his opponent tried to come around from below. When the two flew, it was to continue the conflict on a trunk nearby. Here one backed down as the other retreated backward. Both finally flew in opposite directions; the owner to drum for six minutes. He then attacked the intruder again. The males were still engaged when I left at the end of 50 minutes. The fighting was all silent except for two sharp *ca* notes.

## Courtship and Copulation

A pair of Crimson-cresteds came to a knoll at the edge of woods, near where we lived in Panama, for early morning courtship. The two began a duet of drumming at 06:10 on November 22, each burst a *da-drr*. This *Campephilus*-type of drumming is unlike that of any other woodpecker. After 15 minutes of low bursts, one or two per minute, the male few to his mate. She moved out on a limb giving low notes as he approached. He now mounted in copulation, pecking down at her bill four to five times as he gradually fell to the left. The two were beautiful in the early morning. I think the Crimson-crested the handsomest of woodpeckers.

The copulation indicated that the pair must have a nest nearing completion. I located it a few days later, 400 m away. The female was excavating, but took alarm on seeing me. I found the pair near the hole on returning in the evening. The female flew to it and drum-tapped as her mate alighted below. When he started moving up, she moved down, bending over to fence bills with him (Fig. 48). All now looked well for actual nesting. The male entered the hole for the night and his mate left.

But he was restless. He kept looking out. Finally he came out, never to return. A pair of Collared Araçaris had been watching. For the Crimson-cresteds this was enough. Although the female returned, neither of the pair put up any fight. Four nights later I found the araçaris roosting in the hole.

I now felt that I would see little of the Crimson-cresteds again. But in this I was mistaken. Hearing *kwirr-kwirra*s a few weeks later, I was pleased to see the pair back on the knoll. When the male alighted on the trunk of a slender tree, his mate joined him and the two bent their heads to touch bills. Their red crests were raised to the full and curled forward. The woodpeckers now returned to their original positions, only to swing heads to the other side of the tree and touch bills again, prior to moving where they could have a duet of drumming. The pair had excavated a new nest by this time. But with the usual luck of tropical birds, it was lost later on.

## Nesting

### Crimson-Crested

The pair of Crimson-cresteds on Barro Colorado ceased greeting each other once incubation began. Times between changeovers were long. In waits of one and a half hours and longer I never saw a woodpecker return after leaving. Skutch (1969), in extended waits by the nest of Pale-billeds, noted the female as spending four and a half hours on the eggs and the male as not being relieved again after taking over at noon.

I saw more of the Crimson-cresteds after hatching. The male, after looking out for five minutes, flew out to preen, then reentered to continue brooding. The longest he spent away from the nest in two and a half hours was 10 minutes. I found the pair still brooding a week later. By this time,

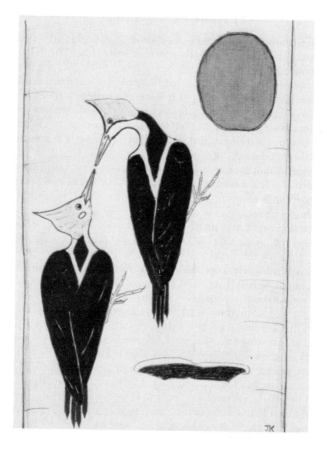

FIG. 48. Female Crimson-crested Woodpecker backs down from nest hole to touch bills with her mate who reaches up toward her.

the female's interest in the nest seemed greatest, for, when not on it, she generally stayed near. The male once stayed away for three hours. Neither of the pair brought visible prey in its bill. On January 30 the male entered the nest while his mate was inside, staying in for a few minutes. On the next day he remained inside with her for five minutes, a rare phenomenon among most woodpeckers, especially in the nesting period.

The male became increasingly apprehensive as nesting progressed. He spent much time looking about and bowing in and out before entering. Whether the predator, if predator it was, that destroyed the nest was in the vicinity, I did not know. On nearly every visit, I noticed a pair of Spectacled Owls perched not far away.

## PALE-BILLED

My wife and I had better luck with Pale-billed Woodpeckers in Guatemala. All three pairs were in late stages of nesting. One nest, particularly favorable for watching, was only 3 m above the ground. Sitting at a distance of 10 m, we noted that on 22 of 35 visits the parents brought white larvae, about 0.6 cm in diameter and 3–4 cm long, in their partly open bills. One thrust at the entrance was enough to transfer the prey to the single nestling. The nestling started chittery notes as soon as it saw a parent, continued them while being fed, and for a bit after the parent had left. In our 13 hours of watching, we witnessed 35 feeding visits of which 18 were by the female and 17 by the male, a very even sharing of activities. Intervals between visits averaged 22 minutes, with variations between none in one and a half hours to six in 36 minutes, all by the male.

### FLEDGING

A second pair also had a single nestling. The nestling was calling *kuk-kuk-kwirr*s as it leaned from its hole one day and on the next day when I saw it fly. On the morning after that, it was still calling the *kuk-kuk-kwirr*s, this time answered with *kwirr-a*s by the male. When the male flew, the fledgling followed. But when the young one came close, the male moved away. This game, kept up for 20 minutes, was, I thought, an effort to lead the young one away into the woods.

### YOUNG AFTER NEST LEAVING

The first juvenile Crimson-crested I encountered on Barro Colorado was on January 31 when continued *k-arr, k-arr* notes led me to it. When its mother gave *kwirr-a*s and flew, it followed. I later found it close beside her as she dug for grubs.

I was watching a male digging in a well-rotted stub on January 22 when a female, adult in plumage, alighted close by. She made no effort to feed herself, just preened lightly and made *k-da, k-da* begging notes. The male paid no seeming attention until, finding an extra large grub, he leaned over and fed her. Then a second female arrived. Unlike the first one, she fed herself and was, it seemed, the mate of the male. The male did not feed the begging female again. She foraged for herself occasionally, but kept so close to the tail of the male in the next hour as, at times, to be almost touching it. It seemed that she was a young one of the year before. While this is a long time for a woodpecker to stay with its parents, my observation fits descriptions by Short (1970) for the Crimson-crested in Argentina and of Tanner (1942) for the Ivory-billed.

### COMPARISONS WITH THE IVORY-BILLED

The main similarities between Pale-billed and Crimson-cresteds, and the Ivory-billed Woodpeckers are that: (*i*) the neotropical species are relatively tame and easy to approach; (*ii*) their main form of courtship is bill-touching; and (*iii*) their drumming is what Tanner (1942) called for the Ivory-billed, a two-part *bam, bam.* In other similarities (*iv*) the parents fed nestlings large white grubs, and (*v*) a young Crimson-crested in adult plumage was found accompanying its parents a year after it was probably fledged.

I have wondered, from these similarities, whether, were more study possible, the Crimson-crested and Pale-billeds might not prove to be as close a counterpart of the Ivory-billed as the Lineated of the Pileated Woodpecker, which is closer than one might expect from plumage differences.

## METHODS OF COMMUNICATION

### DRUMMING, TAPPING, FLIGHT NOISE

*Drumming.*—Drumming of the two species is a strong blow, followed by a vibratory roll, *da-drr.* The double drums come at rates of one or two a minute, three per minute being a fast rate. Single *da-drr*s enable members of a pair to keep in touch and duets of them, continuing for up to 20 minutes, may appear at heights of courtship. Still louder drumming, against a resonating stub, is usually related to conflict.

*Drum-tapping.*—The *Campephilus* species have a rapid form of tapping, identical with that of the Lineated and Pileated Woodpeckers, used at the rim of a nest hole (Fig. 49), or deep down inside, at changeovers during excavation.

*Wing noises.*—The woodpeckers can fly silently. They can also make a heavy sound in flying even short distances that doubtless informs one of a pair where the other is going. Noisy flights were also heard in conflicts.

### VOCALIZATIONS

*Alarm notes.*—Notes indicating moderate disturbance, as when I came close to a nest, were *ca* and *ca-wa-rr-r.* A sharp, high-pitched *ca* was the only vocalization heard in several conflicts. Shrill, piping, *put, put, putta*s were given by both sexes in high excitement and were kept up for minutes at a time. On the whole, however, the *Campephilus* species were relatively silent birds, giving way to alarm less frequently than the sympatric Lineateds.

*Intimate notes.*—Low notes, expressive of closeness of pair bonds, were given, among other times, prior to coition and to changeovers in excavating. Variations included *wuk, wuk; wrr, wrr; wun, wun;* and *uh, uh.*

*Breeding call.*—A tree frog-like *kwirr, kwirr-ah.*

### DISPLAYS

*Bill-touching.*—The woodpeckers of a pair bent toward each other at the time of most active courtship, with crests raised and often curled forward, to touch bills, tip to tip, or along half their lengths in a kind of fencing.

FIG. 49. Female Crimson-crested Woodpecker drum-taps at rim of recently completed nest hole as mate approaches.

Allen and Kellogg (1937, p. 168) wrote that as a female Ivory-billed climbed up a pine toward her mate, "he bent his head downward and clasped bills with her."

## LITERATURE CITED

ALLEN, A. A., AND P. P. KELLOGG. 1937. Recent observations on the Ivory-billed Woodpecker. Auk, **54**: 164–184.

BOCK, W. J., AND W. D. MILLER 1959. The scansorial foot of woodpeckers with comments on the evolution of perching and climbing feet in birds. Amer. Mus. Novit., no. 1931, 45 p.

CODY, M. L. 1969. Convergent characteristics in sympatric species: a possible relation to interspecific competition and aggression. Condor, 71: 222–239.

KILHAM, L. 1972. Habits of Crimson-crested Woodpecker in Panama. Wilson Bull., 84: 28–47.

——. 1977a. Nesting behavior of Pale-billed Woodpeckers in Guatemala. Auk, 94: 773–774.

——. 1977b. Pale-billed Woodpeckers robbed of nest hole by Collared Araçaris. Auk, 94: 774–775.

SHORT, L. L. 1970. Notes on the habits of some Argentine and Peruvian woodpeckers (*Aves, Picidae*). Amer. Mus. Novit., no. 2413, 37 p.

SKUTCH, A. F. 1969. Life histories of Central American birds. **III.** Pacific Coast Avifauna (Cooper Ornith. Soc.), no. 35, 580 p.

TANNER, J. T. 1942. The Ivory-billed Woodpecker. Res. Rept. no. 1, Nat'l Audubon Soc., New York. 111 p.

# 11

## SOME ASPECTS OF BEHAVIOR AND MORPHOLOGY

## HEAD-SCRATCHING AND WING-STRETCHING

The Heinroths (1924–1926) state that most passerines scratch their heads "indirectly" by lowering one wing and passing the foot over it, and that woodpeckers do the same unless wishing to clean a corner of the bill. Both in the aviary and in the field, however, I have found that woodpeckers always scratch their heads directly, i.e., without lowering the wing (Fig. 50). I observed this almost daily in the aviary. Something noted particularly was that a woodpecker may pass its bill over the oil gland, at the base of the tail, then rub a foot with its bill, a way, it seemed, of transferring oil to the head by way of scratching. Relatively few groups of birds, according to Nice and Shantz (1959), scratch by the direct method. Among woodpeckers that I have seen scratching directly are Hairies, Downies, Pileateds, Red-cockadeds, Red-bellieds, Red-headeds, sapsuckers and flickers.

Scratching in birds is a way of preening feathers that cannot be reached with the bill. Although it may serve an immediate purpose in relieving irritation, as when flickers on the lawn in Florida scratched with one foot, then the other, its main function is probably keeping down ectoparasites.

Another behavior is the leg-wing stretch, so-called for most birds, because the leg on the same side is stretched out with the wing, while the bird stands on the other foot (Eibl-Eibesfeldt and Kramer, 1958). A situation noted in the aviary was that woodpeckers do not do this. They stretch the wing down, but a leg does not follow. One has, however, to be in a good position to see this. The foot on the same side as the wing can be moved a short way and this is deceiving. The movement is to secure a fresh grip as the wing goes

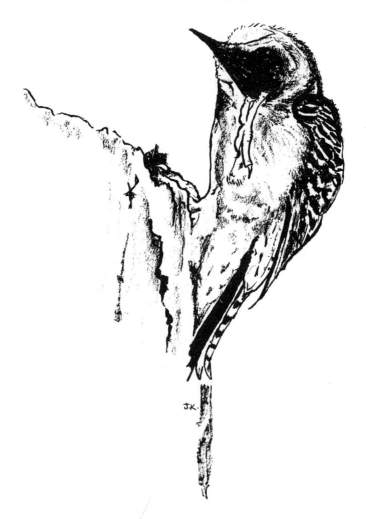

FIG. 50. Red-bellied Woodpecker scratching head directly without lowering wing (from a photograph).

down by itself. I think that woodpeckers do this wing-stretch in an atypical manner because they are unable to cling or stand readily with one foot, a maneuver easy for birds in other groups. Red-bellieds are unusual in stretching both wings backward and downward simultaneously (Fig. 51), while keeping both feet planted. These stretches are often followed by a "double wing-neck stretch" (Fig. 52) (Stickel, 1965).

FIG. 51. Female Red-bellied Woodpecker doing a modification of the synchronized leg-wing stretch common to many birds. In woodpeckers, both feet remain planted, but in Red-bellieds both wings may be extended backward and downward simultaneously.

## PLAY

It is difficult to define play (Ficken, 1977) and, in consequence, much of what birds do as such is probably missed. A helpful generalization of Marler and Hamilton (1967:193) is that a "lack of 'seriousness' is a key quality." This lack was a feature of what I observed with woodpeckers. Their play came at times when they were idle, with nothing pressing to do. It fell under three categories, all corresponding to a major pattern of the 'serious' side of their lives.

### DODGING

An advantage to studying the roosting habits of woodpeckers is being in the woods in the first hour of a day when they are most lively. An expression of this is what I call playing "dodgeball." A female Hairy, on December 13, started dodging behind a tree trunk on coming near a flock of redpolls.

Fig. 52. Sapsucker performing a double wing-neck stretch.

When they flew, she swung around again, with wings stretched straight backward, as if trying to keep the trunk between herself and the smaller birds. Another Hairy, on a following morning, was well up in an oak. When four Pine Grosbeaks alighted on the ground, the woodpecker dropped to a limb above to play at dodging. I witnessed dodging two more times that winter, once with Black-capped Chickadees and once with Pine Grosbeaks. In all instances the birds providing the stimuli were harmless ones, showing no signs of attack or even interest. They served merely as releasers, providing the Hairies with occasions to dodge as if before an imaginary enemy.

I have observed Downies playing in the same way. A male White-breasted Nuthatch was singing on March 2, with his mate only a short distance away, when a female Downy came between and started dodging before the male. The Downy flew away after a few moments, only to return and dodge some more. Neither species showed any aggressiveness. A juvenile Downy dodged before a chickadee, and later, two nuthatches. The mother of the juvenile had dodged when close to a chickadee (Fig. 53) the week before. Although it is conceivable that wild juveniles learn to play from parents, my hand-

FIG. 53. Downy Woodpecker dodging about in play, with a chickadee acting as a releaser.

raised Downies and Hairies dodged from an early age. Dodging was an almost daily event after I turned on the lights in the aviary in the morning. One of my Downies often started dodging on the underside of a log when a sapsucker flew over. I noted this behavior only in minutes after the lights were turned on and never later in the day. There was no sign of hostility. The Downy usually held its wings straight out behind its back, closing them intermittently as it shifted about. Use of the wings in this way gave speed and agility.

It should be emphasized that wings were never extended sideways as in threat displays. This was brought out with the female Pileated. She was very playful at dodging and might wave her wings, as well as extending them backward, when a flicker flew overhead. She often raised her crest as she moved her head and long neck to peer around at her fancied assailant. Later in the day, a flicker might fly close without being noticed.

The Pileated looked up one morning to find a Red-bellied in an aggressive pose just above her. She immediately went into a threat display, wings held out horizontally and somewhat back, rapping on a log as she did so. This was a "serious" response to an aggressive threat.

Several of our Hairies were kept in an aviary with Red-breasted Nuthatches. The Hairies never dodged opposite to each other or to the Downies, but they did so to the nuthatches, following their every move as they flew about, sometimes for as long as 3–4 minutes.

When two of our younger Hairies were ready to fledge, I placed them in a large aquarium. Here one dodged about an upright stick before a house fly. It thus seemed as on previous occasions that small "assailants" made the best releasers.

Our handraised sapsuckers were the only woodpeckers to play dodgeball with each other. A possible explanation is that juvenile sapsuckers, unlike the other woodpeckers that I have studied, stay together in summer as a family group. I have never observed dodging in flickers. This may be because they are largely ground feeders and, in consequence, are less adept at shifting about tree trunks.

## ERRATIC FLIGHTS

A second form of play is erratic flight in which woodpeckers suddenly loop in, out, and around trees. This might be regarded as being merely a form of exercise, except that it occurs most frequently at the same time as dodging and may even follow it directly. A Hairy on January 30 dodged before a chickadee, then flew off in erratic flight. This type of flight is a form of dodging on the wing, as if the woodpecker were being pursued by a hawk. I have noted it in the field for Hairies and Downies, as well as for sapsuckers, flickers, Red-cockadeds, Pileateds, and Red-bellieds.

Morse (1975) gives a closer description of what I have witnessed in his account of "erratic flights" of European Goldcrests and Treecreepers. Although most of the flights he witnessed were without provocation that he could discover, two, one for each of the species, were when pursued by a Sparrowhawk. The flights then, Morse found, were no different from ones performed under other circumstances.

Humphries and Driver (1967) indicate that erratic displays are widespread among both vertebrates and invertebrates. "When attacked by predators," they wrote (p. 1767), "many prey animals do not flee in a straight line; their behavior is highly erratic and unpredictable, taking the form of zigzagging, looping, spinning, or wild bouncing."

## PLAY VERSIONS OF COURTSHIP

While my handraised flickers and Red-bellieds did not carry on dodgings and erratic flights, they did manifest a sense of play in other ways. As already discussed, flickers perform bill-waving dances both in courtship and against rivals. Our handraised juveniles began dancing within three weeks of fledging and continued to do so as a daily event that I interpreted as play. Many of these dances, as seen among wild flickers in the fall, might be interpreted in the same way, if the birds were immatures.

Adult Red-bellieds do much tapping in the wild, beginning in midwinter. A handraised female, that was very tame, did so on various objects when she was three months old, both to me, when I entered the aviary, and to a female Pileated in the same cage. The tapping of Red-bellieds may thus be like the dances of flickers, an integral part of adult courtship that is performed by juveniles as play.

### STORAGE OF MISCELLANEOUS OBJECTS

Red-bellied Woodpeckers spend much time storing food in fall and winter. Our handraised Red-bellieds, seemingly as play, stored objects of no apparent value. When I gave a female a bent nail, she spent five minutes trying to insert it into various holes, hunching her shoulders forward as she did so. Toothpicks, clips, and even small wads of paper elicited similar behavior. The Red-bellieds also stored objects of their own. A male loosened a sliver of wood, arranged it to point forward in his bill, then flew about the aviary in search of a storage place. He was preparing to store a small chip on April 6, when his mate took it from him and flew off with it. Only one other woodpecker in the aviary stored miscellaneous objects. This was a sapsucker that tried to store a chip of wood in six different holes before finding one that was suitable. This seemed peculiar, because I have never seen sapsuckers storing anything in nature. It was not until years later that I learned, from a note by Conner and Kroll (1979), that sapsuckers store food in nature.

Storage of odd objects has also been described for Acorn Woodpeckers. Ritter (1921:4) stated, as his opinion, that "the [storing] instinct sometimes goes wrong to the extent of storing pebbles instead of acorns, thus defeating entirely the purpose of the instinct." It is not always easy, however, to perceive the purpose of what animals are doing. Play, for example, may not be a case of instincts gone wrong so much as a way of developing and practicing skills against a time when an animal may need them for survival. Play, according to Eibl-Eibesfeldt (1970), is learning.

### DISCUSSION

Play, in general, has been less described among birds than mammals. Thorpe (1956), however, thinks that true play is widespread among birds, being best known for hawks, hornbills, ravens, and a few others. So far I have encountered no references to play among woodpeckers. My handraised ones were an asset to watching it.

One reason was that I had a chance to observe them early in the morning when they were most exuberant. A second asset was tameness. Not all of my captives were tame, for some of them became moderately wild, in spite of my having taken them from the nest at an early age. It was those that were the most tame, and least disturbed, that were the most playful. This suggested that even if a woodpecker is not disturbed enough to fly away in the presence of an observer, he may be wary enough, in the woods, not to play while being watched. This may account, in part, for the paucity of accounts of play among wild birds. A third reason that captives offer opportunities is that animals play when they have nothing else to do. My woodpeckers, being provided with food, shelter, and an absence of predators, had more time for idling than they would have had in the wild.

Among definitions of play, I find that of Armstrong (1947:304) especially apposite. "Surplus vitality," he writes, "may manifest itself in many ways which are commonly described as playful when, apart from the exercise involved, and their function in providing a means of expression for exuberant energy, they do not directly serve some biological end." The idea of surplus energy is one that I find particularly applicable because most of my observations were made early in the day. Armstrong continues that play may "acquire value as, for instance, when playful combats . . . serve as training for serious fighting in later life." He might have added "for escape from predators" as well as for serious fighting. I might also comment on the notion that only young birds play. Both dodging and erratic flights are activities of juvenile and adult woodpeckers. They are a practice of evasive tactics—ones that may be needed instantly when a predator strikes.

Hairy and Downy Woodpeckers swing under limbs and dodge behind trunks when in combat with others of their own kind. Being somewhat solitary they do not play with each other, possibly because play, even though not serious, might be taken as such by a conspecific. This may explain why these woodpeckers seek out chickadees or other harmless species for practice.

A final conclusion is that play among woodpeckers, as among birds in general, is worthy of more attention than it has received. If play is left out, it is possible that something of importance has been omitted from any study of their total way of life.

## PLUMAGES OF HAIRY AND DOWNY WOODPECKERS

### ADAPTIVE VALUES OF COLOR PATTERNS

Downies and Hairies are similar in plumage, even though they are not sibling species. One might think that plumage differences would be needed to insure reproductive isolation. But the two differ so widely in feeding habits, time of onset of breeding behavior, and type of pairbond, as well as in size, that plumage differences would not appear needed. What is of interest is why the two should look so much alike.

The white underparts of both species are not particularly striking in months when leaves are on the trees. It is only when breeding seasons begin in winter that the effectiveness of the white of throat, breast and belly becomes apparent. I have often noticed that when a Hairy or a Downy is drumming high in a tree, as often happens on early mornings in late winter, the rising sun catches the white and sends a gleam that one can see from a distance. The most active drumming of courtship and territory is in these first hours when the sun is low and slanting. White under these circumstances may be especially effective as a releaser of territorial and sexual behavior. One might note that White-breasted Nuthatches, that also carry on a winter courtship high in trees, also have underparts that are gleaming white.

The patterns on the backs of Hairies and Downies are generally disruptive and concealing. There is probably some compromise, for the pattern has to serve both in summer, when leaves are on the trees, as well as in winter, when the trees are bare. Demonstration that these back patterns are effective is difficult. The account of Thompson (in Bent, 1939), is therefore of interest. "I once saw a goshawk pursuing a Downy Woodpecker, when the latter darted through a tuft of foliage and flattened itself close upon the body of a thick oak bough, where it remained motionless as the bark itself. The hawk alighted on the same bough within two feet of its intended victim, and remained sitting there for some minutes, evidently looking in vain for it. The woodpecker was stretched longitudinally on the bough, its tail and beak close to the bark, its black and white speckled feathers looking like a continuation of the wrinkles and lichen."

A convenient feature of the plumages of Hairies and Downies is that no two of them have patterns on the back of the head that look alike—an asset to the identification of individuals. Downies have equally individual patterns on the undersides of their tails, as I have noticed when parents are hanging down, within nest holes, to feed their young. Mrs. E. W. Brooks (pers. comm.) has recorded over 50 different undertail patterns in banding operations. As mentioned by Short (1982) complex patterns with many possible variations are characteristic of the genus *Picoides*.

A pattern of Hairies and Downies that can be disruptive is that of their heads. This is when one of them is looking from a nest or roost hole with head drawn back. The black and white lines radiating from the base of the bill then suggest a snake-like creature ready to strike. One cannot see the eyes, for they are concealed in the black bands that run through them. In their place one sees the ends of white bands that look more like eyes than the real ones. This effect is increased when the feathers of the crown are raised. Should one put a finger to the hole, as I have done in the aviary, the woodpecker strikes out with lightening speed.

Black patches concealing the eyes are found in Hairy and Downy Woodpeckers, as well as in Red-breasted Nuthatches and Black-capped Chickadees. A feature of these hole-nesters, which are sympatric in the north, is that they excavate their own nest holes. This means that the holes fit their head size and that they are thus better able to defend them. White-breasted Nuthatches and Tufted Titmice lack black eye patches. These birds are alike in using natural cavities for nesting, ones with entrances larger than their body size. Such entrances are difficult to defend directly. In this situation, White-breasted Nuthatches have evolved elaborate systems of defense by other means.

It is curious that most of the European woodpeckers of the genus *Picoides* (the Great, Middle, and Lesser, as well as the Syrian and White-backed Woodpeckers) lack concealing black bands over the eyes. It would be interesting to know if these species are exposed to different selection pressures, or nest in a different fashion, than their American counterparts. One selection pressure not found in Europe is the raccoon. Raccoons are effective predators of hole-nesting birds. There could, therefore, be selection for any feature that might aid in defense against them.

Another feature of Hairies and Downies is that there is no difference between the sexes except for a small red patch at the back of the head. This lack of any marked sexual dimorphism is characteristic of many woodpeckers. Among them males and females share the tasks of nesting more equally than do most passerines. Both sexes of woodpeckers can fight in defense of roost as well as nest holes against rivals of their own species, without regard to sex. In such contests, it is advantageous to the female to look essentially like the male. It puts her on a more equal basis. It is helpful to this situation that the sexual marker is at the back of the head of the male and cannot be seen readily as two contestants face each other. In bill-waving dances, where heads are bent back sharply, nuchal patches are especially difficult to see.

## ATTRACTION OF DOWNY TO HAIRY WOODPECKERS

This phenomenon is, I think, related to the similarities in plumage. A female Downy flew to within 30 cm of a male Hairy working on the limb of an oak. She paused, came close, then flew away. There were no signs of hostility or other emotion in 16 incidents of this sort that I witnessed. A Hairy pecked mildly when a Downy came close, on two occasions, but this was more a preservation of individual distance than an attack.

In another type of approach, a female Downy came to within 8 cm of where a female Hairy was working, watched for a minute, then left. When the larger woodpecker flew away, the Downy returned to inspect the place where the Hairy had been. This was the only time I saw evidence of interest in a specific feeding place. In 15 of 16 incidents where I saw Downies fly to Hairies, they either fed close by for a short time or only paused before moving on. Food did not seem to be involved. There was no evidence, furthermore, that sex played a role. A male Downy was just as apt to fly to a male as to a female Hairy and the same was true of a female Downy. Fourteen of the 16 episodes, however, did take place between January and June, in months that included the breeding seasons of both species.

Several interpretations are conceivable. The sight of the larger species actively feeding may have roused the curiosity of the smaller one. My impression, however, is that it is similarity of plumage that leads Downies to approach Hairies. A Hairy may well, at first glance, look like an oversized Downy. The Downy, therefore, is roused by a super-normal stimulus, much as Oyster-catchers are attracted to oversized eggs. Cody (1969) has advanced the idea that when two sympatric species of woodpecker look alike, there should be an increase of aggressiveness between them. But I have seen no evidence of this with Hairies and Downies. Downies attack Hairies when the latter come close to roost or nest holes, but no more than they would attack any other woodpecker.

## BLACK-CROWNED MORPHS AMONG FEMALE YELLOW-BELLIED SAPSUCKERS

Although I can make no guess as to actual incidence, I have encountered 12 Black-crowned morphs among female sapsuckers in New Hampshire. Of seven nests found in 1967, the females at three were black morphs. I tried, at the time, to detect behavioral differences between black and red-crowned females, without success. One black-crowned female, however, achieved something that I have seen with no other woodpecker. After losing one mate in the mid-nesting period, she attracted another who helped to feed the young.

A question is why black-crowned morphs should be maintained in populations of sapsuckers. Although pleiotropy could be involved, with some other character being the object of selection, I theorize that the black-crowns are there because males prefer them as breeding partners. Here it is helpful, I think, to consider situations among wood warblers (Parulidae). Skutch (1957) was first to note that while species endemic to Central America are apt to be sedentary and monomorphic, with both sexes having brightly colored plumages, species migrating to temperate zones tend to be sexually dimorphic with females selected for neutral or dull plumage. A number of selection pressures may be active. One, commonly suggested, is that a neutral plumage protects a female and her nest from exposure to predators. Selection pressures, however, can be multiple. Hamilton (1961) believes that the sexual dimorphism of the warblers has a primary function in speeding up territorial and pairbonding behavior. This is in species that, being migratory, have only a few months in which to breed.

Situations among the species of sapsuckers of the superspecies *varius* appear to be remarkably parallel to those described for the wood warblers. The species that is the most brightly colored, the Red-breasted Sapsucker, is sexually monomorphic as well as being sedentary or migratory only to a minimal degree, while sexual dimorphism is present in the Red-naped and Yellow-bellied species, forms that are migratory. Of the two, the Yellow-bellied is the more migratory and is the more dimorphic. Black-crown morphism among females is only encountered in the latter species. A question is whether

FIG. 54.  Male sapsucker (right) scratching chin directly. Female sapsucker (left) fluffing body feathers. Given a choice, the male chose this drab female, practically a juvenile in plumage, as a mate.

the morph may not represent a change in the direction of a duller plumage for females.

I was impressed with this possibility in the aviary. As narrated previously, I had four sapsuckers, all siblings and handraised the year before. One was a male, the other three females. These latter formed a hierarchy; the one brightest in plumage, a typical breeding female, being dominant and a very dull female, hardly different from a juvenile, subordinate to the others.

The male chose the dullest female for a mate (Fig. 54). The two were taking interest in a nest site when I decided to test his preference by removing all of the females. After a few days, I reintroduced them one at a time. When I reintroduced the brightest female, the male attacked her, but when the dull female was returned, he greeted her with courtship displays.

In regard to Hamilton's (1961) theory, I wonder if it does not apply even better to the Yellow-bellied Sapsucker than to warblers. One can argue that dull-colored females are selected for by way of protection on the nest. With sapsuckers this does not hold, for they cannot be seen when within their cavities. I think that male Yellow-bellied Sapsuckers prefer black-crowned females because, without red crowns, they look less like rival males. An increase in sexual dimorphism may thus promote closer pairbonds and, *pari pasu*, greater degrees of nesting success.

## COLORS AS RELEASERS OF SEXUAL BEHAVIOR

The placing of varied species of woodpeckers together in one aviary led to unexpected results. One was the way patches of color in one species acted as sexual signals in others. Our observations centered on a lone female Pileated. As narrated earlier, the crest of a Pileated, male or female, is of the same fiery red and silky texture as the feathers on the forehead, crown, and nape of a male Red-bellied Woodpecker. My male Red-bellied treated the female Pileated as a rival male. A female Red-bellied, on the other hand, made advances to the Pileated as if it were a male of her own kind. The attacks of the male Red-bellied became so persistent that I had to remove the Pileated. Having seen how relentless he became, I was interested in Kinsey's (1945) report of a handraised Acorn Woodpecker. Males of this species also have red crowns. Kinsey's male was exceedingly tame to begin with, but one day it made a vicious attack on the face of the lady who looked after it. The attack, it was discovered, was set off by her wearing a red bandana on her head. "Subsequent tests with various red objects," wrote Kinsey, "sent the . . . woodpecker into a perfect frenzy of excitement and caused him to repeatedly attack such objects."

Another reaction involving our Pileated was her attraction to a female sapsucker. Here the white throat and red crest of the sapsucker, plus the combination of black bands radiating from the base of the bill, suggested the markings of a male Pileated. This interaction and that of the Red-bellieds were specific, for none of the other woodpeckers in the aviary, Hairies, Downies, or flickers, were ever involved.

Were my observations and those of Kinsey artifacts of captive birds? Tinbergen (1958), while watching a lone female Red-necked Phalarope in Greenland, found that she responded repeatedly to Lapland Buntings, Ringed Plovers, and Purple Sandpipers, as though they were males of her own kind, but not to Snow Buntings. The first three species, Tinbergen observed, were of "about the same size and general color" as the phalarope.

In 1954, I watched a somewhat similar type of interaction when a male Pied-billed Grebe made repeated attacks on a Ring-necked Duck, but not on other ducks or waterfowl that came to his pond. Ring-necks, as seen from a distance, have markers like those of a male Pied-billed, including a black one on the bill.

Some situations appear to predispose to interspecific responses. One is a lowering of threshold that takes place as a breeding season advances, in a lone bird without a mate. This was true of my lone female Pileated as well as for the lone female phalarope of Tinbergen. As for the male Red-bellied and the male Acorn Woodpecker, it may be that confinement, at close quarters, makes males in a breeding condition more belligerent. Against this is the result of an experiment performed by Selander and Giller (1959:118) with the head of a female Red-bellied Woodpecker, separated from a museum skin and stuck up close to the nest hole of a pair of wild Red-bellieds.

The male attacked, separated the front part of the head and flew off with it. All that remained was a ball of cotton and a tuft of red feathers. To the author's surprise, the wild female Red-bellied returned to attack this, continuing until the red feathers disappeared. "These observations," it was concluded, "suggest that the red feathers of the head are of paramount importance in releasing aggressive behavior."

## LITERATURE CITED

ARMSTRONG, E. A. 1947. Bird display and behavior. Oxford Univ. Press, New York. 431 p.

BENT A. C. 1939. Life histories of North American woodpeckers. Bull. U.S. Nat'l Mus. **174**: 1–334.

CODY M. L. 1969. Convergent characteristics in sympatric species: a possible relation to interspecific competition and aggression. Condor, **71**: 222–239.

CONNER, R. N., AND J. C. KROLL. 1979. Food-storing by Yellow-bellied Sapsuckers. Auk, **96**: 195.

EIBL-EIBESFELDT, I. 1970. Ethology, the Biology of Behavior. Holt, Reinhart and Winston, New York. 530 p.

EIBL-EIBESFELDT, I., AND S. KRAMER. 1958. Ethology. The comparative study of animal behavior. Quart. Rev. Biol., **33**: 181–211.

FICKEN M. S. 1977. Avian play. Auk, **94**: 573–582.

HAMILTON, T. H. 1961. On the functions and causes of sexual dimorphism in breeding plumage characters of North American species of warblers and orioles. Amer. Nat. **95**: 121–123.

HEINROTH, O., AND M. HEINROTH. 1924–26. Die Vögel Mitteleuropas. Vol. I. H. Bermühler Verlag, Berlin. viii + 339 p.

HUMPHRIES, D. A., AND P. M. DRIVER. 1967. Erratic display as a device against predators. Science, **156**: 1767–1768.

KILHAM, L. 1954. Repeated territorial attacks of Pied-billed Grebe on Ring-necked Duck. Wilson Bull., **66**: 265.

———. 1959. Head-scratching and wing-stretching of woodpeckers. Auk, **76**: 527–528.

———. 1968. Reproductive behavior of White-breasted Nuthatches. I. Distraction display, bill-sweeping, and nest hole defense. Auk, **85**: 477–492.

———. 1972. Reproductive behavior of White-breasted Nuthatches. II. Courtship. Auk, **89**: 115–129.

———. 1974a. Interspecific actions of sexual signals among handraised woodpeckers. Avicult. Mag., **80**: 104–108.

———. 1974b. Play in Hairy, Downy, and other woodpeckers. Wilson Bull., **86**: 35–42.

KINSEY, E. C. 1945. Nesting of the California Woodpecker in captivity. Aviculture, Nov/Dec., 328–332.

## BEHAVIOR AND MORPHOLOGY

MARLER P., AND W. J. HAMILTON III. 1966. Mechanisms of animal behavior. John Wiley, New York. 771 p.

MORSE, D. H. 1975. Erratic flights of Goldcrests *Regulus regulus* and Treecreepers *Certhia familiaris*. Ibis, **117**: 379–382.

NICE, M. M., AND W. E. SCHANTZ. 1959. Head-scratching movements in birds. Auk, **76**: 339–342.

RITTER W. E. 1921. Acorn-storing by the California Woodpecker. Condor, **23**: 3–14.

SELANDER R. K., AND D. R. GILLER. 1959. Interspecific relations of woodpeckers in Texas. Wilson Bull., **71**: 107–124.

SHORT, L. L. 1982. Woodpeckers of the world. Delaware Mus. Nat. Hist. Monogr. Ser., no. 4, 676 p.

SKUTCH A. F. 1957. Migratory and resident warblers in Central America, pp. 275–285. *In* The Warblers of America. Devin-Adair, New York.

STICKEL, D. W. 1965. Wing-stretching of Red-bellied Woodpeckers. Auk, **82**: 503.

THORPE, W. H. 1956. Learning and instinct in animals. Harvard Univ. Press, Cambridge. 493 p.

TINBERGEN, N. 1958. Curious naturalist. Basic Books, New York. 280 p.

# 12

## SUMMARY AND CONCLUSIONS

## AGONISTIC BEHAVIOR

### TERRITORY

Territorial conflicts between males at the onset of a breeding season, are largely limited to displays along a segment of common boundary. They are generally mild unless intensified by the arrival of a female. The bill-waving dances of Hairies and Downies may continue for an hour or more. Here it is possible that emotion fortifies learning. A woodpecker may not soon forget a place where it has fought for an hour. Once a breeding season is underway, only the area around a nest is defended. The main purpose of large, initial territories is to insure that each pair has an area of woodland in which to search for a nest site.

Although males do most of the fighting, females may participate or at least accompany their mates, a situation especially true among Hairies and Pileateds. An occasional female can be the first to establish the eventual breeding territory. In Maryland I followed a female Hairy that did an enormous amount of drumming one fall in attracting a male to her territory which she defended against other females. The only clear territorial conflicts that I have witnessed with Red-bellied Woodpeckers were also between females.

### Relations of Territorial to Courtship Behavior

Territorial conflicts occur in the same weeks as early courtship and the two activities can stimulate each other. Two male Hairies that resorted to the same bit of common boundary, one February, were regularly accompanied by their mates. Although the females stayed back and did not participate, they were sexually aroused. This was shown by the *jeek* vocalizations made as they flew to their mates during lulls in the conflict. On several occasions there were attempts at copulation two months before nesting.

It may seem strange that the chief displays used in territorial conflicts, the bill-waving dances for flickers and Pileateds, and the bobbing dances for sapsuckers, should also be used in courtship. But this dual use of a display is far from rare among birds (Howard, 1929:72). The dances of woodpeckers are conciliatory in essence. The bill, instead of being held fixed and pointed straight at an opponent, as when a woodpecker is about to meet or launch a physical attack, is held up and waved, a posturing that cancels any possibility of its being used as a weapon. Just as the song of a passerine may serve, at one time, to attract a mate and to warn a rival, so the message conveyed by a dance varies according to the sex of the woodpecker being faced. Bill-wavings among Hairies and Downies are simpler in being used only in conflicts.

### Defense of Nests

Male and female woodpeckers may cooperate in guarding nests, one staying inside until relieved by its mate. I have seen this with a pair of Hairies when starlings came regularly to the top of their nest tree and with a pair of sapsuckers, when a gray squirrel rested in a hole nearby. I have also noted it for a pair of Pileateds when a pilot black snake lived in their nest stub for five days. At times of more immediate danger, a male may take over the guarding entirely. A male Hairy did so when a red squirrel kept coming near his hole. It is not always possible, however, to predict which sex will be the more active in defending a nest. When a gray squirrel came to the vicinity of a Pileated nest on Sapelo, it was the female that kept attacking it, even though the squirrel, heavier than she, attacked her several times. Her mate, after facing the squirrel only once, left and did not return. The male's leaving may have represented an economy of effort. There is no use of both of a pair attacking an enemy if one partner can handle the job alone. When a Barred Owl came close to a sapsucker's nest near the time of fledging, the male became much excited and remained so for a half hour. His mate, in the meantime, went on feeding the young as though nothing unusual was happening.

### Which of a Pair is Stronger?

I have twice had occasions for comparing the fighting abilities of the sexes of woodpeckers. One was when a male sapsucker started an excavation a meter above that of a pair of Hairies. The female Hairy grappled with the sapsucker and was completely defeated. Her mate, coming a little later, fought in the same manner, but emerged the victor. The sapsucker never returned. Male Hairies are 12–22 percent heavier than females, according to Short (1982), and have bills that are 10–16 percent longer. These measurements could make a difference.

I watched a lone Pileated on Sapelo attack and defeat a mated pair at their nest. The severest conflict was at the entrance. Here the lone male jabbed at the female, then forced his way in and, after a scuffle, drove her out. Male Pileateds, like male Hairies, are larger than females. Among only a few birds does the male construct the nest, or most of it, and roost there at night. A reason for this among woodpeckers may be that males, being stronger, are better fitted to excavate a cavity as well as to defend it.

## LIMITS TO FIGHTING

Woodpeckers can, in some cases, give up a nest without resistance. I have noticed this for Crimson-crested and Pale-billed Woodpeckers in relation to araçaris and Skutch (1969) for Golden-naped Woodpeckers beset by tityras. It is possible that the woodpeckers were exhibiting an innate wisdom rather than timidity. Araçaris as well as tityras might be regarded as being professional pirates. They are geared to win. Starlings can also be regarded as professionals. I have often thought in watching Hairies, Red-bellies, and flickers struggling against them, that they would do better to give up sooner. They always lose. But starlings are newcomers and woodpeckers may not have had time to evolve in relation to them. There are ways of avoiding them, of which one is to nest within woods among leafy branches and another, as pointed out by Troetschler (1976), is to stagger nestings. Starlings are synchronous breeders, all nesting at one time. Woodpeckers, with more flexibility, are relatively safe if they excavate holes when starlings are busy with young of their own.

Aggressive behavior can be wasteful of time and energy. Carried beyond useful limits it could become dysgenic. There are times when it becomes so as I discuss below under Stress, Crowding, and Abnormal Behavior. But under usual circumstances, woodpeckers are not particularly aggressive birds. They fight only when there is some benefit in doing so. Red-headeds are among the most pugnacious of woodpeckers and have warning colors to go with their pugnacity. But their aggressiveness, over most of a year, is directed to birds that steal their stores. When I watched twelve Red-headeds packed into small territories for eight fall, winter, and spring months, I witnessed almost no intraspecific conflicts. The energies of the Red-headeds were directed particularly at Red-bellieds that also live on acorns. Yet on their breeding grounds, where the two species are not in competition, they get along peacefully, as I have noted in South Carolina and Selander and Giller (1959) in Texas.

## SUMMARY AND CONCLUSIONS

### STRESS, CROWDING, AND ABNORMAL BEHAVIOR

#### SCALING OF BEHAVIOR

Wherever I have studied woodpeckers, north or south, or in the tropics, I have found some pairs going about their nesting quietly while others, living under more crowded conditions, were noisier in relation to drumming, vocalizations, and displays. Both courtship and agonistic behavior were stimulated and this made for good watching. But this has been only up to a point. With too much crowding, as I have noted with Red-headed Woodpeckers in South Carolina, crowding can bring a shift from courtship to fighting. In all such instances there is some failure in the habitat, usually brought on by man. A post-logging decadence that followed World War II, led to an increase of potential nest stubs in New Hampshire and populations of sapsuckers reached a high. Then as stubs became used up and decayed, a shortage set in. With new woods consisting of only young, vigorous trees, no more stubs were available. Under these conditions, a year came when one pair of sapsuckers I was watching could not find a place to nest. They remained on their territory, with the male, seemingly as an outlet for his energies, seeking conflicts with neighbors.

Hairy Woodpeckers suffered the same fate. One of the extreme effects of the failure of the woods was the way one male kept invading the territory of a pair. The owning male always succeeded in driving him back until May 25. On that day the members of the pair had a duet of drumming of the tug-of-war type. It went on for 14 hours. It was the last, extreme, effort of the pair to agree on a nest site, when none suitable was available. By the next day, the pairbond was broken. Thereafter the owning male was completely defeated by the invader at the center of his territory, where he hid in a brush pile. I have watched several pairs of Downies, that after weeks of searching, failed to find a nest site. The males then took to drumming, day after day, until the latter part of June.

#### INTRAPAIR CLASHES

When my handraised female flicker gave up incubating, due to being molested by a sapsucker, her mate, after waiting for her to relieve him, came out of the nest and attacked her relentlessly. This, I thought, was an artificial situation, something that could not have happened in the wild. But, as I have found later, I have not been the only one to encounter pathological behavior during incubation. Skutch (1969) considers Gold-napeds as among the most closely paired of woodpeckers, the male and female sleeping in the nest together. Yet in one nest where incubation began normally, the male, for some unexplained reason, changed and began treating his mate with extreme hostility. Whereas the two had been alternating on the eggs, he now refused to let her enter the nest, spending much of his time chasing her away.

## SUMMARY AND CONCLUSIONS

Lawrence (1967) describes several clashes between members of pairs of Hairy Woodpeckers. When the male of one pair came to relieve his mate on the eighth day of incubation, she pecked out at him viciously and refused to come out. The impasse lasted five minutes. On the first day of incubation in a following year, the male flew from the nest to drive off a male intruder. After a physical clash, he returned to the nest. When his mate came to relieve him 20 minutes later, he flew out, drove her away, and re-entered. His negative attitude, although decreasing, continued throughout incubation.

I think that a key to such cases is that broodiness in birds represents a deep hormonal change. With passerines and many other species this is in the female alone. With woodpeckers, however, both of a pair have brood patches and both are affected. Either sex may be thrown off its course by stressful events occuring during incubation more than during other phases of reproduction.

### ATTACKS ON NESTS BY LONE INDIVIDUALS

Loss of a mate at early stages of breeding may lead to one type of stress. I have no other way of accounting for the attacks of lone individuals on the nests of mated pairs. A female Red-bellied, sometimes carrying food, tried to force her way into the nests of two neighboring pairs in Seneca Swamp. This was in spite of being attacked by the owners. Another instance involved a lone male Pileated on Sapelo. His attacks were so intense that he defeated the owning pair and, for a time, took over their nest. A third experience was not with woodpeckers, but with Casqued Hornbills in Africa. There a lone female attacked a nesting female over a two-month period, then attacked and broke the foot of the fledgling when it emerged. A drive to nest and to raise young has to be strong to succeed. When thrown off its course by the loss of a mate, possibly at an early critical time, the drive may carry on in ways that appear to be destructive.

I have never seen a woodpecker or bird of any kind with a close pairbond attack its mate under usual circumstances. A male Red-breasted Nuthatch may fly at his mate to get her to fly. Then, after a fast, mad pursuit, try to copulate. What might appear to be aggressive is actually the opposite. From having watched many such pursuits with my handraised nuthatches, I think that both sexes, pursuer and pursued, enjoy the chase. With woodpeckers I have rarely seen anything in courtship that bore any semblance to aggressiveness. There are moments, however, when one member of a pair may attack the other. The female Pileated on Sapelo, after battling the lone male in her nest and being ousted, flew at her mate who had been resting not far away. Lawrence (1967) has described a parallel case among Downies, when, following a severe encounter with a red squirrel, a male attacked his mate coming to the nest with food. Emotion worked up in conflict is not easily dissipated. It may, under the stress of the moment, result in a redirected attack, even on a mate, if that is the bird which happens to be nearest.

## DOMINANCE

Dominance of males, as evidenced by supplanting females at food, is a rule among woodpeckers. The resultant spacing out may enable the members of pairs to exploit the resources of their habitat more effectively. Pileateds are somewhat different. Although males displace females, especially when the two are close, females sometimes move to where a male is feeding and he leaves. This may be an expression of their especially strong pairbonds. Hairy Woodpeckers also have strong bonds. Among them sexual differences in feeding decrease the number of displacings, making it easier for the two to travel through woods together.

A reason for male dominance, according to Lorenz (1970), is to keep females behaving like females. If they were not kept suppressed, their potential for male behavior would become manifest. I had an example of this with my handraised flickers. The male was the more active in drumming, inspecting holes, and *we-cup* dances in the fall, his mate appearing subdued. But when I hosed the aviary, the male was terrified. He remained shy and quiet for the rest of the day. As noted on two different days, his mate quickly replaced him as the dominant partner. Male dominance may not be just a matter of displacing. It may also be asserted by the male's lead in drummings, vocalizations, and displays as well as in his preponderant role in nesting. But there is a brief period when the female is dominant. This, as shown when she strikes out at her mate, is when she is laying, as I have noted for both flickers and sapsuckers.

### PARENTAL ACTIVITIES

#### LEAD BY MALE

As parents or prospective ones, male woodpeckers have the most initial drive and play the predominant role in nesting. They seek with breeding calls, drumming, or both to attract a female to a nest site at the start of a breeding season and, when a site is agreed upon, they take the lead in excavating and guarding. A nest becomes the male's roost hole as soon as it is ready. He does all of the incubating and brooding at night and often a major part of it by day. In feeding nestlings, males generally make the most visits and bring the most food, as well as removing most of the fecal sacs. Although nest defense is difficult to quantitate, males, in addition to guarding the nest at night, are the more apt to stay in a nest, by day, in the face of an immediate threat. But, in spite of the lead generally taken by males, the parental system of woodpeckers is far from being ironclad. It is a highly flexible one, a kind of seesaw in which a female does more when a male does less.

#### FLEXIBLE ROLE OF FEMALES

It is generally assumed that males take up a territory at the start of a breeding season, then seek to attract a mate. While this is so for flickers and sapsuckers, where males are first to arrive, it can be difficult to determine for resident species. I followed two female Hairies that were the first ones on what later became the breeding territories. One of them, in Maryland, was extraordinary in doing an immense amount of drumming in the fall. She fought with other females along her territorial borders and attracted a male, who, by midwinter, came to stay. A female in New Hampshire that had lost her mate one year, remained on her breeding territory and attracted a new mate the next. Although males take the greatest interest in trying to establish a nest site and excavating it, they are dependent on the constant approval of their mates. If a mate does not come, a male will call or drum until she does. She is the more particular and conservative of the two. When she ceases to approve of a site, a male goes in search of another. If, after several failures, a breeding season is progressing, a female may take the lead in the search for a new site and do a major part of the initial excavating, as I have seen for Downies.

Males generally take the lead in feeding nestlings. But with Black-backed Woodpeckers and, at times with Hairies, I have found females staying close to nests and making the most visits. At one Hairy nest, the male ceased coming the last week, leaving the female to tend the single nestling alone. Stickel (1965) noted a similar situation with a pair of Red-bellieds. Among nine pairs of Red-bellieds, he found females as attentive to the young as the males in six pairs and more so in three.

The reproductive drives of most birds rise and fall each year. But it is not clear, with woodpeckers, that they fall synchronously. It has seemed with some pairs that the female's interest has continued, like that of the female Hairy feeding her young one alone, when that of her mate has begun to wane. With Pileateds, it is the female that takes the lead in the recrudescence of courtship coming at the end of nesting.

I have especially noted the emergence of females as leaders among flickers. At four nests, it was the female that took the greater interest in the fledging of the young. At one nest, where the parents were still feeding young in July, the male spent much of his time idling by the nest. For three days I did not see him at all. But the most striking example of a female taking the lead was with a pair that started nesting on July 9. Here the female did essentially all of the excavating and incubating. The male visited the nest, but seldom for more than a few minutes at a time.

## Lone Parents

If one of a pair is killed, there appears to be a sexual difference in the prospects of the remaining partner raising the nestlings alone. Of five lone sapsuckers that I followed, three were females and two males. The three females fed their young at exaggerated rates and all of the young died, seemingly of starvation. One of the lone males was killed, but the other, feeding at a slower rate than the females, succeeded in fledging a young one after nine days. Payne (pers. comm.) observed a male Red-headed Woodpecker that cared for two young for 16 days before they fledged. The male's rate of feeding was about the same as the combined rate for himself and mate prior to her death.

A faster rate of feeding was noted for two lone female Hairy Woodpeckers. This was as compared to a lone male in the last five to six days of the nesting period. A faster rate for lone females is apparently not confined to woodpeckers. Smith, et al. (1982), in studies on polygyny in Song Sparrows, found that males aided first mates in raising young, but not those secondarily acquired. The females unaided by males fed their young at faster, less effectual rates. It would seem from these cases that females experience more difficulties as lone parents than males. This, among woodpeckers, may result from males generally taking the lead. Woodpeckers, however, are not always predictable. Lawrence (1967) encountered a lone male sapsucker that fed his young at highly exaggerated rates, at times as fast as once every other minute. He was, however, able to raise young successfully over a period of three weeks.

Males may also be more successful in adopting the young of another nest. A lone female sapsucker that lost her mate one day, had attracted a new one by the next morning. She continued to feed her well-grown nestlings, giving a few *kwee-urk*s but otherwise paying little attention to the new male. He flew to the nest to percuss and tap, as if prospecting a new site, then flew away in courtship flight. On the following morning, early, I saw her in a similar flight, indicating that both participated in an abbreviated courtship. The new male started feeding the young within two days of his arrival. Lawrence (1967) observed the opposite of this situation when a lone male attracted a new female. Although she came to the vicinity of the nest over a 10-day period, she never entered it or fed the young. Her chief response was to carry on courtship by tapping at the entrance and displaying when the male came to feed the nestlings.

It is of interest to compare these situations among sapsuckers with those noted for other birds. Pinkowski (1978) describes a nest of Eastern Bluebirds where the male disappeared and was replaced on the same day by a new male. For the next 11 days this male alternated between courtship and feeding the young, but his feedings were relatively few and erratic. Allan (1979) encountered a somewhat different situation with Dark-eyed Juncos. The original male, killed on the day of hatching, was replaced by a new male on the same day. After a number of copulations over the next three days, the new male started feeding the single nestling on day four. Thereafter he did more than half of the feeding. In all of these cases, whether junco, bluebird, or sapsucker, the replacement male exhibited an accelerated physiological adjustment to his new situation.

A question is why replacement males should have an urge to feed nestlings that are not their own. Here I wonder if arguments about altruism are needed. Male woodpeckers build up a tremendous drive, presumably hormonal, for nesting. If they lose a mate or are unable to find one, they are cut off with energy to spare. A lone female with a nest, if found, provides a natural and satisfying outlet for what would otherwise be a frustrated physical and emotional drive.

## COURTSHIP AND THE PAIRBOND

### PAIRBOND AND NEST SITE

A male sapsucker may start a nest excavation, but no real excavation is made without a mate. A hole, even an indifferent one at the onset of a season, is the center around which a pairbond develops. The initial center, with Red-bellieds, is usually the male's winter roost hole. He initiates a breeding season by calling from it at dawn in midwinter. The female, after a time, answers with a lower call, then flies to him, the two joining in mutual tapping. This flying of the female to the male at dawn is characteristic of a number of woodpeckers. With none, however, is there a ceremony as definite as that of the Red-bellieds and their close relatives the Red-headeds. But these rendezvous at dawn, although they have a look of permanence, break down before long. The female does not come and the male has to search for a new site. With many pairs weeks of trial and error may now set in. The members of a pair agree on a site, as shown by tapping, but as an excavation develops, the female may find something the matter with it. Then the whole process begins again. It is in registering agreements and disagreements that the courtship displays of woodpeckers reach a peak, whether in courtship flights of Downies and Hairies, the winnow flights and bobbing dances of sapsuckers, or the bill-waving dances of flickers with raising of red crests and tilting to show the yellow of underwings and tails. Copulatory behavior can also be a part of early courtship, taking place as early as several months prior to egg laying. But it is more apt to take place as an overflow of emotion arising from a conflict than with any special association with an excavation.

### QUIET AGREEMENT

As a nest approaches completion, woods that have been the scene of lively displays become relatively quiet. No longer disagreeing and in accord, the members of a pair may rest motionless for 20 or more minutes within sight of each other. Silence now expresses the closeness of the pairbond.

What the members of a pair have to communicate, at time of egg laying, is readiness for copulation. A male may drum for his mate to come. At other times copulations take place with few apparent preliminaries. Woodpeckers copulate close to a nest if an open and somewhat horizontal branch is present. Otherwise places vary. A female Downy, instead of flying directly to her mate, may fly first to the hole, then to the copulation branch, as though tying copulation in with attachment to the nest.

## SUMMARY AND CONCLUSIONS

### NESTING AND AFTER

Tapping largely ceases with egg laying. Once the members of a pair start incubating, exchanges between them may be limited to low notes at times of changeovers, a situation continuing for most of the nesting period. In the last days there may be a return to early courtship in a mild form. With nest sanitation finished and the young being fed less, parents have more leisure, a stimulus for scattered drumming, bits of dances, and more intense greetings. This recrudescence of reproductive behavior may become more manifest within two to three weeks of fledging, when the young are independent or partially so. Parents may then start prospecting for a nest hole, with tapping, brief excavating, and even courtship flights. But all of this is transient and dies off within a week or less. Courtship is then at an end with one exception. This is another brief and variable revival on days of suitable weather in midfall.

A noted ornithologist, to my surprise, once remarked that he wondered why birds had to go through such intricate and trying ceremonies in order to reproduce. Why could they not go about the business of nesting without so much fuss? But life is not that simple. For two independent birds to meet and synchronize their physiologies, behavior, and drives for the feat of raising young to fledging in a relatively few weeks, means development, at least in woodpeckers, of a strong pairbond, a bond flexible enough to meet the threats and hazards of a fluctuating environment. This is something that cannot be built up overnight. A gamut of special vocalizations, ceremonies, and displays have evolved to effect the change. They are all needed and watching them, for me, has always been the annual peak of my woodpecker studies.

### LITERATURE CITED

ALLAN, T. A. 1979. Parental behavior of a replacement male Dark-eyed Junco. Auk, **96**: 630–631.

HOWARD, H. E. 1929. An introduction to the study of bird behaviour. Cambridge Univ. Press. 135 p.

KILHAM, L. 1973. Reproductive behavior of the Red-breasted Nuthatch. I. Courtship. Auk, **90**: 597–609.

LAWRENCE, L. DE K. 1967. A comparative life-history study of four species of woodpeckers. Ornith. Monogr. (Amer. Ornith. Union), no. 5, 156 p.

LORENZ, K. 1970. Companions as factors in the bird's environment, p. 101–258. *In* Studies in Animal and Human Behaviour. Vol. 1. Harvard Univ. Press, Cambridge.

PINKOWSKI, B. C. 1978. Two successive male Eastern Bluebirds tending the same nest. Auk, **95**: 606–607.

SELANDER, R. K., AND D. R. GILLER. 1959. Interspecific relations of woodpeckers in Texas. Wilson Bull., **71**: 107–124.

SHORT, L. L. 1982. Woodpeckers of the world. Delaware Mus. Nat. Hist. Monogr. Ser., no. 4, 676 p.

SKUTCH, A. F. 1969. Life histories of Central American Birds. III. Pacific Coast Avifauna (Cooper Ornith. Soc.), no. 35, 580 p.

SMITH, J. N. M., Y. YOM-TOV, AND R. MOSES. 1982. Polygyny, male parental care, and sex ratio in song sparrows: an experimental study. Auk, 99: 555–564.

STICKEL, D. W. 1965. Territorial and breeding habits of Red-bellied Woodpeckers. Amer. Midl. Nat., 74: 110–118.

TROETSCHLER, R. G. 1976. Acorn Woodpecker breeding strategy as affected by starling nest-hole competition. Condor, 78: 151–165.

# APPENDIX I

## Raising and Care of Captive Woodpeckers

The longer natural parents can do the feeding of their young the better. Woodpeckers taken from a nest within three to four days of fledging will still become tame if handled properly. A number of our nestlings, however, were nearly naked, with only a few pin feathers, when we removed them from the nest. We kept these smaller nestlings, to start with, in a cereal bowl lined with tissue and placed them in a dark cabinet after feeding. The darkness, simulating that of a natural nest cavity, kept them quiet between feedings.

A convenient way to feed small nestlings is to impale a piece of meat, raw hamburger or better chicken, on a toothpick, then dip the piece in water to get rid of its stickiness. Nestlings have oral flanges (Fig. 55) at the base of their lower mandibles, structures that are particularly developed in woodpeckers and other hole-nesting birds. Wiping these with the toothpick causes the nestlings to open their bills widely and beg. If feedings are not too frequent, young will beg spontaneously. This is the ideal situation. Each nestling knows when it has had enough. After feeding, probing the region of the vent with the toothpick may cause the nestling to pass a fecal sac.

Fig. 55. Young Red-headed Woodpecker showing oral flange at base of lower mandible.

233

Fig. 56. Male flicker shooting tongue into a rotting log, brought in moist from the woods.

In feeding the objective is to give a maximum amount of protein. This can be done with raw meat being used as a mainstay. But just meat is not enough. Whole animals of some kind are seemingly essential. We have used parts of previously killed and cut up suckling rats or mice, thus providing a mixture of blood, viscera, bone, fat, and probably vitamins and other materials needed to build body structures. Insects are ideal if available. We have kept mealworms (*Tenebrio* sp.) alive the year around, increasing their numbers each spring in order to have a supply.

One rule about feeding birds is never to give water. Parents do not do so in nature. If water is given, it is almost sure to go down the wrong way, enter the lungs, and cause pneumonia.

All of our adult woodpeckers, from flickers and Pileateds to sapsuckers and Hairies and Downies, fed on much the same diet. Mainstays were suet, half oranges, and each morning some bread soaked in a commercial vitamin mixture. This I fed by hand as a way of taming the birds, for they were especially fond of it. We fed our woodpeckers peanut hearts when we lived in Maryland. These are, unfortunately, difficult to find in some places. They make excellent food. The flickers and Pileated took up the small pieces on their long sticky tongues as if dealing with so many ants.

I always kept 20–25 cm of forest loam and old leaves on the floor of the aviary, stocking it with earthworms. The flickers (Fig. 56) were adept at feeding on them and even Hairies, that do not do so to any extent in nature, learned to dig them out. I maintained the worms by burying the orange peels, which are excellent for this purpose if the proper decay organisms are in the soil. When they were, the worms were able to use the peels within a short time.

A rewarding but cumbersome way of feeding the woodpeckers was to bring in rotting logs from the woods. Not all logs contain insects. One can learn by dissecting what kind of logs are best. The best logs I found were thoroughly damp and rotten enough, in places, to dig into. Logs are of little value if either too hard or too soft and rotten. The woodpeckers took an immediate interest in any new log and it was a spectacle to see them all working, each after the manner of its kind.

Only two species of hole-nesting birds bred successfully in the aviary. These were the Red-bellied Woodpecker and the Red-breasted Nuthatch. Parents need a large, daily supply of insects. The only stable source that I have found is mealworms. In addition to these I used a commercial insect trap, a device with a circular fluorescent light, a motor, and a black cloth bag. The motor creates a suction that draws the insects down through the center of the light. On warm, favorable nights, we sometimes collected a handful of assorted insects, including moths.

Among other requisites for woodpeckers, whose bills grow continuously, are logs that offer some resistance. The logs can be hard and dry, but not so hard that the woodpeckers will be unable to knock off splinters and dig holes. Woodpeckers do this with gusto even on logs containing no insect prey. Logs serve to keep them active during the day as well as keeping their bills worn to the proper size. Our aviary, on many mornings, sounded like a carpenter shop, as chips accumulated on the floor below.

Woodpeckers drink water and like to bathe in it. Hence I always kept a sloping bird bath in the aviary, cleaning it and filling it with fresh water daily. I also used a hose to water the bottom of the aviary. This was not only to keep it from getting dry and dusty, but also to make it suitably moist for the earthworms.

Keeping the woodpeckers supplied with hollow logs or bird houses for roosting at night was always a problem, for the woodpeckers often knocked them to pieces. I had, in consequence, to keep patching the boxes with aluminum.

My aviaries were of no one size. In Maryland I used an indoor, one-car garage, and in New Hampshire, I had two small aviaries built inside a greenhouse attached to my library, and another on a porch leading from it. These latter aviaries were convenient in enabling me to keep an eye on the woodpeckers while working at my desk. All of these aviaries had to be lined with a tough plastic to protect the walls of the house. Woodpeckers love to dig into plaster, even on the ceilings. Other sides of the aviaries were of turkey wire.

FIG. 57.   Female Red-bellied Woodpecker facing rival in an adjacent cage.

I have preferred to have my aviaries indoors. This was not only for convenience of watching, but also because of hazards involved in open, outdoor aviaries. Stray cats, dogs, people, or odd neighborhood excitement, as well as the presence of wild Hairy or other woodpeckers, can be over-exciting to captives. When excited they bat back and forth against the wire, making study of breeding or other behavior impossible. All of our aviaries were well enclosed. The birds, of course, need some chance to look out. Small windows high up are sufficient for this, especially if sunny enough for the woodpeckers to sun-bathe.

A difficulty with my aviaries was that I never had enough of them. The woodpeckers and nuthatches I kept got along well together, for the most part, in summer, fall, and early winter. But once breeding seasons began,

FIG. 58. Female Red-bellied about to feed young in aviary; mealworm in bill.

all sorts of intra- and interspecific clashes began to appear. This meant that I had to subdivide aviaries to keep individuals and species from harming each other. In spite of these difficulties, the Downy Woodpeckers and flickers mated, laid and incubated eggs and as mentioned, the Red-bellied Woodpeckers and Red-breasted Nuthatches raised young successfully. Figures 55–58 are photos showing some of the woodpeckers and their activities in the aviary.

# APPENDIX II

## SCIENTIFIC NAMES OF VERTEBRATES AND PLANTS

### VERTEBRATES

Araçari, Collared, *Pteroglossus torquatus*
Araçari, Fiery-billed, *Pteroglossus frantzii*
Blackbird, Eurasian, *Turdus merula*
Blackbird, Rusty, *Euphagus carolinus*
Bluebird, Eastern, *Sialia sialis*
Bobwhite, Northern, *Colinus virginianus*
Cardinal, Northern, *Cardinalis cardinalis*
Chachalaca, Plain, *Ortalis vetula*
Chickadee, Black-capped, *Parus atricapillus*
Chickadee, Carolina, *Parus carolinensis*
Creeper, Brown, *Certhia americana*
Duck, Ring-necked, *Aytha collaris*
Duck, Wood, *Aix sponsa*
Flicker, Northern, *Colaptes auratus*
Flycatcher, Pied, *Musicapa hypoleuca*
Goldcrest, *Regulus regulus*
Goshawk, Northern, *Accipiter gentilis*
Grackle, Common, *Quiscalus quiscula*
Grebe, Pied-billed, *Podilymbus podiceps*
Greenfinch, *Chloris chloris*
Grosbeak, Pine, *Pinicola enucleator*
Grouse, Ruffed, *Bonasa umbellus*
Hawk, Cooper's, *Accipiter cooperi*
Hawk, Red-shouldered, *Buteo lineatus*
Hawk, Sharp-shinned, *Accipiter striatus*
Hawk, Sparrow, *Accipiter nisus*
Heron, Green, *Butorides striatus*
Hornbill, Black-and-White Casqued, *Bycanistes subcylindricus*
Huia, *Heteralocha acutirostris*
Hummingbird, Ruby-throated, *Archilochus colubris*
Jackdaw, *Corvus monedula*
Jay, Blue, *Cyanocitta cristata*
Jay, Brown, *Cyanocorax morio*
Junco, Dark-eyed, *Junco hyemalis*
Kingbird, Eastern, *Tyrannus tyrannus*
Kinglet, Golden-crowned, *Regulus satrapa*
Kite, Hook-billed, *Chondrohierax uncinatus*
Marmoset, *Oedipomidas geoffroyi*
Mockingbird, Eastern, *Mimus polyglottos*

Nuthatch, European, *Sitta europaea*
Nuthatch, Red-breasted, *Sitta canadensis*
Nuthatch, White-breated, *Sitta carolinensis*
Owl, Barred, *Strix varia*
Owl, Spectacled, *Pulsatrix perspicillata*
Pika, *Ochotona princeps*
Pygmy-Owl, Ferruginous, *Glaucidium brasilianum*
Raccoon, *Procyon lotor*
Redpoll, Common, *Carduelis flammea*
Robin, American, *Turdus migratorius*
Robin, British, *Erithacus rubecula*
Sapsucker, Red-breasted, *Sphyrapicus ruber*
Sapsucker, Red-naped, *Sphyrapicus nuchalis*
Sapsucker, Yellow-bellied, *Sphyrapicus varius*
Screech-Owl, Eastern, *Otus asio*
Skunk, Eastern, *Mephitis nigra*
Snake, Pilot Black, *Elaphe obsoleta*
Sparrow, House, *Passer domesticus*
Sparrow, Song, *Melospiza melodia*
Squirrel, Flying, *Glaucomys volans*
Squirrel, Gray, *Sciurus carolinensis*
Squirrel, Red, *Tamiasciurus hudsonicus*
Thrush, Hermit, *Catharus guttatus*
Tit, Blue, *Parus caeruleus*
Tit, Great, *Parus major*
Titmouse, Tufted, *Parus bicolor*
Tityra, *Tityra* sp.
Treecreeper, *Certhia familiaris*
Weasel, *Mustela* sp.
Woodpecker, Black, *Dryocopus martius*
Woodpecker, Black-backed, *Picoides arcticus*
Woodpecker, Crimson-crested, *Campephilus melanoleucos*
Woodpecker, Downy, *Picoides pubescens*
Woodpecker, Golden-naped, *Melanerpes chrysauchen*
Woodpecker, Great Spotted, *Picoides major*
Woodpecker, Hairy, *Picoides villosus*
Woodpecker, Hoffman's, *Melanerpes hoffmanni*
Woodpecker, Lesser Spotted, *Picoides minor*
Woodpecker, Lewis', *Melanerpes lewis*
Woodpecker, Lineated, *Dryocopus lineatus*
Woodpecker, Middle Spotted, *Picoides media*
Woodpecker, Pale-billed, *Campephilus guatemalensis*
Woodpecker, Pileated, *Dryocopus pileatus*
Woodpecker, Red-bellied, *Melanerpes carolinus*
Woodpecker, Red-cockaded, *Picoides borealis*

Woodpecker, Red-crowned, *Melanerpes rubricapillus*
Woodpecker, Syrian, *Picoides syriacus*
Wren, House, *Troglodytes aedon*

## PLANTS

Ash, White, *Fraxinus americana*
Aspen, Quaking, *Populus tremuloides*
Balsa, *Ochrona limonensis*
Beech, American, *Fagus grandifolia*
Birch, Paper, *Betula papyrifera*
Birch, River, *Betula nigra*
Birch, Yellow, *Betula lutea*
Butternut, *Juglans cinerea*
Camphor-tree, *Cinnamomum camphora*
Dogwood, Flowering, *Cornus florida*
Elm, American, *Ulmus americana*
Grape, Wild, *Vitis* sp.
Greenbriar, *Smilax laurifolia*
Gum, Black, *Nyssa sylvatica*
Hackberry, Common, *Celtis occidentalis*
Hemlock, Eastern, *Tsuga canadensis*
Hornbeam, Hop-, *Ostyra virginiana*
Locust, Black, *Robinia pseudoacacia*
Maple, Red, *Acer rubrum*
Maple, Silver, *Acer saccharinum*
Maple, Sugar, *Acer saccharum*
Myrtle, Wax, *Myrica cerifera*
Oak, Pin, *Quercus palustris*
Oak, Red, *Quercus rubra*
Palm, Royal, *Roystonea* spp
Pine, Loblolly, *Pinus taeda*
Pine, White, *Pinus strobus*
Poison ivy, *Rhus radicans*
Poplar, Swamp, *Populus heterophylla*
Sycamore, *Platanus occidentalis*
Sumac, *Rhus* sp.
Walnut, Black, *Juglans nigra*
Woodbine, *Parthenocissus quinquefolia*

A CATALOG OF SELECTED
# DOVER BOOKS
IN ALL FIELDS OF INTEREST

# A CATALOG OF SELECTED DOVER
# BOOKS IN ALL FIELDS OF INTEREST

CONCERNING THE SPIRITUAL IN ART, Wassily Kandinsky. Pioneering work by father of abstract art. Thoughts on color theory, nature of art. Analysis of earlier masters. 12 illustrations. 80pp. of text. 5⅜ × 8½.                23411-8 Pa. $3.95

ANIMALS: 1,419 Copyright-Free Illustrations of Mammals, Birds, Fish, Insects, etc., Jim Harter (ed.). Clear wood engravings present, in extremely lifelike poses, over 1,000 species of animals. One of the most extensive pictorial sourcebooks of its kind. Captions. Index. 284pp. 9 × 12.                23766-4 Pa. $10.95

CELTIC ART: The Methods of Construction, George Bain. Simple geometric techniques for making Celtic interlacements, spirals, Kells-type initials, animals, humans, etc. Over 500 illustrations. 160pp. 9 × 12. (USO)        22923-8 Pa. $8.95

AN ATLAS OF ANATOMY FOR ARTISTS, Fritz Schider. Most thorough reference work on art anatomy in the world. Hundreds of illustrations, including selections from works by Vesalius, Leonardo, Goya, Ingres, Michelangelo, others. 593 illustrations. 192pp. 7⅛ × 10¼.                20241-0 Pa. $8.95

CELTIC HAND STROKE-BY-STROKE (Irish Half-Uncial from "The Book of Kells"): An Arthur Baker Calligraphy Manual, Arthur Baker. Complete guide to creating each letter of the alphabet in distinctive Celtic manner. Covers hand position, strokes, pens, inks, paper, more. Illustrated. 48pp. 8¼ × 11.
24336-2 Pa. $3.95

EASY ORIGAMI, John Montroll. Charming collection of 32 projects (hat, cup, pelican, piano, swan, many more) specially designed for the novice origami hobbyist. Clearly illustrated easy-to-follow instructions insure that even beginning papercrafters will achieve successful results. 48pp. 8¼ × 11.        27298-2 Pa. $2.95

THE COMPLETE BOOK OF BIRDHOUSE CONSTRUCTION FOR WOOD-WORKERS, Scott D. Campbell. Detailed instructions, illustrations, tables. Also data on bird habitat and instinct patterns. Bibliography. 3 tables. 63 illustrations in 15 figures. 48pp. 5¼ × 8½.                24407-5 Pa. $1.95

BLOOMINGDALE'S ILLUSTRATED 1886 CATALOG: Fashions, Dry Goods and Housewares, Bloomingdale Brothers. Famed merchants' extremely rare catalog depicting about 1,700 products: clothing, housewares, firearms, dry goods, jewelry, more. Invaluable for dating, identifying vintage items. Also, copyright-free graphics for artists, designers. Co-published with Henry Ford Museum & Green-field Village. 160pp. 8¼ × 11.                25780-0 Pa. $8.95

HISTORIC COSTUME IN PICTURES, Braun & Schneider. Over 1,450 costumed figures in clearly detailed engravings—from dawn of civilization to end of 19th century. Captions. Many folk costumes. 256pp. 8⅜ × 11¾.        23150-X Pa. $10.95

STICKLEY CRAFTSMAN FURNITURE CATALOGS, Gustav Stickley and L. & J. G. Stickley. Beautiful, functional furniture in two authentic catalogs from 1910. 594 illustrations, including 277 photos, show settles, rockers, armchairs, reclining chairs, bookcases, desks, tables. 183pp. 6½ × 9¼. 23838-5 Pa. $8.95

AMERICAN LOCOMOTIVES IN HISTORIC PHOTOGRAPHS: 1858 to 1949, Ron Ziel (ed.). A rare collection of 126 meticulously detailed official photographs, called "builder portraits," of American locomotives that majestically chronicle the rise of steam locomotive power in America. Introduction. Detailed captions. xi + 129pp. 9 × 12. 27393-8 Pa. $12.95

AMERICA'S LIGHTHOUSES: An Illustrated History, Francis Ross Holland, Jr. Delightfully written, profusely illustrated fact-filled survey of over 200 American lighthouses since 1716. History, anecdotes, technological advances, more. 240pp. 8 × 10¾. 25576-X Pa. $10.95

TOWARDS A NEW ARCHITECTURE, Le Corbusier. Pioneering manifesto by founder of "International School." Technical and aesthetic theories, views of industry, economics, relation of form to function, "mass-production split" and much more. Profusely illustrated. 320pp. 6⅛ × 9¼. (USO) 25023-7 Pa. $8.95

HOW THE OTHER HALF LIVES, Jacob Riis. Famous journalistic record, exposing poverty and degradation of New York slums around 1900, by major social reformer. 100 striking and influential photographs. 233pp. 10 × 7⅞.
22012-5 Pa $10.95

FRUIT KEY AND TWIG KEY TO TREES AND SHRUBS, William M. Harlow. One of the handiest and most widely used identification aids. Fruit key covers 120 deciduous and evergreen species; twig key 160 deciduous species. Easily used. Over 300 photographs. 126pp. 5⅜ × 8½. 20511-8 Pa. $2.95

COMMON BIRD SONGS, Dr. Donald J. Borror. Songs of 60 most common U.S. birds: robins, sparrows, cardinals, bluejays, finches, more—arranged in order of increasing complexity. Up to 9 variations of songs of each species.
Cassette and manual 99911-4 $8.95

ORCHIDS AS HOUSE PLANTS, Rebecca Tyson Northen. Grow cattleyas and many other kinds of orchids—in a window, in a case, or under artificial light. 63 illustrations. 148pp. 5⅜ × 8½. 23261-1 Pa. $3.95

MONSTER MAZES, Dave Phillips. Masterful mazes at four levels of difficulty. Avoid deadly perils and evil creatures to find magical treasures. Solutions for all 32 exciting illustrated puzzles. 48pp. 8¼ × 11. 26005-4 Pa. $2.95

MOZART'S DON GIOVANNI (DOVER OPERA LIBRETTO SERIES), Wolfgang Amadeus Mozart. Introduced and translated by Ellen H. Bleiler. Standard Italian libretto, with complete English translation. Convenient and thoroughly portable—an ideal companion for reading along with a recording or the performance itself. Introduction. List of characters. Plot summary. 121pp. 5¼ × 8½.
24944-1 Pa. $2.95

TECHNICAL MANUAL AND DICTIONARY OF CLASSICAL BALLET, Gail Grant. Defines, explains, comments on steps, movements, poses and concepts. 15-page pictorial section. Basic book for student, viewer. 127pp. 5⅜ × 8½.
21843-0 Pa. $3.95

MY BONDAGE AND MY FREEDOM, Frederick Douglass. Born a slave, Douglass became outspoken force in antislavery movement. The best of Douglass' autobiographies. Graphic description of slave life. 464pp. 5⅜ × 8½.     22457-0 Pa. $7.95

FOLLOWING THE EQUATOR: A Journey Around the World, Mark Twain. Fascinating humorous account of 1897 voyage to Hawaii, Australia, India, New Zealand, etc. Ironic, bemused reports on peoples, customs, climate, flora and fauna, politics, much more. 197 illustrations. 720pp. 5⅜ × 8½.     26113-1 Pa. $15.95

THE PEOPLE CALLED SHAKERS, Edward D. Andrews. Definitive study of Shakers: origins, beliefs, practices, dances, social organization, furniture and crafts, etc. 33 illustrations. 351pp. 5⅜ × 8½.     21081-2 Pa. $7.95

THE MYTHS OF GREECE AND ROME, H. A. Guerber. A classic of mythology, generously illustrated, long prized for its simple, graphic, accurate retelling of the principal myths of Greece and Rome, and for its commentary on their origins and significance. With 64 illustrations by Michelangelo, Raphael, Titian, Rubens, Canova, Bernini and others. 480pp. 5⅜ × 8½.     27584-1 Pa. $9.95

PSYCHOLOGY OF MUSIC, Carl E. Seashore. Classic work discusses music as a medium from psychological viewpoint. Clear treatment of physical acoustics, auditory apparatus, sound perception, development of musical skills, nature of musical feeling, host of other topics. 88 figures. 408pp. 5⅜ × 8½. 21851-1 Pa. $8.95

THE PHILOSOPHY OF HISTORY, Georg W. Hegel. Great classic of Western thought develops concept that history is not chance but rational process, the evolution of freedom. 457pp. 5⅜ × 8½.     20112-0 Pa. $8.95

THE BOOK OF TEA, Kakuzo Okakura. Minor classic of the Orient: entertaining, charming explanation, interpretation of traditional Japanese culture in terms of tea ceremony. 94pp. 5⅜ × 8½.     20070-1 Pa. $2.95

LIFE IN ANCIENT EGYPT, Adolf Erman. Fullest, most thorough, detailed older account with much not in more recent books, domestic life, religion, magic, medicine, commerce, much more. Many illustrations reproduce tomb paintings, carvings, hieroglyphs, etc. 597pp. 5⅜ × 8½.     22632-8 Pa. $9.95

SUNDIALS, Their Theory and Construction, Albert Waugh. Far and away the best, most thorough coverage of ideas, mathematics concerned, types, construction, adjusting anywhere. Simple, nontechnical treatment allows even children to build several of these dials. Over 100 illustrations. 230pp. 5⅜ × 8½.     22947-5 Pa. $5.95

DYNAMICS OF FLUIDS IN POROUS MEDIA, Jacob Bear. For advanced students of ground water hydrology, soil mechanics and physics, drainage and irrigation engineering, and more. 335 illustrations. Exercises, with answers. 784pp. 6⅛ × 9¼.     65675-6 Pa. $19.95

SONGS OF EXPERIENCE: Facsimile Reproduction with 26 Plates in Full Color, William Blake. 26 full-color plates from a rare 1826 edition. Includes "The Tyger," "London," "Holy Thursday," and other poems. Printed text of poems. 48pp. 5¼ × 7.     24636-1 Pa. $3.95

OLD-TIME VIGNETTES IN FULL COLOR, Carol Belanger Grafton (ed.). Over 390 charming, often sentimental illustrations, selected from archives of Victorian graphics—pretty women posing, children playing, food, flowers, kittens and puppies, smiling cherubs, birds and butterflies, much more. All copyright-free. 48pp. 9¼ × 12¼.     27269-9 Pa. $5.95

THE BEST TALES OF HOFFMANN, E. T. A. Hoffmann. 10 of Hoffmann's most important stories: "Nutcracker and the King of Mice," "The Golden Flowerpot," etc. 458pp. 5⅜ × 8½. 21793-0 Pa. $8.95

FROM FETISH TO GOD IN ANCIENT EGYPT, E. A. Wallis Budge. Rich detailed survey of Egyptian conception of "God" and gods, magic, cult of animals, Osiris, more. Also, superb English translations of hymns and legends. 240 illustrations. 545pp. 5⅜ × 8½. 25803-3 Pa. $10.95

FRENCH STORIES/CONTES FRANÇAIS: A Dual-Language Book, Wallace Fowlie. Ten stories by French masters, Voltaire to Camus: "Micromegas" by Voltaire; "The Atheist's Mass" by Balzac; "Minuet" by de Maupassant; "The Guest" by Camus, six more. Excellent English translations on facing pages. Also French-English vocabulary list, exercises, more. 352pp. 5⅜ × 8½. 26443-2 Pa. $8.95

CHICAGO AT THE TURN OF THE CENTURY IN PHOTOGRAPHS: 122 Historic Views from the Collections of the Chicago Historical Society, Larry A. Viskochil. Rare large-format prints offer detailed views of City Hall, State Street, the Loop, Hull House, Union Station, many other landmarks, circa 1904–1913. Introduction. Captions. Maps. 144pp. 9⅜ × 12¼. 24656-6 Pa. $12.95

OLD BROOKLYN IN EARLY PHOTOGRAPHS, 1865–1929, William Lee Younger. Luna Park, Gravesend race track, construction of Grand Army Plaza, moving of Hotel Brighton, etc. 157 previously unpublished photographs. 165pp. 8⅞ × 11¾. 23587-4 Pa. $12.95

THE MYTHS OF THE NORTH AMERICAN INDIANS, Lewis Spence. Rich anthology of the myths and legends of the Algonquins, Iroquois, Pawnees and Sioux, prefaced by an extensive historical and ethnological commentary. 36 illustrations. 480pp. 5⅜ × 8½. 25967-6 Pa. $8.95

AN ENCYCLOPEDIA OF BATTLES: Accounts of Over 1,560 Battles from 1479 B.C. to the Present, David Eggenberger. Essential details of every major battle in recorded history from the first battle of Megiddo in 1479 B.C. to Grenada in 1984. List of Battle Maps. New Appendix covering the years 1967–1984. Index. 99 illustrations. 544pp. 6½ × 9¼. 24913-1 Pa. $14.95

SAILING ALONE AROUND THE WORLD, Captain Joshua Slocum. First man to sail around the world, alone, in small boat. One of great feats of seamanship told in delightful manner. 67 illustrations. 294pp. 5⅜ × 8½. 20326-3 Pa. $4.95

ANARCHISM AND OTHER ESSAYS, Emma Goldman. Powerful, penetrating, prophetic essays on direct action, role of minorities, prison reform, puritan hypocrisy, violence, etc. 271pp. 5⅜ × 8½. 22484-8 Pa. $5.95

MYTHS OF THE HINDUS AND BUDDHISTS, Ananda K. Coomaraswamy and Sister Nivedita. Great stories of the epics; deeds of Krishna, Shiva, taken from puranas, Vedas, folk tales; etc. 32 illustrations. 400pp. 5⅜ × 8½. 21759-0 Pa. $8.95

BEYOND PSYCHOLOGY, Otto Rank. Fear of death, desire of immortality, nature of sexuality, social organization, creativity, according to Rankian system. 291pp. 5⅜ × 8½. 20485-5 Pa. $7.95

A THEOLOGICO-POLITICAL TREATISE, Benedict Spinoza. Also contains unfinished Political Treatise. Great classic on religious liberty, theory of government on common consent. R. Elwes translation. Total of 421pp. 5⅜ × 8½. 20249-6 Pa. $7.95

BRASS INSTRUMENTS: Their History and Development, Anthony Baines. Authoritative, updated survey of the evolution of trumpets, trombones, bugles, cornets, French horns, tubas and other brass wind instruments. Over 140 illustrations and 48 music examples. Corrected and updated by author. New preface. Bibliography. 320pp. 5⅜ × 8½. 27574-4 Pa. $9.95

HOLLYWOOD GLAMOR PORTRAITS, John Kobal (ed.). 145 photos from 1926–49. Harlow, Gable, Bogart, Bacall; 94 stars in all. Full background on photographers, technical aspects. 160pp. 8⅜ × 11¼. 23352-9 Pa. $9.95

MAX AND MORITZ, Wilhelm Busch. Great humor classic in both German and English. Also 10 other works: "Cat and Mouse," "Plisch and Plumm," etc. 216pp. 5⅜ × 8½. 20181-3 Pa. $5.95

THE RAVEN AND OTHER FAVORITE POEMS, Edgar Allan Poe. Over 40 of the author's most memorable poems: "The Bells," "Ulalume," "Israfel," "To Helen," "The Conqueror Worm," "Eldorado," "Annabel Lee," many more. Alphabetic lists of titles and first lines. 64pp. 5³⁄₁₆ × 8¼. 26685-0 Pa. $1.00

SEVEN SCIENCE FICTION NOVELS, H. G. Wells. The standard collection of the great novels. Complete, unabridged. First Men in the Moon, Island of Dr. Moreau, War of the Worlds, Food of the Gods, Invisible Man, Time Machine, In the Days of the Comet. Total of 1,015pp. 5⅜ × 8½. (USO) 20264-X Clothbd. $29.95

AMULETS AND SUPERSTITIONS, E. A. Wallis Budge. Comprehensive discourse on origin, powers of amulets in many ancient cultures: Arab, Persian, Babylonian, Assyrian, Egyptian, Gnostic, Hebrew, Phoenician, Syriac, etc. Covers cross, swastika, crucifix, seals, rings, stones, etc. 584pp. 5⅜ × 8½. 23573-4 Pa. $10.95

RUSSIAN STORIES/PYCCKNE PACCKA3bl: A Dual-Language Book, edited by Gleb Struve. Twelve tales by such masters as Chekhov, Tolstoy, Dostoevsky, Pushkin, others. Excellent word-for-word English translations on facing pages, plus teaching and study aids, Russian/English vocabulary, biographical/critical introductions, more. 416pp. 5⅜ × 8½. 26244-8 Pa. $7.95

PHILADELPHIA THEN AND NOW: 60 Sites Photographed in the Past and Present, Kenneth Finkel and Susan Oyama. Rare photographs of City Hall, Logan Square, Independence Hall, Betsy Ross House, other landmarks juxtaposed with contemporary views. Captures changing face of historic city. Introduction. Captions. 128pp. 8¼ × 11. 25790-8 Pa. $9.95

AIA ARCHITECTURAL GUIDE TO NASSAU AND SUFFOLK COUNTIES, LONG ISLAND, The American Institute of Architects, Long Island Chapter, and the Society for the Preservation of Long Island Antiquities. Comprehensive, well-researched and generously illustrated volume brings to life over three centuries of Long Island's great architectural heritage. More than 240 photographs with authoritative, extensively detailed captions. 176pp. 8¼ × 11. 26946-9 Pa. $14.95

NORTH AMERICAN INDIAN LIFE: Customs and Traditions of 23 Tribes, Elsie Clews Parsons (ed.). 27 fictionalized essays by noted anthropologists examine religion, customs, government, additional facets of life among the Winnebago, Crow, Zuni, Eskimo, other tribes. 480pp. 6⅛ × 9¼. 27377-6 Pa. $10.95

THE INFLUENCE OF SEA POWER UPON HISTORY, 1660–1783, A. T. Mahan. Influential classic of naval history and tactics still used as text in war colleges. First paperback edition. 4 maps. 24 battle plans. 640pp. 5⅜ × 8½.
25509-3 Pa. $12.95

THE STORY OF THE TITANIC AS TOLD BY ITS SURVIVORS, Jack Winocour (ed.). What it was really like. Panic, despair, shocking inefficiency, and a little heroism. More thrilling than any fictional account. 26 illustrations. 320pp. 5⅜ × 8½.
20610-6 Pa. $7.95

FAIRY AND FOLK TALES OF THE IRISH PEASANTRY, William Butler Yeats (ed.). Treasury of 64 tales from the twilight world of Celtic myth and legend: "The Soul Cages," "The Kildare Pooka," "King O'Toole and his Goose," many more. Introduction and Notes by W. B. Yeats. 352pp. 5⅜ × 8½.
26941-8 Pa. $7.95

BUDDHIST MAHAYANA TEXTS, E. B. Cowell and Others (eds.). Superb, accurate translations of basic documents in Mahayana Buddhism, highly important in history of religions. The Buddha-karita of Asvaghosha, Larger Sukhavativyuha, more. 448pp. 5⅜ × 8½. ,
25552-2 Pa. $9.95

ONE TWO THREE . . . INFINITY: Facts and Speculations of Science, George Gamow. Great physicist's fascinating, readable overview of contemporary science: number theory, relativity, fourth dimension, entropy, genes, atomic structure, much more. 128 illustrations. Index. 352pp. 5⅜ × 8½.
25664-2 Pa. $7.95

ENGINEERING IN HISTORY, Richard Shelton Kirby, et al. Broad, nontechnical survey of history's major technological advances: birth of Greek science, industrial revolution, electricity and applied science, 20th-century automation, much more. 181 illustrations. ". . . excellent . . ."—Isis. Bibliography. vii + 530pp. 5⅜ × 8¼.
26412-2 Pa. $13.95

*Prices subject to change without notice.*

Available at your book dealer or write for free catalog to Dept. GI, Dover Publications, Inc., 31 East 2nd St., Mineola, N.Y. 11501. Dover publishes more than 500 books each year on science, elementary and advanced mathematics, biology, music, art, literary history, social sciences and other areas.